SUCCE

AS A COACH

INSIGHTS FROM THE EXPERTS

EDITED BY JONATHAN PASSMORE

Succeeding as a Coach
Insights from the Experts

© Pavilion Publishing & Media

The authors have asserted their rights in accordance with the Copyright, Designs and Patents Act (1988) to be identified as the authors of this work.

Published by:
Pavilion Publishing and Media Ltd
Blue Sky Offices
25 Cecil Pashley Way
Shoreham by Sea
West Sussex
BN43 5FF

Tel: 01273 434 943
Email: info@pavpub.com
Web: www.pavpub.com

Published 2021

A catalogue record for this book is available from the British Library.

ISBN: 978-1-914010-26-2

Pavilion Publishing and Media is a leading publisher of books, training materials and digital content in mental health, social care and allied fields. Pavilion and its imprints offer must-have knowledge and innovative learning solutions underpinned by sound research and professional values.

Editor: Jonathan Passmore
Production editor: Mike Benge, Pavilion Publishing and Media Ltd
Cover design: Tony Pitt, Pavilion Publishing and Media Ltd
Page layout and typesetting: Emma Dawe, Pavilion Publishing and Media Ltd
Printing: CMP Digital Print Solutions

Contents

Foreword

Although in a relatively short period of time coaching has evolved to become a multi-billion dollar business prospering in every part of the world, our profession is still facing existential challenges due to its nature as a fragmented practice with non-unified global standards. Therefore, I truly welcome this book as it offers a holistic approach to coaching.

We live in interesting times: today we witness that humanity faces more and more stress due to a changing socio-economic environment coupled with challenging issues like climate change and digital transformation. I believe that as coaches we are lucky to be well equipped to deal with such challenges. And our wisdom comes with an important responsibility; we need to act as agents for change to let the people we touch better deal with issues in their lives. All these developments add meaning to our responsibility as practitioners of coaching to raise the standards and the level of expectation of our practice for the benefit of society.

It's hard to imagine what historians in fifty or a hundred years' time will be writing about the 2020-21 global pandemic. Most likely the way we react to what has happened will determine the impact of this crisis. I'm sure that humanity will win this battle despite all the damage, but at the same time we will be obliged to develop new psychological strategies to cope with the changes in our lives.

As practitioners of coaching we have an important role to play. Our communities expect us to provide care, support, compassion, kindness, reality checks, and encouragement to those who require these things. We also need to take care of ourselves, and find the most appropriate ways to deploy our competencies for the benefit of society.

We contribute by shaping a better tomorrow for our communities, by focusing on our inclusive approach, by engaging in non-judgemental dialogues fuelled with empathy, compassion, courage and curiosity, and by adhering to the best standards in every aspect of our lives. I believe that today's challenges require open minded, compassionate, curious, brave, transparent, non-judgmental and emotionally connected leadership.

It looks like the time for coaching to shine has come.

Dr Riza KADILAR
EMCC Global President
Amstelveen, April 2021

Introduction

Succeeding as a Coach offers both new and experienced coaches insights from the practices of more than a dozen highly experienced executive coaches with over 100 years of coaching experience between them, all in short, bitesize chapters.

The book is divided into 50 chapters across five sections. The first section offers ideas about how to prepare and plan for sessions, from using mindfulness to insights on tripartite contracting. The section also covers topics less frequently explored in coaching titles such as the chemistry meeting, how to select a coach training provider and also how to set up and market your coaching business.

In the second section the focus is on starting the coaching relationship. This section covers aspects of the coach's mindset such as compassion, forming an attachment and a listening mind, as well as topics such as cross-cultural work, effective goal setting, how to refer clients experiencing mental health issues and how to manage personal disclosures.

The third section focuses on the core of a coaching session with core communication skills such as active listening, powerful questions, reflections and summaries, as well as exploring the use of psychometrics and eco-coaching.

The fourth section focuses on ending the coaching session, such as how to manage time across the session, how to give and receive high-quality feedback, how to manage notes and how to manage GDPR, as well as how to effectively close a session.

The final section examines post-session issues from supervision to reflection, as well as developing wisdom as a coach, how to go about developing your own personal coaching philosophy and how to build a coaching culture in your team or organisation.

The short nature of the chapters hopefully provides the essential ingredients to enable most coaches to add ideas to their existing practice through the 50 coaching hacks included in the book.

Prof Jonathan Passmore

About the Editor

Professor Jonathan Passmore

Jonathan is a chartered psychologist, executive coach, coaching supervisor, author and professor of coaching. He has written widely with more than 30 books and 100-plus scientific articles and book chapters. He was listed in the top eight global coaches in the Thinkers 50 Marshall Goldsmith list, in the top 30 Global Coaching Gurus, was the director of the Henley Centre for Coaching, Henley Business School, University of Reading, UK and is now Senior VP Coaching at the global coach firm CoachHub.

About the Contributors

Dr Tim Anstiss

Tim is a medical doctor who works as a consultant focusing on health and well-being improvement, a visiting tutor at Henley Business School and writes on coaching, change and motivational interviewing.

Michel Beale

Michael is a Marshall Goldsmith Stakeholder Coach, a visiting tutor at Henley Business School and an expert in supporting coaches in business development.

Julia Carden

Julia is a fellow of the CIPD, member of the BPS, an accredited EMCC coach, and a visiting tutor at Henley Business School.

Prof David Clutterbuck

David is visiting professor of the Henley Business School, a prolific author and co-founder of the EMCC.

Karen Foy

Karen is an ICF credentialled coach and Coach Mentor, EMCC coach supervisor and is a member of Coaching Faculty at Henley Business School.

Prof Alison Hardingham

Alison is a professor at the Henley Business School, author of *The Coach's Coach*, and an executive coach and psychotherapist.

Dr Elizabeth Houldsworth

Liz is a researcher, author and member of Coaching Faculty at Henley Business School.

Karen Izod

Karen is a visiting tutor at the Henley Centre for Coaching, a change consultant and author of several books including *Resource-ful Consulting* and *Mind-ful Consulting*.

Ann James
Ann is a visiting tutor on the Henley PCEC programme, a Henley-trained and ICF-accredited coach and supervisor.

Nancy Kline
Nancy is a visiting tutor at the Henley Centre for Coaching, Henley Business School, and author of *Time to Think* and *More Time to Think*.

Jenny King
Jenny is a chartered psychologist and independent consultant and coach.

Sarah Leach
Sarah is a member of Coaching Faculty at Henley Business School, author, and an ICF PCC accredited professional coach.

Dr Ruth E Price
Ruth is a chartered psychologist, certified coach, and a member of Coaching Faculty at Henley Business School.

Prof. David Pendleton
David is professor of leadership at Henley Business School, and author of several texts on leadership including *Leadership: All you need to know.*

Philippe Rosinski
Philippe is a consultant, visiting tutor at the Henley Business School, and author of several books including *Coaching across Cultures* and *Global Coaching.*

Aboodi Shabi
Aboodi is a regular speaker at coaching conferences, a contributor to Coaching at Work, an ICF PCC credentialled coach, and a member of Coaching Faculty at Henley Business School.

Tracy Sinclair
Tracy is a Professional Certified Coach (PCC), Coaching Supervisor, Mentor Coach and ICF Assessor, a member of Coaching Faculty at Henley Business School, and author of *Becoming a Coach.*

Anna-Marie Watson
Anna-Marie is a trained outdoor instructor, ultra-sports athlete, and an accredited ICF coach who specialises in outdoors coaching.

John Whittington
John is visiting tutor at Henley Business School, founder of CoachingConstellations.com, and the author of *Systemic Coaching & Constellations.*

Glossary, abbreviations and terms

AC   Association for Coaching

APA   American Psychological Association

APECS   Association of Professional Executive Coaches and Supervisors

BPS   British Psychological Society

EMCC   European Mentoring and Coaching Council

ICF   International Coaching Federation

Client   We use the word client in this book to refer to the person or people working with the coach, as opposed to the person (organisation) paying

Sponsor   We use the word sponsor to refer to the person (usually a representative of an organisation) who has asked for the coaching or is paying

SECTION 1: PRE-COACHING

Chapter 1:
How can I set up a successful coaching practice?

Michael Beale

Introduction

While most coach training programmes teach you how to coach, few tell you how you can make a living from the new skills you have acquired. Maybe this is because most coaching schools are run by trainers, not successful coaches. We believe that being able to set up and run a successful coaching practice is as much about the skills of running a business as it is about the skill of coaching. This chapter explains the nuts of bolts of how to go about setting up your practice and how to win your first few clients.

Starting the journey

When I speak to coaches who have set up and established successful coaching practices, they invariably make two observations. First, it was much harder than they originally thought; and second, they're really glad they had the discipline and perseverance to continue.

The closest metaphor I've found to starting a coaching business is Joseph Campbell's metaphor of the hero's journey in his book, *The Hero with a Thousand Faces* (Campbell, 2017). Overcoming the challenges in developing your own businesses will not only help you develop yourselves, but it will help you establish a genuine connection with the opportunities and challenges faced by your clients. They've become heroes and heroines who can also inspire you in your own journey.

To successfully set up a coaching business, you need to:

1. Get the clients you want.

2. Work *on* the business as well as *in* the business.

3. Develop and look after yourself – remember, when you start your business, you're the most important resource the business has.

Setting up a coaching business

When you've thought through the challenges and questions that follow, you'll be in a significantly stronger position to set up and run your business. You'll have set yourself up for success.

Legal and statutory considerations

There are multiple company structures, and these vary across the world. Commonly used structures for coaching businesses include setting up as a:

- **sole trader** – where you are responsible for the business's debts

- **partnership** – where you share any debts with the other partners

- **limited company** – where the company's debts are separate, but you're responsible for more detailed reporting and have additional responsibilities.

However, before you decide which of these to pursue, speak to coaches in the country in which you operate. Different legal structures face different tax obligations, they require different insurance arrangements, and their employment relationships may also vary. Considering which suits you and your business partners is a key initial decision. Your accountant is a good place to start when considering what the right option is for you; alternatively, most governments provide information online (see, for example, in the UK: www.gov.uk/set-up-business).

Key questions about your business

When thinking about your business and its structure, a number of questions are worth considering:

1. **Purpose:** The clearer you are about your purpose, the more motivated you will be. Why do you want to set up a coaching practice? This may be obvious but writing it down can help to clarify your thoughts. Is it about income, lifestyle, helping others, working with your partner? Is it for you? Your clients? Your community? Your country? Humanity?

2. **Vision:** The clearer you are about your vision, the clearer you'll be about the direction you need to take to get there. When the business is really successful what will you see? What will you hear about it from others? How will you feel? How will you know when you have been 'successful'?

3. **Plan:** A plan helps you to be effective and efficient. What are the steps on the route to achieving your vision? What resources do you already have and what do you still need? How will you prioritise between competing demands on your time and resources? What is your plan if something goes wrong? What is your exit strategy from the business?

4. **Activity:** Activity creates the motion that moves you in the direction of your goal. What do you need to do on a daily, weekly and monthly basis to get there?

5. **Review:** How are you going to review your progress? How are you going to make sure that you learn from events? Many regions in the UK provide business mentoring. Is one available in your region?

As a rule of thumb, 80% of your time should be spent on the first item in this list i.e. activity that moves you towards your customer and client vision; 20% of your time should be spent on the other elements. This is much easier when you've thought through all the other elements before you start trading.

What else?

It's best to come up with initial top-level answers to these questions, and then to look in detail at four key areas of your business:

1. Customers and clients.

2. Finance.

3. Processes.

4. People – capability and learning.

Each area deserves its own plan and metrics.

Customers and clients

Attracting customers and clients is a key area of the business. Basically, without quality, paying clients, you don't have a sustainable business. So the sooner you plan and start implementing your plan to attract and maintain clients, the better. You can explore more about this topic in the next chapter, *How can I market my coaching business?*

Finance

When starting a business, the key measure is normally cash flow. Cash flow is critical; not being able to cover your monthly expenses leads to bankruptcy. When starting a business, it's worthwhile to have enough cash and reserves to last at least twelve months, to enable the business to become cash positive.

It's also worth reverse engineering all the elements that impact cash flow, so you understand what levers you have. For example, the price you charge clients can have a significant positive impact on cash flow; clients going bankrupt or not paying can have a negative impact on cash flow.

Similarly, many successful coaches keep their day job, or run a part-time practice as they scale up their income. Having a mixed portfolio can be a very useful way to start.

It's also good practice to keep expenses as low as possible, until you have fully tested what works. Avoid spending large sums on an expensive website, brand, business card, letter head and so on. This gives the impression of activity but can be a distraction from winning the first five clients. Our advice would be to make your client income fund these one by one. Clients do not buy coaches just because of their website or business card. Of course, a nice business card or easy-to-find website, with some case studies and resources, is helpful to build credibility, but more important than any of these is the power of speaking to potential clients directly.

Processes

The processes you develop will impact your business. These include habits and routines, as well as the formal processes: from how you manage personal data (see more about this in the chapter: *How can coaches and leaders better manage personal data?*) to how you contract with your clients (see more about this in the chapter: *How should I contract for a coaching assignment?*).

In J D Meier's book, *Getting Results the Agile Way* (Meier, 2010), he suggests there are three keys to improve the results you get. These are time, energy and technique. The best way to get results from your use of these three resources is to plan out your week in advance and build in key routines. Choose three key outcomes for every day, and three priorities for each week. Add in a short review to the end of each day, and at the end of every week.

In addition, there may be times during the day when you have both discipline and creativity. There are also times when you may be best focusing on routine tasks, and other times when it would be best not to work at all as you're more likely to make mistakes or are simply less productive. Making the right choices about how you use your resources can enhance your productivity.

As a minimum, you'll need an accounting system (this could be as simple as a spreadsheet), a customer relationship management (CRM) system to keep track of customers (again, a spreadsheet or database can meet this need for small companies), and a means of keeping up to date with legal and statutory requirements.

People – capability and learning

When you start a business, you're its key resource. Think carefully about your core skills and capabilities. What are they? How can you maximise your use of them? What other skills or resources do you need to put in place, now or in the future? Depending on the size of your business and your skills, these may include a bookkeeper, an administrator or a marketeer.

Conclusion

Many coaches find establishing a successful and profitable coaching business a lot more time consuming and challenging than they originally thought. However, they are almost all delighted that they persevered. They find that their coaching practice gives them financial and geographical freedom together with a truly satisfying and long-lasting career.

Following the suggestions in this chapter will enable you to overcome these challenges much more easily. We recommend that you start planning your business as early as possible, and give yourself enough time to test, refine and implement your plan.

References

Campbell, J (2017) *The Hero with a Thousand Faces*. Novato, CA: New World Library.

Meier, J D (2010) *Getting Results the Agile Way*. Innovation Kirkland, WA: Playhouse LLC

Chapter 2:
How can I market my coaching business?

Michael Beale

Introduction

Do you want more clients? Better paying clients? In an increasingly competitive environment with more trained coaches vying for business, securing the right kind of clients can be a challenge even for the best trained coach. Many coaches now hold an accredited coaching qualification, a university diploma or master's degree in coaching. But one key commercial differentiator between all these trained coaches is their understanding of their market and ability to communicate their services through branding and marketing to their chosen audience. If you don't have a marketing and branding plan, this chapter can help you reflect on why and how to create one.

Why is marketing important?

Coaching is a business that has a relatively low cost of entry, is personally rewarding and – when successful – leads to time, financial and geographic freedom. It's also highly competitive, with an estimated four out of five coaching businesses not succeeding. Therefore, it's important that you maximise your chances of success.

One of the ways in which you can significantly improve your likelihood of success is by developing your approach to branding and marketing to attract clients. It's worth remembering that without clients you don't:

- generate revenue
- learn how to create value
- generate your own case studies and testimonials.

> ## Table 2.1: Key steps in branding and marketing
>
> The key steps in branding and marketing are:
> 1. market research
> 2. brand position
> 3. establish your target market and client proposition
> 4. establish your approach to pricing
> 5. reach out to and/or attract clients
> 6. establish and implement a sales process
> 7. review and improve what you do.

Branding and marketing your coaching business

A warning: It's always better to start aligning the seven elements above before you start your business. Once you've established your business, it's often expensive both in time and money to significantly change them.

An interesting challenge when carrying out the following steps is that one answer will often impact your approach to the others. It's therefore recommended that you come up with some initial approaches to each, and then repeat the process in more depth.

Additionally, markets are always evolving, and from time to time you need to check that what you first came up with still produces the results you want.

Step 1: Market research

A simple and effective way to research your market is to use Marshall Goldsmith's feedforward approach (Goldsmith, 2008).

Ideally, reach out initially to six or so prospective clients who genuinely interest you, then ask them your own version of this question:

> *"I'm developing a coaching business where I'm looking to give my clients particularly good value. If you were me and were starting a coaching business, what are the top two areas you would focus on to attract and keep quality clients?"*

Whatever they say, genuinely thank them for their input and write their response down. The idea is to end up with a list of 12 ideas for consideration, which will help you with what comes next.

Step 2: Brand position

There are a number of brand positions for a coaching business, for example:

- commodity coach (like an Uber taxi)
- specialist coach (by market niche or geography)
- connector coach (you don't coach, instead you introduce others)
- brand name coach (clients buy the brand, not you)

Each has advantages and disadvantages. For example, a commodity coach (at least in theory) has a wide market to exploit but will need to be exceptionally price-competitive. A brand-name coach will need time to build their brand and will only have a restricted market, but they will have the advantage that they can charge what they want.

It's important to decide where you are as you start your business, and where you want to end up.

Step 3: Establish your target market and client proposition

You need to be clear about who your ideal clients are and how they'll benefit.

Curiously, as Seth Godin (2018) notes, it can be useful to start with the smallest viable market (not the largest). A small, well-targeted group can both significantly benefit from the service you offer and be able to pay you.

Step 4: Establish your approach to pricing

You can be free, or you can charge by time, value or brand. Given that coaches charge between zero and £250,000 for a programme, for a single client, you have a lot of options. You can find out more about pricing in the chapter: *How much should I charge my clients?*

Step 5: Reaching out to and/or attracting clients ('prospecting')

There are four basic approaches to prospecting for new clients:

1. Hunting (traditional selling) – where you directly reach out to prospective clients.
2. Attraction (social media, books, speaking) – where you develop content and attract followers who will buy from you when the need arises.

3. Nurturing – developing relationships with a few key buyers and influencers in your target market so, as in point 2, they will buy from you when you stimulate a need or a need arises.

4. Paying – where you pay commission or a fee to third parties who bring you prospects or business.

Each approach can work well. In my experience, most successful coaches develop a significant expertise in at least one of these areas.

Step 6: Establishing and implementing a sales process

Your sales process is the steps you go through from prospecting, through agreeing a contract to setting up a programme in such a way that the client is likely to receive the most value from it. The actual process will depend on your target market and whether you're targeting individuals or influencers who are buying for organisations.

Table 2.2 The sales process

A typical sales process would be:
- Prospect
- Build rapport and trust
- Qualify
- Discovery phase (detail of what the client wants, how to get there etc)
- Proposal
- Handle objections
- Agree contract and set up to succeed
- Implementation
- Develop referrals and case studies.

It's important that you demonstrate the right behaviours for each stage, and that you can successfully guide the client through all the stages.

Step 7: Reviewing and improving what you do

I suggest three different sets of measurement criteria to ensure you continually get better at what you do:

1. Your input – when you start a business, it's your input and effort that gets you started.

2. Key metrics e.g. the number and value of clients, together with metrics that represent aspects that are important to your clients. These enable you to track the results your clients get.

3. Feedback and feedforward from your clients and other stakeholders – this will enable you to keep track of the relationship you have with your clients.

All three will help you continually improve what you do, and lead to an ongoing successful coaching business.

Conclusion

All businesses need to market themselves, and due to the low cost of entry it is more important for a coaching practice than for many other businesses.

In preparing to market your business, develop a clear approach to these seven areas:

1. Market research

2. Brand position

3. Client proposition

4. Pricing

5. Attracting clients

6. Establish a marketing review process

7. Continually improve how you market.

If you approach each in the right way, you will develop a thriving and profitable coaching practice.

References

Goldsmith, M (2008) *What Got You Here Won't Get You There*. London: Profile Books

Godin, S (2018) *This is Marketing*. London: Penguin Business

Weiss, A (2008) *Value-Based Fees*. San Francisco, CA: Pfeiffer

Meier, J D (2010) *Getting Results the Agile Way*. Kirkland, WA: Innovation Playhouse LLC

Chapter 3: How can I look after myself when starting a new business?

Michael Beale

Introduction

Starting a coaching business involves the legal requirements of setting up a business, clarifying its purpose and vision, building a website and brand identity, developing financial systems such as invoicing and payment tracking, establishing organisational policies such as managing personal data, and developing a marketing plan. In the excitement of addressing these external challenges, it's easy to forget that you are by far the most important resource your business has. As such, one of the key factors of success is how you look after yourself.

Looking after yourself

In their book *Magic in Practice* (2015), Garner Thomson and Khalid Khan observe that some people can engage fully with the day-to-day challenges of work and life while somehow remaining impervious to stress and its effects. This is particularly useful and relevant when starting a new business.

They outline six psychological modulators that make a difference:

1. Social support and connectedness.
2. A sense of control.
3. Predictability.
4. Positive expectancy.
5. Meaning and purpose.
6. Releasing stress.

We've developed each of these in relation to setting up a successful coaching practice.

Social support and connectedness

It's important that you develop social support that is in addition to, and separate from, your clients. A personal board of directors can help in this process. This might include someone who can act to coach you, one or more mentors with skills in different areas and, of course, a supervisor.

A sense of control

When you start a business, there are many things – potential clients, the economy and competitors – that are not directly under your control. It's therefore important you take charge of those elements that are under your control, namely where you invest your time and energy, and the techniques you use.

As we noted in Chapter 1, Meier (2010) suggests that time, energy and the techniques you use are three keys to improving the results you get. This involves planning each day's and week's priorities, reviewing the outcomes achieved, and making the best use of the different times of each day for different tasks, reflecting your energy levels.

Predictability

We all work best with our own individual balance between high predictability and low predictability. If you choose clients and assignments that are totally predictable it can become boring. If you choose clients and assignments that are totally unpredictable it can become very stressful. The art is to choose the portfolio balance that suits you best.

Positive expectancy

Believe your glass is always half full. Try to recognise the positive outcomes in events, in your clients and in yourself. You can strengthen your expectancy by taking time out to reflect on what you've already achieved and what you're already grateful for. Admitting and addressing the right problems is also key to your success. It's useful to allocate some time to consider challenges that might occur and how you can minimise their impact. While it may appear counterintuitive, thinking through the first actions you would take if the worst happened to your business can be useful. You can then totally focus on what you need to do to make your business work. Develop a mindset that you can make the very best out of the good things that happen, while having the resilience to make the best out of anything that doesn't go to plan.

Meaning and purpose

In addition to a vision of where you want your business to be in several years, it's worth being clear about what running your business does for you personally. It's also likely to increase your motivation if you have a purpose for your business that's bigger than you.

Releasing stress

It's worth developing hobbies that you can include as part of your new business development. These can help dissipate the stress of running your own business and may provide the social element, which can sometimes be missing if you are setting up a business by yourself.

It's also worth developing some form of exercise routine. As most small businesses work from home, it can be tempting to sit and work all day without a break. However, you could schedule a lunchtime walk into your day. This provides a useful break, encourages movement and provides a period to reflect on what you have achieved, and what your priorities are for the remaining part of the day.

In addition, activities such as cycling, running, swimming and aerobics provide physical elements to help balance the sedentary nature of sitting at a desk for hours. Yoga, meditation or mindfulness can provide similar exercise for the mind. Whatever options you choose, do consider the social aspects that can come from groups, such as an exercise class, a book group or an evening language class.

The quantity and quality of the food we eat and the quality of sleep we get also have a significant impact on our performance. While coffee and chocolate are stimulants, you may be better off in the long run eating a banana and drinking water with a slice of lemon.

Finally, while it's tempting to think about using the evening for email or social media, the screen and associated cognitive engagement will, for many people, negatively affect the ability to sleep. Instead, try to avoid screen time for two hours before you settle down to sleep; instead read a book or, better still, exercise or meditate.

Practical application

A good way to apply the above is to score yourself between nought and five for each of these six psychological modulators.

Table 3.1 Six psychological modulators.

Factor	Score (0-5)
Social support and connectedness	
Sense of control	
Predictability	
Positive expectancy	
Meaning and purpose	
Releasing stress	

As you reflect on your scores, consider which would be most useful for you to get better at. Develop a plan to improve those that are worth improving, then commit to reviewing your scores on a daily, weekly or monthly basis.

Conclusion

Dalio (2017) suggests that you become stronger by solving problems. He argues that if you set big goals, you will encounter big challenges. By looking after yourself on the journey, you are best placed to meet and overcome the challenges you will encounter on your journey.

As you move forward, keep in mind this five-step process to solve problems and achieve the results that you want:

1. Have clear goals.
2. Identify and don't tolerate problems.
3. Diagnose problems to get to their root cause.
4. Design a plan.
5. Push through to completion.

If you look after yourself, you can develop the internal resources to solve problems, increase the chances of your business succeeding and increase your own personal success and fulfilment.

References

Dalio, R (2017) *Principles*. London: Simon and Schuster

Meier, J D (2010) *Getting Results the Agile Way*. Washington, WA: Innovation Playhouse LLC

Thomson, G and Khan, K (2015) *Magic in Practice*, (2nd ed). London: Hammersmith Books Limited

Chapter 4:
How should I select a coach training provider?

Jonathan Passmore

Introduction

The coaching market is crowded. There are dozens, possibly hundreds, of companies offering training. But how can you select the right course for you? How can you avoid courses that are excellent at selling, but neglect the classroom experience? How do you know which are quality assured and independently accredited? This chapter aims to demystify the whole process of choosing a coaching course by exploring a range of criteria you can use when facing choices. Of course, there is not one simple range of criteria; different courses will suit different individuals' needs, but being clear about what is most important to you will help you make the best choice.

Why are you seeking training?

When thinking about coach training, and which provider to choose, the best place to start is with yourself: what do you want to achieve from undertaking a coaching qualification? For most people, it is that they want to train to become a professional coach and set up their own business.

Of course, that is not the only possible reason. It may be because they are being trained to be an internal coach, or because they are commissioning training for others in their organisation and want to review the options available. Each of these individuals will have slightly different needs. However, a small number of people are interested in coaching either as a journey of personal self-discovery, or because they are interested in the science of coaching (and, of course, these reasons are not mutually exclusive). Whatever is true for you, the starting point is to be clear about your own reasons.

The next question is to consider what qualifications you have already. If you have a master's degree, for example, then gaining a further post-graduate degree might not be a motivating factor for you. Instead, you may simply be looking for the coaching skills themselves, or for professional accreditation.

The final self-reflection question to guide you in choosing a course regards what type of work you anticipate undertaking after your course. A health coach, an executive coach, and a careers coach may all benefit from slightly different training pathways.

What criteria should you look for in a provider?

The starting point when looking for training is to undertake a search for providers based in your area or in locations that you are prepared to travel to. A search engine is a good starting point for this, but also check out the professional coaching body websites for accredited providers. Links to the Association for Coaching (AC), the European Mentoring and Coaching Council (EMCC) and International Coaching Federation (ICF) are provided at the end of this chapter. Finally, local coach networks may provide a useful source of options.

It may initially be helpful to produce a longlist of potential providers (perhaps 5–8 of them) and to evaluate each one based on a set of criteria. Table 4.1 sets out 12 key questions to help you reflect and to define your criteria. These questions can help in narrowing down your list of potential providers to a shortlist of just two or three.

Table 4.1: 12 key questions to ask

1. What's the evidence for the claims made in the PR material?
2. Is there a balance between theory and practice?
3. What models are taught on the programme?
4. What's the student/tutor ratio?
5. How many hours are delivered face to face?
6. What academic qualification does the course offer?
7. Which professional bodies is the course accredited by?
8. What resources are included in the course fees?
9. What coaching experience do the trainers have?
10. What types of people attend this programme in an average cohort?
11. What other benefits do the fees include?
12. How much does it cost?

Marketing materials

It is worth reviewing the marketing materials of training providers, but you should also try to get behind the claims. Always be cautious about providers who promise the Earth. Ask yourself: what's the evidence? Do they have any research to support the claims they make? I once came across a coaching provider whose claim was that they offered 'the best coaching programme in the world'. Fortunately for them, the claim was made in a country where trading standards rules were lax. I imagine they had not reviewed all the coaching courses in the world against a set of pre-defined criteria and conducted detailed analysis to support their number-one ranking. More likely they just said it. Look for schools whose claims are supported by evidence.

Theory or practice?

Most courses are heavily weighted towards practice. For most participants this is good – most are looking to learn to be a coach, rather than to undertake a comprehensive exploration of a body of knowledge. But even for those who want to become professional coaches, it is important that tutors possess a sound understanding of psychological theory and coaching research. What references do they make to recent research studies they use on the programme (examples might include those listed in Table 4.2). Look for schools that make use of research to inform their teaching.

Table 4.2: Examples of recent coaching research

- Athanasopoulou, A and Dopson, S (2019) A systematic review of executive coaching outcomes: Is it the journey or the destination that matters the most? Leadership Quarterly, 29 (1), 70–88
- Bozer, G and Jones, R J (2018) Understanding the factors that determine workplace coaching effectiveness: A systematic literature review. European Journal of Work and Organizational Psychology, 27 (3), 342–61
- Grover, S. and Furnham, A. (2016) Coaching as a Developmental Intervention in Organisations: A Systematic Review of Its Effectiveness and the Mechanisms Underlying It. Plos One. https://doi.org/10.1371/journal.pone.0159137
- Jones, R J and Bozer, G (2018) Advances in the psychology of workplace coaching. Applied Psychology: An International Review, 67 (4), 768–72
- Jones, R J, Woods, S A and Guillaume, Y R F (2016) The effectiveness of workplace coaching: A meta-analysis of learning and performance outcomes from coaching. Journal of Occupational and Organizational Psychology, 89 (2), 249–77
- Theeboom, T, Beersma, B and van Vianen, A E (2014) Does coaching work? A meta-analysis on the effects of coaching on individual level outcomes in an organizational context. The Journal of Positive Psychology, 9 (1), 1–18

Eclectic approach

A few schools still teach only one coaching approach. However, having a single model in your coaching, no matter how good it may be, is like having a single tool in your toolkit. As the law of the instrument (or 'Maslow's hammer') states: 'If the only tool you have is a hammer, everything looks like a nail'. Of course, every client is different, and the best-trained coaches combine a range of different approaches into what is commonly described as an eclectic or integrated approach. Look for schools that teach three or four different models.

Student/tutor ratio

In cultivating the skills of coaching, learners should be observed and given feedback throughout the course. This is hard to do if the student/tutor ratio is 30:1, or even 15:1. The lower the ratio, the more opportunity you have to be observed, to receive feedback and to build a relationship with the tutor and your colleagues. However, you don't want a class so very small that there is no one to learn from apart from the tutor. There is real value in observing others as well as reflecting on your own performance. Look for ratios of between 6:1 and 10:1.

Face-to-face delivery

There has been a growth of video and online providers. Yet experience suggests that it is very hard to learn coaching solely by watching pre-recorded material or reading notes. A blended learning approach provides the best of all worlds: learners can engage with tutors live in the room, review key learning though a virtual learning environment and also extend their knowledge by reading books and research papers. Look for a provider who offers learning in the classroom supported by more in-depth learning online.

Qualification and accreditation

There is a diverse range of coaching qualifications. Some provide their own certificates. In such cases, ask if the course is recognised by any professional body or university. As a general rule, its best to stay clear of those only providing a certificate of attendance, unless it's a one-day taster course.

Most providers' programmes are accredited by one or more professional coaching bodies, such as AC, EMCC or ICF. Find out which ones have given accreditation to the programme you are considering, and what this accreditation offers you. Think about which professional body, or bodies, will best equip you to achieve your goals. Look for courses that provide you with both a qualification and a professional body accreditation.

Resources

It's worth finding out what resources are available to support your studies. Some providers will make available a printed set of their teaching slides. Others may provide a workbook, while others (mainly universities) will provide access to books, journals and other learning resources through their library – which is likely to be both a physical space and an online resource. It's important to ask what added value these supporting resources offer you in addition to the core course materials. Look for courses that provide comprehensive materials to help you deepen your knowledge.

Experience

Coaching experience makes a big difference. Ask your tutors about this. What experience do they have in leadership positions? What experience do they have of coaching the types of people you want to coach? What's their reputation in the field? Get the names of the tutors who will be delivering your course. Undertake an internet search to find out more about them and their experience. Look for a provider with tutors whose experience and skills are most relevant to your aspirations.

Participants

The other participants can also make a difference to your learning experience. Ask about the typical profile of the participants. Are they mainly fifty-year-old company directors or twenty-one-year-old graduates? Are they mostly women or men? What advantages would this group of fellow participants bring you? Would they be fun to engage with? What knowledge would they bring to the classroom? How would they enhance your network? Look to identify a course that attracts people whose experience and network will add to your overall learning experience.

Benefits and costs

The last, but by no means least, important area to explore is cost. How much does the programme cost? Is it within your budget? Price is not always a sign of quality. At the same time, rarely are good things cheap. The most important consideration is value: what value will the provider's brand add to your personal brand? What additional benefits – such as professional body membership, access to other events and access to additional resources – are provided? You may not value these highly at the start of the course, but try to imagine what they will add over the long term when comparing costs and expected outcomes. Look to select a course that is within your budget, but provides the maximum added value in terms of brand, additional resources and depth of study.

Table 4.3: 10 look-outs

1. Look for schools whose claims are supported by evidence.
2. Look for schools that make use of research to inform their teaching.
3. Look for schools that teach three or four different models.
4. Look for student/tutor ratios of between 6:1 and 10:1.
5. Look for a provider who offers classroom learning and more in-depth learning online.
6. Look for courses that provide a qualification and a professional body accreditation.
7. Look for courses that provide comprehensive materials to help deepen your knowledge.
8. Look for a provider with tutors whose experience and skills are relevant to your aspirations.
9. Look for a course with people whose profiles and networks add to the learning experience.
10. Look to select a course that is within your budget, but provides maximum added value in terms of brand, additional resources and depth of study.

Making your final decision

Once you have a shortlist, you can further narrow it down by approaching the providers, and asking if you can observe a sample teaching session or visit the training spaces they use. Additionally, you may want to talk in more detail to individual tutors to get a sense of their experience, and how you will fit.

Conclusion

While you will have your own set of questions and your own criteria for selecting a course, as a consumer of coaching education you can afford to be quite demanding. You should be clear with yourself about what you want to get out of the programme. This can help you clarify the criteria against which you are making your selection. In the end, aim to select the highest-quality provider that offers you the most benefits within your budget.

References

Athanasopoulou, A and Dopson, S (2019) A systematic review of executive coaching outcomes: Is it the journey or the destination that matters the most? *Leadership Quarterly*, 29 (1), 70–88

Bozer, G and Jones, R J (2018) Understanding the factors that determine workplace coaching effectiveness: A systematic literature review. *European Journal of Work and Organizational Psychology*, 27 (3), 342–61

Grover, S. & Furnham, A. (2016) Coaching as a Developmental Intervention in Organisations: A Systematic Review of Its Effectiveness and the Mechanisms Underlying It. *Plos One*. https://doi. org/10.1371/journal.pone.0159137

Jones, R J and Bozer, G (2018) Advances in the psychology of workplace coaching. *Applied Psychology: An International Review*, 67 (4), 768–72

Jones, R J, Woods, S A and Guillaume, Y R F (2016) The effectiveness of workplace coaching: A meta-analysis of learning and performance outcomes from coaching. *Journal of Occupational and Organizational Psychology*, 89 (2), 249–77

Theeboom, T, Beersma, B and van Vianen, A E (2014) Does coaching work? A meta-analysis on the effects of coaching on individual level outcomes in an organizational context. *The Journal of Positive Psychology*, 9 (1), 1–18

Professional membership websites

Association of Professional Executive Coaching and Supervision: https://www.apecs.org

Association for Coaching: www.associationforcoaching.com/

British Psychological Society - Coaching Division: https://www.bps.org.uk/member-microsites/special-group-coaching-psychology

European Mentoring and Coaching Council: www.emccouncil.org/

International Coaching Federation: https://coachfederation.org/

Chapter 5:
How can therapists become business coaches?

Alison Hardingham

Introduction

Many therapists are interested in becoming coaches. They see the parallels between what they do and what coaches do. Therapists marvel at how much more coaches can charge, and envy the status and freedom that such higher rates could bring them. As the old joke goes: 'What's the difference between coaches and therapists? About £200 an hour.'

It is not just about money though. Therapists see an opportunity to develop their career in a direction that not only plays to many of their existing strengths, but is also still about helping people, about working one-to-one, and which holds the promise of being less emotionally taxing than therapy. Many of them extend their professional lives to include coaching. They find it energising to work with some high-functioning executive clients while still working as therapists with patients who need, even if only temporarily, more time and support.

There are also good reasons why the coaching profession would welcome therapists who have added to their training and expertise the coaching skill set. There is a real and costly growth in mental health issues in society generally. One in four adults will experience a mental disorder each year (Golding & Diaz, 2019). As awareness of mental health grows too, coaches who are also therapeutically trained find that they are well-placed to respond to organisations that are concerned about some of their most high-functioning executives. There are also coaching clients who choose to benefit from a therapeutic approach at times, yet would be reluctant to incur what many still perceive as the stigma of formal therapy.

This chapter provides practical advice on how therapists can become coaches, and on the particular developmental challenges they may have to address. It also identifies the strengths that the therapeutic background and inclination generally provides.

Your motivation

There are many different motivations for becoming a therapist. Some, but not all, are also appropriate for coaching. So, one thing that you need to do is examine anew what your motivations are. Beyond helping, what is it that you find so satisfying in your professional relationship with clients? Which clients do you particularly enjoy working with? And which contexts? What does your work represent to you?

If you are going to move into coaching, you will probably need to find contact with high achievers stimulating. Many of them will be heads of their organisations, and many will hope with your help to become even more confident and capable.

Also, since many of your coaching clients will be working in business, and much of your work will be helping them to build more effective working relationships, you will find it helpful if you are interested in, and excited by, that world. You will have the opportunity to play a small part in helping the wheels of commerce turn more smoothly. If big business leaves you cold, you may need to think again about executive coaching.

Of course, you might like to consider working only for organisations that have a purpose, which does interest and excite you. For example, many successful executive coaches work exclusively for the not-for-profit sector.

A third area you will benefit from thinking about is the activities you most enjoy in your professional life. Some of these will be less evident in coaching. For example, you will not generally be required to care for or look after your clients, beyond an underlying and clearly demonstrated compassion and trustworthiness. But you will be required to match your clients' sometimes fast pace and high energy, as well as encourage reflection. Your expertise will be offered from an equal position; you will not have the authority of a diagnosis or the respect accorded to someone who 'knows best' (Vaughan-Smith, 2007).

You also need to become aware of all the diverse ways in which coaches can provide services to their clients. Clients will not typically attend your consulting room. You may have to travel to meet them; you may find yourself in a variety of offices and even coffee bars and hotel lobbies. You may be required to coach by Zoom or phone; this kind of virtual working is commonplace in coaching. You may be contacted by email in between sessions.

The 'real' client

This next point is connected with your motivation, although it is also a skill set that can be learned.

In coaching, the person who pays the bill (which as we have seen is substantial) has a clear right and responsibility to dictate the terms under which the coaching will be carried out. How comfortable will you be negotiating with the representatives of the employing organisation, building those relationships in a way that supports your coaching work? When there are conflicts of interest (on confidentiality, on scope of the work, for example), will you be able and willing to enter into discussions that clarify your position, protect the interests of the person you will be coaching, and also satisfy that most important of stake-holders, the client's organisation?

Transferrable skill

Now we come to one of the main reasons why you can have confidence in your abilities as a coach. Your therapeutic background has already provided you with a core competence in coaching. Indeed, in many forms of therapy it is difficult to discern any difference between what the therapist is doing and what a coach would do. This similarity is noted in the description of Emily doing the 'homework' set by her psychiatrist in Alastair Campbell's semi-autobiographical novel, *All in the Mind* (Campbell, 2008). You have been trained to listen, and probably have a natural aptitude for it; you summarise accurately; you notice the language your client uses, their metaphors, the words they repeat; you bring a focused attention to all aspects of your client's presence. You show empathy, and indeed have expertise in the whole relationship-building process, for you know how vital it is to the therapeutic endeavour. You can challenge without becoming confrontational; you know when to offer support and how to stay detached. You are used to exercising professional judgement while staying open to the complexity and unpredictability of another human being.

You have probably spent years in therapy yourself, and so your self-awareness is likely to be high. You can use your own responses to guide you in your work. You may be less likely than many coaches who have not had the benefits of your training to become caught up in a destructive dynamic with your client.

You will understand the importance of supervision and know how to use it. You will be ethically aware, and in all likelihood be acquainted with your own biases and stereotypes. You will have some skills in managing these and ensuring they don't compromise your work.

All these things, and more, are consequences of your therapeutic background, and all will be strengths in winning and doing coaching work.

In addition, you may already have a specific skill set on which you can draw in coaching. Many of the tools of coaching have come from therapy. Cognitive behavioural therapy, for example, can be revised as cognitive behavioural coaching; brief solution-focused therapy as solution-focused coaching; and psychodynamic, Gestalt, and person-centred approaches have also generated rich seams of coaching expertise (Passmore, 2021; Cox *et al*, 2011). You do not have to deny your existing skill set, but rather adapt it to meet the challenge of your new clientele and context. You will be a richer, deeper coach as a result.

Conclusion

Business coaching, as we have seen, is not for every therapist. It is a distinctive practice, with its own demands and pressures. You clearly need to engage in a process of reflection along the lines of the questions posed in this chapter, and possibly have an experience of coaching for yourself. If you are still convinced that this is a direction you want to move in, then you can move forward, confident in the knowledge that for many therapists it has proved a valuable and sensible extension of their expertise.

References

Campbell, A (2008) *All in the Mind*. London: Hutchinson.

Cox, E, Bachkirova, T and Clutterbuck, D (eds) (2010) *The Complete Handbook of Coaching*. London: SAGE.

Golding, E and Diaz, P (2019) *Mental Wealth: an essential guide to workplace mental health and wellbeing*. New York: MorganJames.

Passmore, J (2021). *The Coaches Handbook: The complete practitioner guide for professional coaches*. Abingdon: Routledge.

Vaughan Smith, J (2007) *Therapist into Coach*. Maidenhead: OUP.

Chapter 6:
How can I use mindfulness to prepare for each session?

Jonathan Passmore

Introduction

Mindfulness has become a popular concept, with growing evidence about its positive benefits for health and performance both generally (Parsons *et al*, 2016) and at work (Passmore, 2019). At its heart, mindfulness involves a state of non-judgemental presence that can enhance any relationship.

In coaching, mindfulness can help both the coach and the client. There are four main benefits in coaching. Coaches can benefit from being more present and working non-judgementally with each client, undertaking a mindfulness meditation or body scan before each session. By acting with mindfulness during their coaching sessions they can be more aware of themself, their client and their environment. Thirdly, mindfulness brings the benefit of helping the coach manage the stress of working one-to-one with clients. Finally, clients too can benefit from mindfulness, the coach can enable the client to share details of the concept and encourage clients maybe through a homework activity to introduce the practice to their daily routine and reflect on its impact.

What is mindfulness?

The term mindfulness is derived from a translation of the Buddhist term *sati*. Sati combines aspects of awareness, attention and remembering, which are conducted with non-judgement, acceptance, kindness and friendliness to oneself and others.

A number of writers have offered definitions of mindfulness over the 2,500 years of its history. In the 21st century, one of the best-known writers on the subject, John Kabat-Zinn, suggests it is a way of paying attention on purpose in the present moment and non-judgementally:

> *Mindfulness is simply a practical way to be more in touch with the fullness of your being through a systematic process of self-observation, self-inquiry and mindful action. There is nothing cold, analytical or unfeeling about it. The overall tenor of mindfulness practice is gentle, appreciative, and nurturing.*

(Kabat-Zinn, 1991: 13)

What are the benefits?

Over the past three decades, research has begun to reveal the benefits of using mindfulness, and these findings have coincided with a growth in the number of published papers exploring both the science and application of the practice. These academic papers suggest that mindfulness meditation contributes to physical and psychological well-being.

Research has shown that mindfulness has benefits that can be applied across a range of scenarios, from mental health and depression to cancer care, heart disease, pain management and reduction in blood pressure. However, possibly less well known are the cognitive benefits that mindfulness practice seems to confer. Research in this area has shown positive effects on general brain performance, including working memory and cognitive attention, specifically: stability (Smallwood & Schooler, 2015), control (Ocasio, 2011) and efficiency (Neubauer & Fink, 2009).

While most early studies have focused on health care, there are a small and growing number of organisational studies. A critical review of this literature by Good *et al* (2016) and Passmore (2019) has revealed that in addition to the health literature, there is a growing literature about workplace mindfulness. These reviews reveal that the largest single area for organisational application remains well-being, but possibly more interesting is the evidence of the spread of mindfulness through organisations from tech giants such as Google, to more traditional organisations, such as the US Army.

How can mindfulness help in coaching?

It has been argued that mindfulness practice delivered through coaching can offer similar benefits to those gained through training, with mindfulness benefiting both the coach and the client. These benefits may arise in four ways: preparing for coaching, maintaining focus in coaching, managing emotions in coaching and teaching clients mindfulness (see Table 6.1).

Table 6.1: Potential benefits of mindfulness in coaching

- helping the coach to prepare for coaching
- helping maintain focus in a session
- helping the coach manage emotional responses
- teaching the technique to clients

(Passmore & Marianetti, 2007)

One challenge most individuals face, not just coaches, is the challenge of the wandering mind. The coach may be moving from one client's premises to another, or from one Zoom call to the next. In these situations, the wandering mind can result in the mind gravitating back to the previous call, or drifting off to consider the next issue. Mindfulness offers a practical way of putting such demands aside and focusing on the here and now.

Mindfulness can also be useful for the coach in helping maintaining focus in an individual session. With coaching sessions of an hour to two, the wandering mind can draw the coach away from full attention in the session.

A third challenge faced by the coach is the relationship, specifically the emotions created from client engagement. These may be attraction or revulsion towards the client, or their behaviour, leading to risks of collusion or damage to the coach–client alliance. Mindfulness provides a resource enabling more awareness of these natural human emotional responses, and from these the ability to better manage them appropriately.

Finally, as with training, the coach may wish to share with the client some of the science of mindfulness or tools to use by themselves. This may come about if clients ask or are curious about mindfulness.

Mindfulness for coaches

There are a wide number of mindfulness techniques and practices that coaches can use (Passmore & Amit, 2017). Three of these are summarised in Table 6.2. These practices can be used at work, sitting at a desk, or applied to other everyday situations to help improve focus and workplace performance.

Table 6.2: Three practices for mindfulness	
Identifying environmental distractions	This exercise is a suggestion on how we can become clearer about what is disturbing our attention and how this impacts on our level of concentration, and our productivity/personal relationships.
STOP	This exercise is a suggestion to help us become more proactive by stopping and choosing mindfully how we want to continue with our day. It's something we can do that does not require much time.
Being the observer	Rumination is a common human trait. It can happen especially when the client is upset about something that has happened or a conversation that went wrong. When the client over-identifies with their thinking, they can become anxious and stressed. The exercise is aimed to help clients acknowledge that they are not their thoughts, and their thoughts are not the truth.

One practice that can be particularly useful as a coach is the 'lobby body scan' (see Table 6.3). This can be completed in fewer than five minutes and used while waiting for a meeting or in your office waiting for colleagues to join you on a conference call.

Table 6.3: The lobby body scan

Step 1	Find somewhere comfortable to sit, and create a posture of erectness and dignity.
Step 2	Start to observe the breath – the in-breath and the out-breath. Follow this for eight or nine cycles of slowly breathing in and out; filling the lungs and slowing exhaling, before starting the cycle again.
Step 3	Start to be aware of what's going on in the body: any pains, tensions or sensations. Be open to these sensations, not judging them or seeking to explain them, but simply being aware of their existence.
Step 4	Direct the breath to any areas of tension or stress, and allow the breath to hold, caress and surround any uncomfortable sensations, allowing these sensations to dissolve or subside. Taking each place of tension or stress in turn, and directing eight or nine breathes into each place, or as many as feels appropriate, until each subdues.
Step 5	Start to broaden the breath and become aware of the sensation of the whole body, sitting erect and dignified in the chair.
Step 6	Take that closing sensation into the next part of the day.

Conclusion

The growing science base for mindfulness has confirmed its value as a practice that can support well-being, but its impact on cognitive performance also makes it a useful tool for coaches, as well as managers in organisations. Practice such as a four-minute body scan or STOP can easily be introduced to daily routines to improve performance.

References

Good, D, Lyddy, C, Glomb, T, Bono, J, Brown, K, Duffy, M, Baer, R, Brewer, J and Lazer, D (2016) Contemplating mindfulness at work: An integrative review. *Journal of Management* 42 (1) 114–42.

Kabat-Zinn, J (1991) *Full Catastrophe Living: Using the Wisdom of Your Body and Mind to Face Stress, Pain, and Illness*. New York: Delta Trade Paperbacks.

Neubauer, A C and Fink, A (2009) Intelligence and neural efficiency. *Neuroscience and Biobehavioral Reviews* 33 1004–23.

Ocasio, W (2011) Attention to attention. *Organization Science*, 22, 1286–96.

Parsons, C, Crane, C, Parsons, L, Fjorback, LO and Kuygen, W (2016) Home practice in mindfulness based cognitive therapy and mindfulness-based stress reduction: A Systematic literature review and meta-analysis of participant mindfulness practice. *Behaviour Research and Therapy* 95 29-41. DOI: 10.1016/j.brat.2017.05.004.

Passmore, J and Amit, S (2017) *Mindfulness at Work: The Practice and Science of Mindfulness for Leaders, Coaches and Facilitators*. New York: Nova Science.

Passmore, J., and Marianetti, O. (2007). The role of mindfulness in coaching. *The Coaching Psychologist*. 3(3), 131-138.

Passmore, J (2019) Mindfulness at organisations: A critical literature review (Part 1). *Industrial and Commercial Training* 51 (2) 104-113 https://doi.org/10.1108/ICT-07-2018-0063.

Smallwood, J and Schooler, J W (2015) The science of mind wandering: Empirically navigating the stream of consciousness. *Annual Review of Psychology* 66 487–518.

Chapter 7:
How can I help my client prepare for coaching?

Ann James

Introduction

There's no training for clients: no certificate, no manual, no accreditation that prepares them for the work they are about to do. As coaches, it's deeply ingrained in our learning that the most effective coaching happens when the relationship is equal and collaborative. In this guide, we offer some thoughts on how you can help your clients to get the most from their coaching by helping them to prepare.

How does a 'prepared client' make a difference?

Recall for a moment your first ever experience of working with a coach – of being the client in the relationship. You may have felt excited, eager to get on with the progress that you wanted to make, or maybe a little anxious, unsure about what to expect from your coach, the process and yourself. Now, as an experienced coach, it's worth reflecting on what you wish you'd known then so that you can support your clients as they prepare for your work together.

How the client arrives at and engages with coaching will have an impact on the 'feel' of the session, the working relationship, the coaching outcomes and, ultimately, the return on expectation enjoyed by the individual or sponsoring organisation. But how can we help our clients achieve that state of readiness?

What can help clients to arrive ready?

As a client, especially someone new to it, preparing to embark on a programme of coaching can be a bit of a blank page. There's no rulebook. Experienced coaches are likely to each have their own way of supporting the client's preparation. As a minimum, there will be a broad agreement around the work to be done (often referred to as the 'contract'), and possibly some exchanges of emails or conversation before the work begins. Once the work is under way, it might flow from one session to the next with little onus upon the client to consciously and deliberately prepare for each session.

So how do we introduce some structure and direction while respecting the client's ownership of the agenda?

Let's look at preparation as it might play out at different stages in the work.

Preparation for the whole relationship

Before the coaching kicks off, you will probably have conversations with your future client, with the person commissioning the work (if the work is within an organisation) and possibly with the individual's sponsor or line manager. These might formally come together in a multiparty contact meeting (Foy, 2021).

The first stage of preparation happens here. Your client's voice might be just one of several articulating goals, aspirations and agendas for the coaching – and theirs is not necessarily the loudest.

The clarity and quality of contracting at this stage sets the scene for the client's entire experience: it establishes the scope of the work, activates the mandate to get on with it, defines boundaries and makes explicit the protocols for how everyone will behave.

In Table 7.1 we have included important areas you might discuss.

Table 7.1: Discussion points

- The client's overarching goals and hopes for the coaching: what do they want to be different afterwards?
- Your commitment to their success: what do they need from you in order to get the most from the coaching?
- Managing bumps in the road: how will you both deal with any frustrations or difficulties that crop up in your relationship?
- Managing other stakeholders: what would be the red-flag issues that require reference back to the sponsor or manager?
- Topics that are in or out of bounds: what if the conversation takes an unexpected turn?
- Keeping it safe and ethically sound: does your client understand what you mean by confidentiality and its limitations?

Preparation for individual sessions

We tend to think of each session as the specific segment of time in the diary (typically up to a couple of hours) that we spend in a scheduled conversation with our client. It can be useful to reframe this to include some time for preparation on the part of the client, as well as the coach.

A coaching conversation will rarely, if ever, pick up from where it was left. Things will have moved on, so encourage your client to think about their starting point for the approaching session. But remember, it's not their job to meet any need you may have to be filled in on what has happened since you last met.

In Table 7.2 we offer some questions you could offer clients in advance of each session.

Table 7.2: Client pre-coaching questions

- What are your reflections on your progress so far?
- What challenges have you encountered?
- What do you want to bring to our next conversation?
- Why is this a priority for you?
- How do you feel about this topic?
- What would be a good outcome of the session?
- What could distract you from engaging fully with the next session?
- How will you manage any distraction?

Preparation for ending

Coming to the end of a coaching relationship is a significant event for many clients. We all have different responses to endings and this could be a challenging transition for your client. You have been a source of consistent support, empathy and attention for them, attributes that they might not readily have access to elsewhere. Talk to them about what their future needs might be and identify ways in which they can access resources and support from elsewhere. In Table 7.3 we have set out some useful questions for clients to consider as they move forward beyond the coaching relationship.

Table 7.3: Useful questions

- Who could be a trusted sounding board or 'buddy' to give you ongoing support?
- What do you need in order to stay motivated and hold yourself to account?
- Where could you find other resources to support you?
- How will you know you're making progress?

The legacy of preparation

A decision to engage with coaching is a significant commitment of time, energy and financial resources, and often occurs during a period of challenge and uncertainty. By going that extra mile and actively encouraging your clients to prepare well, you will help them extract every bit of value from the time you have together; more than that, they will develop habits that will continue to serve them well long after your work together is done.

Conclusion

In this chapter I have set out ways coaches can help their clients to prepare for a session. Preparation is an essential task in coaching and can help clients get the best value from their session and the wider coaching process.

References

ICF (2019) ICF Core Competencies. Available at: https://coachfederation.org/core-competencies (Accessed 28 October 2020).

Foy, K. (2021). Contracting in coaching, pp344-354. In J. Passmore, (ed.) *The Coaches Handbook*. Abingdon: Routledge.

Chapter 8:
How much should I charge my clients?

Jonathan Passmore

Introduction

Most people are attracted to coaching to make a difference, as well as to make a living. While most coach training programmes focus on the skills to enable people to make a difference, little is mentioned about the commercial aspects of coaching. How do coaches run a business: marketing, selling, contracting and charging? How much to charge is one of the most frequently asked questions by coaches new to the market. As almost no coaches place details of the prices on their website, knowing what others charge is a tricky call. In this chapter we will review details about what others charge, as well as help you think through what you should charge.

What should I charge for my services?

Most new coaches emerge from coach training having completed 20, 50 or 100 hours of coaching. They may have coached colleagues at work, extended family and members of their professional network. Most of the time this coaching is at pro-bono rates: free.

This might sound a sensible strategy. The new coach wants to practise and get clients to give up their time to be coached as the new coach practises their skills. They are not yet sufficiently skilled and charging feels unethical. But is this the right approach? What else could the new coach do, and how can more experienced coaches have a plan to increase their fees to the right level.

For new coaches, we suggest they begin with the end in mind. By this, we mean the new coach should decide, even before embarking on their coaching development journey, who they hope to coach and what they hope to charge once they are qualified.

Getting started

It may be helpful to think about the development journey as a series of steps. Of course, each individual varies in their pace of development, and development is incremental. But consider the following steps: nought-50, 50-150, 150-500, 500-plus hours.

In the first phase (nought-50 hours) the new coach should aim to practise on people who they never expect to charge and who they feel comfortable testing out new techniques and tools. This prevents the new coach undermining their future business and allows them to experiment. This group could include fellow coaching students, students on other programmes such as an MBA, or the manager of a local charity, who would never have access to coaching if it was not free. Whichever you choose, it's a good idea to make clear you are in training.

In phase two (50-150 hours) you are starting to develop your skills. You might choose at this point to offer your services to one or more bigger charities. You could offer to coach 15-30 managers, giving you experience of coaching different people and lots of coaching hours. Or you could aim to secure clients from your local community. For the charity, this may be a continuation of the pro-bono offer. For the local community, you could offer a special offer, with the rate you plan to charge, maybe £100, discounted for the first six sessions to £50 per hour, and target one specific outlet, for example a local magazine. You could advertise in the magazine and include a code that is a one-off promotion. However, in this phase avoid targeting your wider chosen market. The rate you set now will influence how clients will see you in a year, and may limit your ability to charge the appropriate rate for the sector.

In phase three (approximately 150-500 hours) you can start to think about getting serious. By this stage you probably will have completed your training, and you may have secured a professional accreditation. These badges give you credibility in the eyes of clients. This may be the point that you start to implement your charging plan. However, you may not feel confident to set your fees at the full rate, but if you do decide to set these lower, aim for only 10-15% below your target rate, as increasing prices by 30% or 50% can raise questions from clients.

In the final phase (approximately 500-plus) you should be aiming to move your prices to the full market rate. You might do this over two steps, maybe two consecutive years where on 1 January you increase your rates by five or seven per cent.

But how much should I charge?

The reality is that rates vary widely between £50 to £2,000 per hour. They vary between countries, and usually reflect two factors: the economic strength of the country (ability to pay) and the maturity of coaching in that country (willingness to pay).

They vary between sectors, with some sectors of the economy able and willing to pay more, such as financial and legal services, while others pay less, charities and retail. They also vary between individuals. Between these are government bodies, health and Small and Medium-sized Enterprises (SMEs).

In a large-scale survey of European coaching practice (Passmore *et al*, 2017), we found no evidence to suggest fee rates were related to coach experience, coach training, or use of supervision. The only factor where there was a clear difference was gender, with men charging more than women. One explanation is that rates are connected to the confidence of the coach. As long as you meet the basic criteria required by the company, and you sound credible, it's possible to command higher rates.

As a general guide, average rates in our research in 2017 ranged between 100-200 euros for private coaching and between 200 and 300 euros for corporate coaching. Generally speaking, rates were higher in Northern and Western Europe and lower in Southern and Eastern Europe. The survey data also revealed that about 10% of coaches charging fewer than 50 euros and a small percentage charging more than 1,000 euros an hour.

These wide variations are less helpful when setting your own rate. We thus suggest when thinking about your rate for private work it might help to review the therapy market: what rates do local therapists charge per session? You can use this information as a guide to set your rate for local private work. For corporate work, build relationships through your professional body with people who provide coaching to your chosen sector, ask them what they charge. Remember to speak to five or six people, not just one or two to build a more rounded picture for the relevant sector rate.

Finally, it is also worth understanding if colleagues are charging the same or different rates for face-to-face and online coaching. Clearly, face-to-face coaching is likely to involve travel time. If you need to travel for two hours to meet a client in a large city, your rate needs to reflect the fact that a two-hour coaching session is in effect six hours for a round trip. Or you need to find ways to cluster coaching sessions together on the same day. This is easier when providing coaching in one organisation for middle managers, than it might be for coaching senior executives with busy travel schedules in different organisations.

How can I put up my fees?

One of the golden rules for business owners is to increase prices when demand outstrips your ability to supply. If you are turning down opportunities because you don't have capacity, this is the time to increase your fees.

Many business owners fear they will lose all their clients. While this might encourage a few to consider other options, it is a sign that your business is doing well and the vast majority of your customers will stay with you if you follow a few simple rules.

Rule one is give your clients as much notice as possible, so that they will have time to get used to the change and, if you are a large supplier, they can adjust their budgets. Rule two is provide some context. If you have won an award, achieved a new qualification, written an article or book, share this information with your clients too, although its best not to directly link these achievements specifically to the price increase.

Develop a rate card

Many coaches provide a range of different services; coaching, team coaching/facilitation, training, supervisor, mentoring. It's likely you have different rates for private clients and corporate clients, as well as different rates for these different services. You may have rates for charities, public sector, medium-size businesses and large corporate organisations. Set these out on a rate card, which will help you to be consistent when submitting proposals for new work.

Conclusion

What's important is to see your coaching practice as a business, as well as a way of making a difference. Being highly skilled in coaching is important, but it's not the only skill to develop. Spend time and effort in developing a business plan (which includes your fee rate), for example where and how you will attract clients, and invest as much time in business development as in continuing to enhance your coaching skills.

References

Passmore, J, Brown, H, Csigas, Z et al, (2017) *The State of Play in Coaching & Mentoring: Executive Report*. Henley on Thames: Henley Business School-EMCC. ISBN 978-1-912473-00-7.

Chapter 9:
How much about myself should I disclose in a coaching session?

Jonathan Passmore

Introduction

Coaching is a confidential service, but how much should we keep confidential about ourselves. Ask most therapists and they will caution against self-disclosure. Ask most leaders or mentors and they are likely to promote the benefits of being authentic, genuine and open. What's the right balance in coaching? In this chapter we will consider how and what self-disclosure may be the right balance in coaching.

Why do some coaches keep information back?

During coach training we are frequently reminded that coaching is not therapy. But coaching has drawn extensively from therapy over the past three decades, including drawing on therapeutic models, such as psychotherapy, gestalt, brief solution-focused therapy and cognitive behavioural therapy, and practices such as the importance of contracting (Passmore, 2021). Many of the best-known coaches also have their background in therapy.

It may thus not be surprising that coaches whose background is in therapy are cautious of self-disclosure. This has its origins in the early days of psychotherapy when self-disclosure by the therapist was seen as negative. Freud and other early psychotherapists believed that the therapist should aim to create a blank canvas on which the client could project their thoughts. This enabled the therapist to explore the client's assumptions and projections about themselves and others. A second argument offered by therapists was that by self-disclosure the therapist risks making the session about them, thus potentially derailing the client's reflection on their own issue. In more recent decades this zero tolerance for self-disclosure has started to reduce. While most therapists remain cautious about what and how they reveal information, there is a recognition that authenticity and warmth are also important features, which contribute to the development of the working alliance.

Why should I disclose information?

This perspective contrasts with the experience of most coaches. While, like therapists, they are attracted to coaching because they care about others and are usually comfortable with their own emotions, they approach coaching from a different perspective. Many coaches have backgrounds in consulting, training, mentoring and leading teams where openness and authenticity are valued and encouraged. Most believe that self-disclosure by the coach can be helpful to clients, as the coach should present themselves as fully human. But is this always the case? How should coaches assess the benefits and the potential pitfalls of self-disclosure? When is self-disclosure useful and when might it be harmful to clients?

Self-disclosure can take two different forms. The first of these is deliberate self-disclosure, which itself has two forms: 'planned disclosure' and 'empathetic disclosure'. The planned disclosure may happen, for example, during the pitch or during the initial contracting meeting with the sponsor. Its best to consider what information you want to release. Not all information will create a positive impact – for example, you may have been made redundant or you may have lost a parent recently. You may be a member of a political party or collect bus numbers. These aspects may risk creating a negative effect, as well as having the possibility the client is as passionate as you about, for example, about buses. Other information is more neutral, such as your qualifications, where you went to university, your coaching experience or where you grew up. Although as we will discuss below, too much information can also be unhelpful.

The second form of deliberate self disclosure is empathic disclosure. This is when we express how we might be feeling in response to our client's story. A client might cry, and we may reflect back our own feeling of sadness in response to their story and their display of emotion. The client may express outrage in response to a situation, such as discrimination or sexual harassment, and we may reflect back an empathetic emotional response. Such deliberate responses contribute to building the coach-client relationship.

A second type of self-disclosure is 'unintended self-disclosure'. This may result from a client's direct question: 'Where do you live?' 'Do you have children?' 'Are you married?' or 'Have you ever lost your job?' In these situations, the coach needs to avoid simply answering the question as they would to a close personal friend. Instead they should consider carefully whether and what personal information to disclose. In the moment this can be difficult, and as a result the coach may share information which, on reflection, they consider was inappropriate.

How should I respond?

If a client asks you a personal question, how should you respond? One way is to simply respond from a position of openness and transparency. At work, many of us are open and transparent about our personal relationships, family and interests. You may judge that you want to adopt the same boundaries as you do at work.

However, you might ask yourself: what purpose does this information serve in what is, after all, a different relationship to one where you are working alongside colleagues in the same team? Do I risk shifting the focus of inquiry from the client to me? If the coach has opinions about how people live their lives, such disclosures may damage the relationship. As a result, an alternative approach advocated by some is for the coach to reflect back the question: "I am wondering why this is important to the client". This has the advantage of exploring the client's curiosity and may lead to a useful insight for the client. However, it risks the coach being seen as evasive or defensive.

A third strategy is to answer in the level of detail you feel comfortable. For example, if asked 'where do you live?' instead of giving the street, you may say a city or a county. When this is followed by a question from the coach, relating to the coaching assignment, most clients pick up this is not the place for personal enquiry. Table 9.1 provides an illustration of how the conversation might proceed.

Table 9.1

Client: Where do you live?

Coach: Oh, I live in Hertfordshire. Now, what's your hope for today's session?

Client: I would like to spend some time talking about...

For coaches who work at home online there is the further challenge that comes from giving access to their personal space. Clients may hear children in a different room, see family photos on a bookshelf or make judgements about the size or decor of their house. As a result, you may like to think about use of a greenscreen or virtual background, and ensure external noises are managed.

A third challenge comes when the coach finds themselves spontaneously sharing information or personal experiences. This may result from the emotional empathy mentioned earlier, when the coach feels moved to share their own story as a means to demonstrate empathy. Occasionally this can be helpful for clients to know they are not alone. However, in the majority of cases this unplanned deep self-disclosure undermines the relationship or detracts from the focus on the client. We suggest these deep disclosures are generally avoided. If the coach does choose to offer a deep disclosure, it may be helpful to take that decision to supervision and examine their intent.

Table 9.2: Deep self-disclosure: Useful questions to explore in self-reflection or supervision
■ What is my intention in sharing this information?
■ How will this information be helpful to my client?
■ When will it be most helpful to share this information?
■ In what way should I share this information?
■ What did I learn about myself as I reflect back on my use of self-disclosure in the session?
■ What is valuable to take to supervision from this experience?

The questions in Table 9.2 can help the coach decide what and how to manage the wish to more deeply disclose, by ensuring they place at the heart of every decision the best interests of their client.

Conclusion

In this chapter we have considered the potential positive benefits and risks of self-disclosure. We have looked at different types of self-disclosure and offered a shorthand guide to help coaches make decisions about whether, what and when to share personal information with their clients. While we have urged caution about deep self-disclosure, we believe that being authentic and open are important parts of coaching, and the coach should focus on being a genuine equal relationship with the clients, while recognising the focus of the session is their client, not their own story.

References

Passmore, J. (2021) *The Coaches Handbook. The complete practitioners guide for professional coaches*. Abingdon: Routledge

Chapter 10:
What makes a successful chemistry meeting?

Jonathan Passmore

Introduction

Chemistry sessions are much talked about in coaching. But what are they? Why have them? And how should one manage them? In this chapter we explore the mystery of the chemistry or discovery session and offer some advice on how coaches can prepare for the session, how they can manage the session to best help their clients and how to use the session as a springboard into the main work of the coaching assignment.

What is a chemistry meeting?

The chemistry meeting, or sometimes called a discovery session, is a pre-coaching, agenda-planning meeting between the coach and client to explore how they might work together. I prefer the use of the latter name, discovery meeting, which signals to the client this is not just about whether we get on together, but helps the client to get a better understand of what they can expect from the coaching relationship.

The meeting might be face to face, or online and tend to be shorted than a typical session which might last 60-90 minutes. A typical discovery session is 30 to 60 minutes, based on an agenda set in advance.

Why hold a chemistry meeting?

The chemistry meeting has three main advantages: It allows clients to make a judgement as to whether they believe they can work with the coach. It allows the coach to make a similar judgment as to whether they feel they can work with the client. It provides a space for a formal contracting conversation. We suggest that for the benefit of both parties there is a no-fault divorce clause in any coaching agreement, where the coach can explain their role, their expectations of the client, logistics, contact arrangements, reporting arrangements and confidentiality. It can also extend to the inclusion of the level of challenge, complaints process and a no-fault-divorce clause, with both parties (at any time) being able to end the relationship, without this being seen as a criticism of the other party.

The final reason is a more technical one. The session allows the coach to make a judgement as to whether they believe they are well placed to help the client. In most situations, a trained coach is well placed to help clients with a wide range of presenting issues. However, on some occasions it becomes clear during a chemistry meeting that the presenting issue is one where a referral to another helping professional may be required – for example, in the case where the client is suffering from a clinical condition and may benefit from a visit to the doctor or therapy before they enter a coaching relationship. Secondly, the coach may make the judgement that the topic is one where a specialist coach, or one with different experience to them, may be better placed to help. Identifying such issues and referring clients is a signal of coach maturity, as opposed to a sign of weakness.

How to manage the meeting?

Before the session it always helpful to think through what you want to achieve from the meeting. Invite your client to prepare by thinking about what their hopes are for the assignment, so this question does not come as a surprise.

Some clients want to use the time to tell their story. In which case, listen without judgement. Try to avoid the temptations to step into coaching mode. Instead, give the client the opportunity to ask you questions about how you might work together or about your previous experience of coaching. We have set out some useful aspects to cover in Table 10.1.

Table 10.1: What should the coach cover?
What is coaching?
What will the coach and what won't the coach do?
Share two or three stories of successful coaching outcomes.
Describe in plain language your coaching philosophy.
Set out how your suggested way of working – session length, frequency, where you will meet, confidentiality and its limits.
Set out briefly your qualifications and professional body accreditation, that you work within a professional code of conduct of ethics, and how clients can complain.

It can also be helpful to ask questions about what the client wants and doesn't want for the coaching. Sometimes clients have a better understanding of what they don't want than what they do want.

While some clients will have had other coaches in the past, for others this might be their first experience. They may be nervous and uncertain about what to expect from you or from coaching. For most clients, the decision to move forward with a coach rests not on how qualified or experienced they are, but on how they feel about them. Coaching is personal and intimate, and the relationship matters. It's thus important during this session to demonstrate how you can create a safe space by demonstrating warmth, humour and a lightness of touch.

What works in the chemistry session?

In some instances, clients are meeting two or three potential clients and thus the chemistry session is a combination of a test drive and a beauty parade. From our experience, what seems to work best is when the coach is relaxed, avoids pushing (or selling), but is focused on understanding the client's needs. They are warm, engaging and try to create a positive, memorable experience, where the client feels heard, understood and believes that there is the potential for change as a result of the coaching relationship. Above all, coaches who look as if they enjoy their work, are relaxed whether they win this assignment or not, and signal they like the client and believe they can work with them, are most likely to end up winning the assignment. But remember, in these beauty parades this is not a judgment of how good a coach you are, just whether you were the right fit for that client at that time. So, whether you are selected or not, don't worry, move on.

Conclusion

The chemistry or discovery meeting is a useful opportunity for both the coach and the client to meet without a focus on the topic, and to check if they can work together. By being warm, relaxed and listening to the client's story, as well as setting out the basics of the coaching relationship, the chemistry session can be a valuable platform from which to start the coaching assignment, ensuring a shared understanding of the focus and the ways of working together.

Chapter 11: Where should I meet my clients?

Jonathan Passmore

Introduction

While most coaches operate from a small home office, others might work as associates for larger coaching companies, while a few might work for larger consulting companies. But whichever it may be, these locations rarely offer an ideal location for client coaching. Home may be too personal, while even large corporate offices present their own challenges. Many coaches ask where is the best place to meet. In this chapter we consider the issue and explore a number of alternatives, each of these may suit different clients, different budget and different privacy needs.

Coaching assignments

Most coaching assignments vary in type and length. Some may be a one-off session; others may be a formal six- or 12-month assignment. The focus of the session may vary between general discussions about improving leadership to providing space for an executive to reflect on a merger or acquisition, or an individual client talking about a general conversation about well-being to a personal discussion about sexual harassment at work. Each client, type of session, and the different session content require the coach to consider both the privacy needs of their client, as well as the image they want to project.

Where shall I meet clients?

Where coaching session should take place is a frequent topic of conversation for both new and well-established coaches. There is widespread agreement that the ideal conditions for the coaching relationship to develop involve meeting in a safe, comfortable space, removed from distractions of everyday life and work. As Nancy Kline notes, we should be seeking to create a physical environment which communicates to our client: 'you matter' (Kline, 1999, p84).

Environmental psychological research also highlights the importance of the physical spaces on our thoughts, feelings and behaviour. This includes considering the type of seating, the spacing of seats, desks and tables, wall colour and images on our walls. Each of these aspects set the tone for the type of conversations that will unfold.

In an ideal world, every coach could have their own private coaching room comfortably furnished reflecting the type of coaching work they undertake and with everything that might be need for session. However, it rarely works in that way.

Coaching from home

Working from a designated space in your own home can be convenient, and can allow you more control over seating and room décor, but as with online coaching, you are inviting your client into your space. As the client enters, they may notice family pictures in your entrance hall, or your style of living: children's toys scattered in the hall or your fanatical attention to order and cleanliness.

One option is to have a separate entrance, or create a separate space. If that's not possible, consider in advance what you wish to disclose to your clients and how you will handle questions such as 'How old are your children?', or 'Where do your children go to school?', which may be triggered by the personal items on display. You will also need to think about any risks and hazards. These may be anything from a loose paving slab on your front step, to cables or a wobbly chair. You will need to ensure you have appropriate insurance should an accident happen on your premises.

Clients will need to know how to find you, where to park, and how to enter the building. If you are running multiple sessions, you will need to think about whether you need to create a waiting area and how to manage family noise, from the dog barking to children and TV noise in another room.

Client workplace

Coaching frequently takes place in the workplace of the client. This has some obvious attractions. It is cheap and removes many of the worries of meeting on your premises. It is also hugely convenient for your client and is usually the option they choose, if asked.

There are some practical concerns that need to be managed. Some clients can find it difficult to switch off from the demands of the office. Emails may be pinging in the background; colleagues may interrupt to talk about a developing issues and phones may ring. What are the rules you need to agree about how such disturbances are managed?

It can also be more difficult to keep a meeting confidential from colleagues, particularly if you are coaching others in the organisation. As a result, the client may find it more difficult than if the session took place in at a neutral space. It's worth talking through these issues with the client during the chemistry meeting or contracting stage, so they can make the right choice and you can agree how they wish to deal with potential interruptions.

Public meeting room

A third option is a public meeting room or space. This may be a room you book in shared offices or in a community facility. This option provides the private space, privacy and time away from distractions that other options suffer. It has the advantage of being anonymous, which for some types of coaching work can be a significant advantage. However, it comes with a cost in terms of a booking fee and also inconvenience in travel time for you and your client.

Coaching out of doors

This is an option that is growing in popularity. Your clients benefit from fresh air and open space, plus gain the bonus of a bit of exercise. It costs nothing. You can walk and coach just about anywhere, and the external environment may provide stimuli for the conversation and new insights.

However, there are a number of downsides; unless you live close to a beautiful location, there is travel time and a cost for you and the client. You will need to plan your route, and think about parking, health and safety and weather. These factors – and a reluctance from some clients, who might see this as not a serious coaching session – are important elements to bear in mind, and mean, in my practice, this is a nice variation rather than a standard feature for most coaching.

Coffee shop or hotel lobby

The coffee shop in an urban area can be ideal, as it's close. However, the volume of comings and goings, and the sitting layout with others being close by, can make these areas less desirable for a private conversation. A second option for a semi-public space is a hotel lobby. This provides more comfortable seating and, often, coffee. Many hotels have made a feature of creating spaces that suit semi-private meetings. Care, though, needs to be taken in selecting the right hotel area, avoiding large TV screens or ones where the seating is located close to check-in and thus the distraction of multiple comings and goings of every guest and their luggage. A final consideration is the nature of the topic and the individual client. If the session or topic is likely to be emotionally charged or the client places a high priority on privacy, it may be important to meet somewhere more private, such as a members' club like the Institute of Directors.

Digital meeting room

A final option, which is growing in popularity, is a digital meeting room. We will explore the challenges and benefits of coaching online in Chapter 37, but this can offer a useful space for sessions. Online sessions are low cost, private and have zero travel costs for both you and your client. The potential downsides include connectivity and the loss of many aspects of face-to-face communication. Connectivity can be an issue – in some parts of the world certain platforms are not available. Broadband speeds vary and can result in the loss of video, delays or frozen screens. These, combined with a loss of much of the body language information we use in face-to-face coaching, can result in a reduction in intimacy and the need for the coach to work harder to build the relationship.

Conclusion

Exploring these issues up front during the contracting or chemistry session is important so that clients understand and consider what is the best option for them. Getting the right location provides the platform from which the coaching work can start. If the client feels comfortable, the coaching relationship has a platform from which to build.

References

Kline, N. (1999). *Time to think*. London: Cassell.

Chapter 12:
How should I contract for a coaching assignment?

Jonathan Passmore

Introduction

Contracts are an essential agreement in the work we do with clients; both the organisational clients who pay for most business coaching, as well as individual clients (clients). Many coaches either do not use assignment contracts at all or rely on a verbal agreement with the client or the organisation. This leads to the potential risk of misunderstanding what coaching is, how we work, what the client or sponsor can expect and what we can expect from them. More importantly, it also fails to provide a means for clients to hold their coach to account: what ethical standards can the client expect, and how should they complain about their coach if they are unhappy? In this chapter we will examine the role of assignment contracts and how coaches can contract with both individuals and organisational clients.

What is a coaching contract?

A contract is an agreement setting out the terms for coaching. In coaching, we might have a number of contracts working simultaneously. In most work, there is a formal agreement between the coach (or their organisation) and the commissioning organisation. This is the legal agreement for the purchase of the service. The organisation may also issue a purchase order (PO) for the work. In addition, the coach is likely to discuss and explicitly agree some key points about the coaching with both the sponsor (the person who has commissioned the coaching) and the client. Each of these agreements may contain various clauses about the coaching and its expected outcomes. However, alongside these, all parties are also following many unspoken agreements about how to interact and work together.

Contracts as frames

One way of viewing this series of contracts is as a series of frames. These frames reflect the expectations the different stakeholders bring to coaching. Some may be written, some spoken, while others are unspoken and may even be outside of the conscious awareness of the parties involved, while still influencing how they interact.

These frames operate at multiple levels. Let's look at each of the frames in turn through the lens of the eight contract frames model (see Figure 12.1).

Frame one (the innermost frame) covers the interactions, moment to moment, in the coaching session. As a social process the coach and client are continually re-contracting, renegotiating the coaching contract. This contract relates to what is happening between them and what each party considers desirable, acceptable and unacceptable behaviours. As an example, the level of challenge that can be brought into a coaching conversation will grow in proportion to the level of trust that exists between the two parties. While this is not explicitly covered in a written contract, each party will have a view about the level of trust and will signal these views through their behaviour. This will influence future moment-to-moment behaviours. If either party breaks this contract, a breach may lead to a rupture of the coaching relationship.

Figure 12.1: Eight contract frames model

A short contracting conversation at the start of each session allows both parties to have a shared understanding of the agenda for the session. For example, does the client want to build on what was discussed last time or deal with a pressing issue that arose yesterday? It can also be helpful for the coach to briefly refer to the key terms of the contract and check nothing has changed for their client. This contracting conversation may take 60 seconds, but provides a useful platform for each session.

Frames three and four are more likely to be written. Frame three covers the agreement between the coach and client, while frame four refers to the agreement with the organisation (if they are funding the assignment).

Many organisations now have formal coaching contracts that the coach is required to sign. If they do not, the coach should offer a written agreement, setting out the terms for the assignment. We suggest in finalising both, a tripartite meeting between coach, client and sponsor will help ensure there is clarity and transparency about the reasons for, and focus of, the coaching assignment. This also provides a platform for a review meeting between all parties at the end of the assignment.

We suggest that these contracts are mediated through a series of other unspoken contracts, or ways of working. These contracts influence how the coach and client interact. All clients working for an organisation (and this is true of coaches, too) operate within an organisational culture. How does this organisation make sense of and respond to customers, colleagues, its regulatory environment and its competitive environment? These are unwritten rules, reflected in 'the way things are done around here' (Deal & Kennedy, 1988). The organisation is also likely to operate within a specific sector, a national culture and within a historical context. These unspoken contracts influence such issues as what people in the organisation wear, how they greet each other and what they can and cannot say to each other – for example, do they wear a tie, a T-shirt or a sword? Do they shake hands, bow or give high-fives? Do they say 'annus horribilis' or 'f***ing awful' to describe a bad year for the business?

Who should I contract with for a coaching assignment?

We advocate tripartite contracting. This is arranging a formal meeting before coaching starts with both the sponsor and the coach. The coach's role in this meeting is more as a facilitator; to set the boundaries for the meeting and for the coaching assignment, encourage both parties to speak about their aims for the assignment, agree a shared set of topics or a general focus and secure agreement for a review meeting at the end of the assignment. As part of this conversation, it is helpful to ensure there is clarity about confidentiality – for example, whether the sponsor is expecting a full, written report at the end of each session, or accepts the coach will keep content confidential (except where there is a risk of serious harm or serious illegality).

The tripartite contracting removes the risk that both sponsor and client want different outcomes from the coaching process, or hold different views about the situation or the performance of the client.

In addition to the commissioning meeting, we would advocate a mid-point review meeting with both parties, assuming the contract is for more than four sessions. This provides the opportunity for the sponsor to feedback to both coach and individual client (employee) their perceptions on progress and to jointly review the agreed coaching agenda. Finally, an end-of-coaching review is also useful as a means of formally closing the assignment and evaluating the impact.

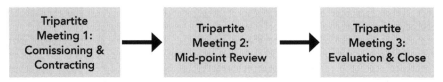

Figure 12.2: The three stages of tripartite contracting

Most larger organisations are experienced purchasers of coaching and many have bespoke contracts for coaching. However, if the contract is a general consulting agreement, we believe there is value in a written agreement setting out the terms for the coaching work, including the number of sessions, length of the sessions, contract value, payment terms and means of redress in cases of dissatisfaction.

Table 12.1: What should be included in a coaching assignment contract?

Elements of a coach–client agreement
- Description of coaching.
- Roles of the coach and client.
- A short description of the coach's way of working.
- Logistics – how, when and where to meet/connect.
- Process for review/taking stock.
- How to end the relationship – including referral arrangements/no-fault divorce clause.
- Statement on confidentiality and its limitations (for example serious illegality and risk of harm).
- Statement on supervision.
- Payment terms (if the client is paying).
- Focus of the coaching – high-level goal or focus.
- Coach's professional membership(s) and ethical code.
- How to complain about the coach.

PROMISE model

Karen Foy (2021) has proposed the PROMISE model as a framework to guide the assignment contracting conversation (see Table 12.2). This framework can be used for either one-to-one contracting or as a guide in a tripartite conversation.

Table 12.2: Promises in the coaching relationship	
Purpose	What brought the person to coaching? What is the work that needs to be done? Often people present with a long-standing issue or concern, but something will have triggered them to take action and seek coaching now. How do they feel coaching will help them?
Relationship	How will you build a partnership for the work to be done? Has the person had coaching before? If so, what worked well and not so well; if not, what do they need to know about you and you about them to build a trusting and effective partnership?
Outcome	What needs to be different at the end of the coaching relationship; how will success be defined? This needs to be highly specific and measurable
Margins	What are the margins or boundaries you are working within? What is up for discussion and what is not? This is particularly important if this work is being sponsored and paid for by a third party. Is there clarity about the boundaries between coaching and other interventions?
In case	This is your opportunity to explore how you will deal, in partnership, with emerging issues or dilemmas. A discussion more easily held in the abstract in advance rather than an embarrassed bargaining discussion when you hit a roadblock. This element of the conversation might start with a 'what will we do if...'
Strategy	What strategy will you agree for the relationship. This should cover logistics such as: when, where and how often you will get together and for how long; cost; cancellations; review process; and any reporting requirements, payment terms and cancellation policies.
Expectations	In order to avoid entering unknowingly into obligations and commitments, we need to have a discussion where we can surface some of our own and our client's expectations in the coaching relationship.
Safety	How can we create a safe working relationship where the client feels supported by their coach and thinking partner to express themselves fully? Confidentiality will be key but where are the parameters? What does the person need to build trust and intimacy? Have you considered the duty of care to your client and others? In short, how you intend to honour their information and well-being?

(Foy, 2021)

Conclusion

Contracting is an essential but often neglected aspect of coaching work. Get it wrong and the coach assignment may start off on the wrong foot. Getting it right by involving all the key parties, and ensuring transparency and clarity, will ensure all parties can work together to provide a bedrock for the subsequent coaching sessions over the coming four, six or 12 months of working together.

References

Deal, T E & Kennedy, A A (1988) *Corporate Cultures: The Rites and Rituals of Corporate Life.* London: Penguin.

Foy, K (2021) Contracting in coaching, pp344-354. In J. Passmore (ed.) *The Coaches' Handbook.* Abingdon: Routledge.

International Coaching Federation (2017) Code of Ethics. Available at: https://coachfederation.org/code-of-ethics (Accessed 19 September 2018).

SECTION 2: STARTING A SESSION

Chapter 13:
How should we start a session?

Jonathan Passmore

Introduction

Contracting for the assignment is an essential component for successful coaching outcomes (see Chapter 12). However, the coach needs to not only formally contract with the sponsor and the individual client for the coaching assignment, contracting needs to happen at each session, and potentially throughout the session, to ensure there is an agreed focus for the work together. In this chapter we will examine the role of session contracts and how coaches can follow a structure to help them ensure each session delivers maximum value to their client.

What is a coaching contract?

In Chapter 12 we reviewed the assignment contract and suggested that tripartite contracting is a useful tool to ensure openness and transparency. We also talked about the multi-layered nature of contracts, and how for an assignment one way to formally contract is the PROMISE model (Foy, 2021).

However, we believe the coach should contract for each session with their client. The contract needs to not only provide a recap of essential elements but provide the platform for the work of the session. In some ways, as we suggested in Chapter 12, it's best to see contracting as a continual process, where the contract is continually being re-made, both consciously and unconsciously. This re-making happens in the session at a formal level when the coach checks in at the mid-point to ensure the client believes the session is on track, and also at the end to close the session (see Chapter 38). But it also happens informally as the coach and client interact through the session, confirming or challenging societal, sectoral and organisational ways of working.

Bennet (2008) suggests that the less formal approach to contracting could lead to higher degrees of trust and, therefore, a more effective relationship. However, there is no empirical evidence to support this assumption. Our view is that a balance is needed between swamping the client with too much information and, on the opposite side, failing to provide the essentials for the coach and client to work together.

Coaches face a number of challenges at the start of a coaching session. For example, when there is small talk at the start of the session, it can be difficult to find the moment to move from small talk to contracting and the session topic. A second common challenge is the client who has two, three or four topics to discuss in the hour. Finally, there is the issue of how to pick-up topics from the tripartite session or previous conversation.

The beginning of a coaching session is thus a case of collecting these threads from these multiple past conversations and agendas, and weaving these together with the client's priorities in the moment to set out a pattern for the client to reflect and select which to move forward with now.

STOKERS

Claire Pedrick (2020) provides a process for coaches to use at the beginning of every coaching session that sets a clear foundation for the work to be done: STOKeRS model. Foy has slighted amended the framework to STOKERS (Foy, 2021).

Claire notes the Stoker is a person who, on the back of a tandem, provides the power, while the 'captain' makes the choice as to where to go. An alternative metaphor, which we prefer, is the person who shovels coal in a steam engine. Again, they provide the power, while the engine driver decides when and where the train goes. The metaphor also works well when we come to the other end of the bookend – closing the relationship (see Chapter 38) on what we call DOUSE.

In both cases, STOKERS and DOUSE offer a framework with possible questions, but this should not be seen as a script. Otherwise, the process becomes mechanical and clients are likley to switch off.

Table 13.1: STOKERS

Subject	'What would you like to focus on?'
	'What is the work you would like to consider today?'
Timing	'Given we have 30 minutes today, what would be a good use of that time?'
	'In the time we have, what part of that would you like to focus on'
Outcome	'What would you like to have at the end of that time?'
	'What would make our time together successful?'
Knowledge	'How would you know you have that outcome?'
	'What would be different at the end of this session?'
Energy	'What makes this important, now?'
Role	'How can we best work together on this?'
	'What would you like from me as your coach?'
Start	'Where would you like to start?'

You will notice confidentiality and ethics are not explicit in this framework. We suggest these are covered in the assignment, but are also worth referencing at the start of each session – reminding the client that these aspects still apply. Such a reference may be in passing and as brief as: '*As before, I will be working under the Global Code of Ethics today and, in terms of confidentiality, I won't discuss or share the contents of the session with others, except if I feel there is a risk of harm to you or others, or in cases of serious criminality where I may have a duty to disclose.*'

Once that element is added, the coach can signal a move to the coaching by asking the subject the question: "So, what would you like to focus on today?" Given that often people have wide-ranging topics or maybe multiple topics, the time element allows the client to consider the most relevant aspects. When there are two or three issues, a coach can prompt a focus by asking how the topics link together – a great way for clients to get thinking from the onset.

The second element to cover is the time available. This often emerges during the discussion of the topic, and enables the client and coach to agree how long they have available and, thus, what can realistically be covered in the time together. As we have noted elsewhere, sessions can vary between 30 minutes and two hours.

The third aspect is the outcome. In the coaching partnership we need a clear objective we are working towards and the client needs to know exactly what success would look like. Checking on outcome and how they will know they have it brings clarity to the conversation. Even if your client says they want to explore a subject and they don't really want action plans at the end you can still help them clarify what they want to know by the end of the session, such as a deeper understanding of a topic, having time to reflect or exploring the pros and cons of different future options.

The fourth element is getting specific with the goal: knowledge. What would be different? How would you know we have been successful in today's discussion?

A key element in this process, and one that has the power to transform the coaching from transactional to transformative, is checking in on the importance or meaning for the client in this topic: why this subject and why now? This can be viewed as the motivation behind the goal. We call this energy (or essence). It's the aspect that provides the urgency for the topic discussion.

The final element in this process is really an opportunity to explore the roles each party will play. What is the individual client expecting from you? What are you expecting from them? How will you work together to achieve the desired outcome? This discussion provides an opportunity to also explore the level of challenge that the client feels comfortable with during the discussion, and gain permission, for example, to call out incongruence, share observations, challenge unhelpful filters, mindsets or beliefs, while appropriately sharing stories and experiences in service of the client moving forward.

The final section of STOKERS is the start. This may seem simple, but this really demonstrates to your client that they are in charge of the process while they are leading the content of this conversation.

In this short conversation, maybe 10 or 15 minutes long, you have started to gather the thread of this conversation. You are holding these threads and, together with your client, you can select which to explore first, returning, maybe at the start of each session to select a different thread and, in so doing, exploring the many pathways and the priorities of your client.

Conclusion

Starting well is an essential ingredient for a successful conversation. Using STOKERS as a framework helps to provide a process to cover off the key ingredients for a successful beginning. The role of the coach is to key these beginning threads, while also holding the end in mind, and helping the client navigate their journey towards their objectives and deeper personal insight.

References

Bennet, J L (2008) Contracting for Success. *The International Journal of Coaching Organisations* 6 (4) 7-14

Foy, K (2021) Contracting in Coaching, pp344-354. In J. Passmore (ed.) *The Coaches Handbook*. Abingdon: Routledge.

Pedrick, C (2020) *Simplifying Coaching*. Maidenhead: McGraw-Hill-Open University Press.

Chapter 14:
How can I use attachment theory to help build better coaching relationships?

Karen Izod

Introduction

'"Curiouser and curiouser!" cried Alice', finding herself in a strange place and wondering what to do next. Being curious is just one response we can make to situations of threat and uncertainty, as we find a balance between our needs for security and reassurance with those for exploration and risk. Attachment theories offer a way of understanding how we typically respond – to people, places, challenges. This chapter will introduce you to patterns of attachment and their significance in the workplace, as well as illuminate some of the dynamics at play between client and coach.

What are attachment patterns?

Attachment theory, developed by John Bowlby (1969), forms part of a range of social theories of human development. Patterns of attachment are understood as arising from the multiple and minute interactions between infant and care giver encountered in our earliest relationships. They build an emotional repertoire that leads to behaviours accompanying us over a lifetime. These patterns of interaction come to the fore as learned and automatic responses when we face threat and anxiety, influencing the extent to which we can make ourselves emotionally available to others and involve others in supporting our emotional needs. Theses feelings of anxiety or fear may be stored in the body, and expressed in physical responses to stress (Fisher, 2017).

Developments in theories of the mind (Fonagy *et al*, 2004) and in the bio-physiological understanding that advances in neuroscience have brought (Damasio, 1994; Porges, 2007) have extended the way in which attachment theories can be brought into an increased range of psycho-social and therapeutic interventions (Flores & Porges, 2017). Their principles can be applied to coaching, particularly where clients need to understand more about how they respond to and behave in challenging situations.

Types of attachment

The experience of being attended to, and having our emotions acknowledged as valid and belonging to us, underpins our ability to reflect, so that we can trust (in varying degrees) our own experiences and develop capacities to be curious and explore. These are evidence of a secure attachment pattern. Where this parental capacity is not available, is intermittent, or beset with anxiety, then we develop less secure, more conflicted mental states, and our modes of being and relating will show signs of ambivalence, fear and dismissiveness. While we will have a strong default pattern of attachment, experience is always shifting and we may move between different patterns of response at any one time.

How are attachment patterns mobilised in the workplace?

Patterns of attachment are easily evoked in workplaces where relationships with authority figures can carry echoes of early parental/carer relationships and may stimulate attachment-based behaviours. Think of being anxious about having to collaborate with a senior figure, challenge a viewpoint or a

Table 14.1: Adult attachment patterns

	Positive view of other	
Positive view of self	**Secure (secure)** Expects others to be available and supportive, and will themselves be available and supportive. Low dependence, low avoidance	**Pre-occupied (anxious ambilvalent)** Is dependent on the acceptance of others and seeks close relations for self-validation. High dependence, low avoidance
	Dismissing (anxious avoidant) Defensively denies the value of close relations and does not expect others to be available for her/him. Low dependence, high avoidance	**Fearful (anxious avoidant)** Is dependent on the acceptance of others but avoids close relations to avoid rejection. High dependence, high avoidance	**Negative view of self**
	Negative view of other	

Adapted from Izod and Whittle, 2014

policy, or face a reorganisation or downsizing. These are all scenarios where a sense of threat or risk to one's well-being can arise; typically, they will trigger a need for security and reassurance, which we can find ourselves responding to in different ways.

Bartholomew and Horowitz (1991) have developed this work to consider how attachment behaviours in adults can include the variables of dependency on, or avoidance of others, together with positive and negative views of self and other.

In adult life we can think of attachment patterns as forming a self-regulation process for how much safety and risk we seek, how much we like routine and the tried and tested, or how much we let ourselves explore and experiment.

How can coaches work with these ideas?

Exploring interaction

From a relational perspective, attachment theories are helpful to the coach as a means of understanding the nuances of interaction:

- How easy/difficult is it for me to turn to friends or colleagues to talk things through or ask for help? What is at stake for me in asking others for support?
- How do I typically respond to others, and what kind of responses do I generally elicit?

Questions such as these help to identify attachment patterns, and yield valuable insights to bring into coaching agendas, where clients are working on issues about their own authority and image, or where they might need to shift their perceptions of others. They are not intended to be either/or questions, but to prompt a range of responses in specific situations and illustrate default positions that might exist. This awareness is valuable in considering how different attachment patterns meet up against each other. Take this scenario:

Ania is putting forward a proposal for a new meeting structure but wants to run it by a colleague before sending it out. She is dismayed when her colleague tells her that she is being overly dependent on her opinion, whereas Ania sees herself as being collaborative.

Helping Ania to explore issues of risk-taking in relation to her attachment pattern (hypothesised somewhere between secure and preoccupied) might then enable her to work out how best to relate to her colleague's opinion of her, and the weight that she also gives to that opinion in relation to her own view of herself.

Exploring place and the working environment

As with people, then so with our environments. Places can bring powerful evocations of early sensory experiences; warmth, cold, security, threat, leading us swiftly into more infantile states of mind, with the feel, smell and sounds of being elsewhere (Izod, 2019). Paying attention to the dynamics of the 'here and now', which is central to working with attachment theories, means thinking about what 'here' is being encountered. Physical and virtual working spaces will have their own particular resonances, particularly the dynamics of being included and excluded, being central or peripheral, that might be being transferred from another time and place, yet having a significant impact on the client's capacities for work.

Working with the emotional resonances raised in attachment work

Working on attachment issues in coaching is reliant on the coach being able to provide a 'secure base' (Bowlby, 1988) from which to explore their experience and help the client avoid rushing into their default positions, so as to develop a broader repertoire of interactions. Paying attention to the contractual basis for the work, the setting and the structure of the sessions all helps to provide an experience of containment both for the client and the coach.

Establishing a relationship that is based on a careful attentiveness and emotional attunement to the client is at the core of working from an attachment perspective. The experience for the client of being listened to, and their experience validated as existing uniquely for them, is fundamental to developing capacities to trust one's own judgement, and with it the capacity to explore new behaviours and to attempt change. Action becomes possible, rather than just thought about.

Exploring the coach–client relationship

Coaching will inevitably entail giving and receiving feedback, and this is where both coach and client can be informed by their attachment patterns (Izod & Whittle, 2014). Learning about one's self, and facing questions as to what has and has not been possible to achieve in a coaching contract is part of the work, and is often accompanied by the dynamics and emotions of ending coaching relationships. The challenge is to find a way to be open to what will surface, without looking for inappropriate reassurances from each other, or apportioning blame.

Conclusion

Working with attachment patterns, both in the client and the coach, supports a dynamic coaching relationship that is concerned with both the content and the process of a coaching session. It is a tool to explore interaction, the nuances of how we find ourselves relating to our working colleagues, and the expectations we have of ourselves and others. With its emphasis on how we regulate ourselves, our thoughts, emotions and beliefs, an attachment perspective particularly supports and encourages a re-examination of how we typically go about interacting with others, and encourages trying out new behaviours in a spirit of experimentation.

References

Bartholomew, K and Horowitz, L (1991) Attachment styles among young adults: a test of a four-category model. *Journal of Personality and Social Psychology* 61 (2) 226–44.

Bowlby, J (1969) *Attachment and Loss Volume 1: Attachment.* London: Hogarth.

Bowlby, J (1988) *A Secure Base: Clinical Applications of Attachment Theory.* London: Routledge.

Damasio, A R (1994) *Descartes' Error.* New York: Grosset-Putnam.

Fisher, J. (2017) Healing the Fragmented Selves of Trauma Survivors: overcoming internal self-alienation. Abingdon: Routledge.

Flores, P J and Porges, S W (2017) Group psychotherapy as a neural exercise: bridging polyvagal theory and attachment theory. *International Journal of Group Psychotherapy* 67 202–22

Fonagy, P, Gergely, G, Jurist, E L and Target, M (2004) *Affect Regulation, Mentalization, and the Development of the Self.* London: Karnac.

Izod, K and Whittle, SR (2014) *Resource-ful Consulting: Working with your Presence and Identity in Consulting to Change* (pp 85–7). London: Karnac.

Izod, K, (2019) 'Here' is where I have a presence. In Ed. Rose, C. *Psychogeography & Psychotherapy: Connecting Pathways.* Monmouth, UK: PCCS Books.

Porges, S W (2007) The polyvagal perspective. *Biological Psychology* 74 (2) 116–43.

Chapter 15:
How can I use compassion in my coaching?

Tim Anstiss

Introduction

Compassion is a motivational state promoted by most world religions, which science now shows confers considerable health, well-being and behavioural benefits on those who cultivate and experience it (Anstiss *et al*, 2020). More than an emotion, compassion has its origins in the mammalian care-giving system. Compassion-focused coaching helps clients to cultivate compassionate brain processes, which can help to counteract the unwanted effects of overactive threat and drive systems. These can have negative impacts on their performance, relationships and well-being, while helping them tap into their strengths of courage, wisdom, caring and meaning-making. In this guide, we will briefly explore emerging scientific understandings about compassion before exploring how to put these insights to work when coaching, guiding and supporting clients, as well as in your own life as a coach.

What is compassion-focused coaching?

Compassion-focused coaching is a form and style of coaching that helps the client cultivate their compassionate mind in order to help them overcome difficulties, suffer less and live their best possible life. It is informed by best practice in an emerging range of compassion-focused approaches, including compassion-focused therapy, compassionate mind training and mindful self-compassion training.

It is a multi-modal approach incorporating a range of strategies, which we have summarised in Table 15.1:

Table 15.1: Strategies

- psychoeducation
- alliance formation
- demonstration and modelling
- Socratic questioning
- working with strengths
- visualisation
- rehearsal
- in-session practice and reflection
- goal-setting
- reframing
- building readiness to change etc

What is compassion?

Compassion is commonly misunderstood as being just an emotion. It is better thought of as a complex motivational state, comprising a range of competencies, sensitivities and skills that comprise a series of factors – see diagram 15.1.

A vast range of definitions have been offered by writers, but, in essence, compassion is '*sensitivity to suffering in self and others, with a commitment to alleviate and prevent it'*.

Diagram 15.1: Aspects of compassion

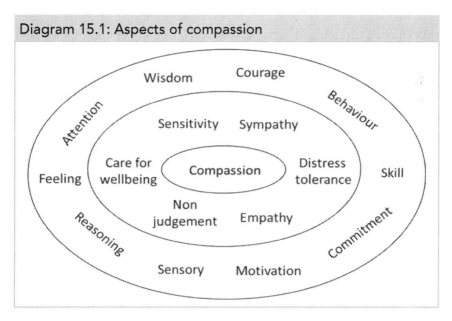

(Adapted from *The Compassionate Mind* (Gilbert, 2009). With kind permission from Constable Robinson).

The concept has its origins in the mammalian care-giving system. Mammals are born less ready to survive than reptiles and parents are very sensitive to indicators of suffering in their offspring, taking steps to prevent and alleviate suffering, sometimes at considerable personal risk e.g. fighting off predators.

The benefits of compassion

We can think of compassion as having three flows – from you to others, from others to you, and from yourself to yourself, with this latter flow being called self-compassion (Anstiss *et al*, 2020). With compassion-focused coaching, in addition to being compassionate toward your client, you are helping the client to tap into the benefits of higher levels of self-compassion, as well as being compassionate towards others and being able to receive compassion from others.

When being compassionate, people may experience such positive emotional states as feeling kind and caring, connected, competent and worthwhile, as well as feeling that they are living more in harmony with their values and using their strengths. They may also gain a sense of achievement, accomplishment and of being part of a team.

Self-compassion involves treating yourself in a similar way to how you would treat a friend who was having a hard time, and seems to be associated with better psychological health and well-being, including lower levels of anxiety, depression, stress, rumination, perfectionism, fear of failure and struggle with unwanted thoughts and feelings. Self-compassionate individuals seem better able to cope with such adversities as academic failure, divorce, childhood maltreatment and chronic pain, while being more likely to look after themselves by making dietary changes, reducing smoking, becoming more active and seeking appropriate medical care (Anstiss, 2016; Anstiss & Gilbert, 2014; Kirby, 2016). Self-compassion may also be associated with such positive states as:

- happiness
- optimism
- wisdom
- curiosity and exploration
- personal initiative
- emotional intelligence
- good relationship functioning.

What does it look like in practice?

The aim of compassion-focused coaching is to guide and help the client to activate, develop and strengthen their compassionate mind. Just as it can take a person several weeks of exercise to notice a change in their physical shape, so too can it take several weeks of practice for a person to notice the benefits of a more compassionate mind.

As a coach, you may start by helping your client to understand aspects of human brain functioning. This may start with a recognition that the human brain has evolved over millions of years, is modular, and that its different modules may not always work in harmony with each other. And this modularity extends to the mind as well as the brain – the mind is also comprised of different parts or modules with each seeming to have its own thoughts, feelings and motivations. This understanding helps to support some other key messages of the approach: That we all have tricky brains, and that many of our difficulties are just not our fault, and our brains are made for us, not by us.

We also share with clients that our minds contain three main emotional regulation systems: threat, drive, and calming. The threat and drive systems aim to help a person detect and escape from threat and danger, and gather resources for the future (shelter, food, mates, status etc) respectively. Sometimes these systems can become overactive and cause problems such as anxiety, burnout, anger, fear of missing out, poor sleep and poor performance. Both the threat and drive system are associated with the sympathetic nervous system. The calm system, or rest and digest system, is associated with the parasympathetic nervous system and can involve feelings of safeness, calm, contentedness, soothing, not-wanting, being comforted, affiliation, acceptance, non-striving and playfulness. Many clients struggle to spend time in this state, unable to tone down their threat and drive systems. By helping clients to cultivate their compassionate mind and direct it to themselves (self-compassion) and even difficult self-parts (e.g. their inner critic, their anxious self, their angry self, etc), compassion-focused coaches can help clients develop improved emotional regulation, life performance and quality of life.

In addition to the psychoeducation outline above – which helps the client to understand the rationale for the approach and develop expectations about what may be involved – the compassion-focused coach guides their clients through a progressive series of exercises and activities to help activate and strengthen the compassion pathways in their brain and help them, over time, become more compassionate both towards themselves, different parts of themselves, and more compassionate to others.

Some exercises are illustrated in Table 15.2

Table 15.2: Compassion exercises
■ Bodily grounding exercises, including practicing a soothing rhythm of breathing, slowing the duration of the in-breath and out-breath. This helps to stimulate the parasympathetic nervous system and encourage feelings of soothing and safeness. This can be accompanied by bringing a gentle smile to the face and imaging a soothing voice tone.
■ Generating an image or feeling of being in a safe place or space, a place which almost welcomes and appreciates you being there.
■ Cultivating a sense of a 'compassionate other', an inner image or felt presence of a benevolent, caring, non-judgmental, wise, understanding other.
■ Cultivating a sense of their 'best compassionate self' – what they are, or have been like, when they have been at their compassionate best. What qualities they want to have. Imagining themselves with and manifesting those qualities.
■ Writing a letter to themselves as if they were writing to a friend struggling with the same issue that they struggle with. And then reading that letter and noticing any feelings which show up.
■ Getting a sense of the characteristic of their critical self-part, their inner critic. Developing the courage to listen to what the critic tells them and trying to discover the fear and any positive intent behind the inner critic's messages. Exploring being compassionate towards the critical self-part (unless it is the voice of an abuser).
■ Cultivating feelings of compassion for people they love and care about (easy), general acquaintances (harder) and people they don't like, don't respect or even hate (harder still).

A range of other exercises to support the development of compassion can be found in *WeCoach* (Passmore *et al*, 2021).

Conclusion

Compassion-focused coaching is a multi-modal form of coaching informed by evolutionary neuroscience. It aims to help the client make better progress in life by cultivating their compassionate mind, their compassionate motivation and self-compassion. It uses many of the same tools and strategies of other forms of coaching, and shares with the client helpful messages, exercises, practices and activities from compassion-focused therapy, compassionate mind training and mindful self-compassion approaches. Coaches themselves may wish to practise these exercises and activities to help them become a better coach and, perhaps, a better human being also.

References

Anstiss, T (2016) Compassion at work. In: L Oades, M Steger, A Fave and J Passmore (eds) *The Wiley Blackwell Handbook of the Psychology of Positivity and Strengths-based Approaches at Work.* Chichester: Wiley.

Anstiss, T, Passmore, J, and Gilbert, P (2020). *Compassion: The essential orientation*. The Psychologist, May (pp38-42).

Anstiss, T and Gilbert, P (2014) Compassionate mind coaching. *In*: J Passmore (ed) *Mastery in Coaching. A Complete Psychological Toolkit for Advanced Coaching*. London: Kogan Page.

Beaumont, E and Irons, C (2017) *The Compassionate Mind Workbook*. London: Robinson.

Gilbert, P (2009) *The Compassionate Mind*. London: Constable.

Kirby, JN (2016) Compassion interventions: The programmes, the evidence, and implications for research and practice. *Psychology and Psychotherapy: Theory, Research and Practice* 90 (3) 1–24.

Passmore, J., Day, C., Flower, J. Grieve, M. and Moon, J. (2021) *WeCoach: The complete handbook of tools, techniques, experiments and frameworks for personal and team development*. London: Libri Press.

Chapter 16:
How can we enable our clients to think for themselves?

Nancy Kline

Introduction

Coaching clients to think is one thing. Coaching them to think for themselves is wholly another. The *for themselves* part changes everything. It can turn our coaching inside out. And it is worth it because the quality of everything our clients do – *everything* – depends on the quality of the independent thinking they do first. Every plan, every decision, every action, relies on the moments when our clients think for themselves – with rigour, imagination, courage and grace. Their independent thinking then becomes the basis of dialogue with others, in turn raising the quality of it all. This chapter focuses on the ways in which the decision to generate our clients' own finest thinking as far as possible can recast the way we coach.

Time for thinking

We have to face this first: most clients expect us to think for them and most of us expect to do exactly that. Neither party says so, but the implicit coaching agreement is, observably, that our clients will think and talk for as long as it takes us to get a beat on their issue, and then we will act. Either we will take a note, or come in with a question of some sort – to clarify, to lead, to challenge, to propose.

The agreement is that, as the coach, we can distract or interrupt the client's thinking whenever we deem valuable. We don't usually crash into the middle of their sentences (though shockingly some of us do), but it is we who are, nevertheless, the ones who determine when it is the right moment for the client to stop talking and for us to start.

Is that a problem? You wouldn't think so. Our clients are generally fine with that. That is what they think they are paying for. They want our thinking, our knowledge, our experience, however it is expressed.

We are fine with that, too. Our clients often tell us that they experience our listening as the finest of their lives, and that they find our knowledge and experience, and our 'take' on their issues, ideas and feelings useful – sometimes life-changingly so.

And why not? They have, since birth, been schooled to devalue their own minds in favour of the minds of 'the experts'. And so have we. Just about the only time we think for ourselves is when we are thinking for others. So as coaches, understandably, we listen to get ready to speak, and then we do.

What is the problem with what is happening here?

Nothing.

The problem is with what is *not* happening.

We are missing gold. We are missing the unthought thoughts of the client. We are missing their unique insight, their crystalline clarification, their spontaneous sweeping away of blocks, their inspired solving of the problem in a way that we could never have thought of.

But does that matter? They are gaining our gold, and that is often rich. True. But we don't know that it will be richer than theirs, because we don't have theirs yet.

We act, though, as if we do. We proceed to insert our thinking before they have fully produced their own. Armed with ours, we close the door to theirs, to insights and ways forward that could have been richer than ours.

Actually, we close the door to more than that. We shut out also our clients' building of respect for their own minds, a form of self-esteem that, in turn, generates better and better thinking. Thus, we stunt their development as a thinker. And that stunts their development as a leader. And that stunts the unfolding excellence of their organisation.

Risk

When we coach by talking whenever we deem best, we have, without knowing it, taken a huge risk. And we have done so after assessing the risk inaccurately. Ordinarily that is an unconscionable act for a professional.

Ordinarily in a high-risk situation we would be considering this question: Could the downside from the loss here be greater than the upside from the gain?

If so, we would pull back and re-think. Certainly, in the investment world, any adviser would do that.

The same principle applies here. We need to face the fact that because we cannot know what our client will think next, we cannot be sure that the downside of the loss of their thinking will not be greater than the upside from the gain of ours. And so we do not take that risk.

We continue the particular quality of listening – generative listening – that can produce the client's own stunning, formerly unformed thinking, which is more valuable than ours would have been.

Help

In that moment when we feel agonisingly certain that our take is needed now, that it is practically a civic duty for us to speak, we can ask ourselves this question:

Do I know *for sure* that what I am about to *say* will be of more value than what my client is about to *think?*

Do we know for certain? No. We can never know that for certain because not even our clients know what they are about to think.

So we have to assess the risk of losing our client's unthought thoughts in favour of gaining our already-thought thoughts. That is not very hard. Because our thoughts are already formed and ready to go, we can offer them the minute the client truly can no longer generate theirs. But if we insert ours too soon, we will never know what theirs would have been, and what new gold will have been lost forever. That risk is potentially monumental.

Changes

Committing to our clients' own thinking changes us. We coach differently. We redefine the singular purpose of our coaching. It is no longer for our clients to benefit from our thinking: it is for them to go as far in their own thinking as they possibly can before they need ours.

The unsettling but profound discovery here is that only they can determine when that is, and so we speak by invitation only – and even then, we first choose questions that will keep them going for themselves. The most pristine question I know for this invitation is: 'What more do you think, or feel, or want to say?' We ask it. They generate more. We ask it again. They generate more. We ask it again. They generate more. That same question registers as new each time. Until it doesn't and they are finished. During that time, we insert not a morsel of our own take; not until they invite us to speak.

Our decision not to insert our thinking until they ask for it means changing the contract with them. They, too, have to opt for the inimitable value of the *unpredictable* product of their own minds, throwing open doors formerly secured by the preference for our thinking over theirs.

Most of all, both of us have to change what we wonder about. We *both* have to wonder how far they can go in their own thinking before they need ours. And how much further than that?

That change means developing the character and sinew of our attention, taking it from reactive to generative. That is an art.

It also means knowing how to ask questions that help them unblock themselves when they are stuck. Those are very different kinds of questions from the ones we employ when our purpose is to guide them somewhere of our own choosing.

We also have to understand and welcome their silences, especially the long ones, the ones in which they often do their most important thinking.

And we have to be willing for an *entire* session to be breathtakingly valuable, and yet contain not a shred of *our* thinking. Not a shred. That takes courage and a ground-breaking commitment to the unleashing of the client's own mind. It also takes distinctive and precisely honed skill.

This, when it becomes our core methodology, can join with our other offerings to construct coaching at its finest.

Conclusion

'Every decision is a sacrifice', said Martha Graham, the great choreographer. She could have been regaling coaches. And we would have done well to listen to her. Every decision we make to speak sacrifices the next unthought thought of the client. That fresh thought might well have changed gloriously the trajectory of the session, even of the life. Do we need to sacrifice that potential for something we already know, something we can offer up later if it is still relevant?

Before we speak, perhaps we need to wonder about that.

References

Brown, P (2012) *Neuropsychology for Coaches*. Milton Keynes: Open University Press.

Kline, N (2015) *More Time to Think*. Cassell Publishers; *The Promise That Changes Everything: I Won't Interrupt You*. London: Penguin Random House.

McGilchrist, I (2011) *The Master and His Emissary*. Yale: Yale University Press.

Stout-Rostron, S (2014) *Leadership Coaching for Results*. Bryanston, South Africa: Knowres Publishing.

Chapter 17:
How can I refer coaching clients to another helping professional?

Jonathan Passmore

Introduction

Coaching is generally a confidential conversation between the coach and their individual client. Confidentiality is an essential ingredient and usually forms part of the contract between the coach and their client. But coaching can be an emotional journey and, on some occasions, it can stir deep emotions within clients. On rare occasions this might create a need to break confidentiality to protect the client, or another person, from harm, or on other occasions to protect the organisation or society from wider wrongdoing. This chapter explores how coaches might manage these rare situations and make appropriate referrals to protect their clients and others.

Is coaching confidential?

Coaching is always described as a confidential process. However, the reality is more complex than this. First, in most commercial coaching assignments, where the organisation has commissioned the coaching, there is an expectation for some feedback or review of the coaching assignment. This can best be managed through a tripartite contracting meeting, and a tripartite review meeting at the end of the assignment.

Apart from the need for the coach to facilitate a review meeting with the client and the sponsor to enable them to jointly review the coaching, there are a few rare occasions when the coach may need to break confidentiality.

This may arise in three situations:

1. Where there is risk of harm to the client.
2. Where there is risk of harm (or actual harm which is occurring or has occurred) to someone else.
3. Where there is serious illegality.

There are also other situations where we may need to refer to another professional to help the client. These referrals may be in cases where the client needs medical help, where a referral to their family doctor or a counsellor would be of benefit. It may also include referrals to another coach if we are not trained or appropriately qualified to manage the presenting issue.

Who to refer?

We may need to make a referral, either with or without the client's agreement. Table 17.1 suggests what circumstances fall into each category.

Table 17.1: Referral guide	
Without client agreement	With client agreement
■ Risk of serious harm to client ■ Risk of serious harm to others ■ Serious illegality	■ Mild depression (or other mental health condition) ■ Physical ill health ■ Issue is outside the skill, training or area of competence of the coach

Mental health issues can range from mild depression to the risk of the client harming themselves. Mental health issues affect around one in four of the adult population in the developed world, and while for the majority of people these vary from short episodes of depression, mental health related issues (suicide) are the most common cause of death for men aged between 20 and 49, and account for 27% of male deaths 20-34 in the UK (UK Government, 2018).

In the case of mild depression or other mental health or physical health issues, coaches should encourage their client to make contact with their family doctor, who is best able to assess and advise them. It can also be helpful for the coach to have the contact number of a counsellor who is willing to accept referrals. This can act as a reciprocal arrangement with the counselling referring coaching cases to the coach.

In some situations, clients may make a statement about their desire or intention to take their own life. As a general guide, the more detailed this statement, the more present and real the danger. In these situations, there may be a need to act outside of the agreement with the client. This may require the coach to make contact with an emergency crisis team, sometimes known in the UK as a Crisis Team or more formally known as the Crisis Resolution and Home Treatment team (CRHT). If this happens the coach should stay with the client until the team arrive.

Table 17.2 lists common signs that may trigger a referral either to a crisis team or to a general mental health professional, family doctor or counsellor.

These are not always signs of depression, or the onset of a mental health problem. Behaviour can be affected by a wide range of circumstances. Coaches need to exercise judgement, taking into account history and situational factors, as well as the factors listed in Table 17.2.

Table 17.2: Signs and symptoms

- Expressed desire and a plan to take one's own life.
- Withdrawal from social relationships/changed interactions during the coaching sessions.
- Significant changes in weight or appearance.
- Disturbed sleep pattern.
- Decline in concentration, focus and/or presence.
- Excessively or repeatedly tearful during sessions.
- Issue or topic continually arises and is preventing progress on the coaching topic.

Additionally, where we need to act to protect the client, we also sometimes need to act to protect others. This may be in situations where the client is making what we judge to be a credible threat to others, or where we become aware of serious illegality. In the latter case this might include serious fraud, large-scale theft or abuse: specific examples might include bribery, insider trading and misrepresentation of information to regulators or other government bodies.

How to refer?

In most cases we should be referring with the agreement of the client. Start by talking the situation through in the session. If you have contracted well at the start, you can refer to what coaching is and what you are qualified to do. By putting the client's needs at the centre, being empathetic and normalising both their feelings and the referral service, most clients are happy to follow their coach's advice in these situations.

In making the referral you may simply give some contact details to the client. However, in more serious or crisis situation, you may need to connect them with the crisis team, a doctor or counsellor. How you do this needs to reflect the needs of the individual client, taking account of their preferences and of how serious you judge the situation.

Conclusion

It is worthwhile stressing that these situations happen only very rarely. Many coaches may go their whole coaching career without the need to make an emergency referral and few make more than one or two referrals to family doctors or counsellors each year. However, being prepared for an emergency will help you to know what to do should the situation arise.

Useful contact numbers and websites (UK only)

For low-level police issues: 101

For emergencies (life-threatening or ongoing situations): 999

For a CRHT team:
- England and Wales: www.mind.org.uk
- Northern Ireland: www.nidirect.gov.uk/services/find-mental-health-organisation
- Scotland: www.nhs.uk/using-the-nhs/nhs-services/urgent-and-emergency-care/nhs-111/

For Samaritans
- (a UK suicide prevention charity): 116 123

For registered therapists/counsellors:
- www.bacp.co.uk/about-therapy/how-to-find-a-therapist/

For local family doctors:
- England: www.nhs.uk/Service-Search/GP/LocationSearch/4
- Northern Ireland: http://servicefinder.hscni.net/
- Scotland: www.nhsinform.scot/scotlands-service-directory/gp-practices
- Wales: www.wales.nhs.uk/ourservices/directory

References

UK Government (2018). Leading causes of death, UK: 2001 to 2018. Retrieved on 24 February 2021 from https://www.ons.gov.uk/peoplepopulationandcommunity/healthandsocialcare/causesofdeath/articles/leadingcausesofdeathuk/2001to2018

Chapter 18:
How can I take account of cross-cultural issues in my coaching?

Philippe Rosinski

Introduction

Weaving culture into coaching and leadership is crucial, not only because cultural diversity is an integral part of our reality, but because when coaches and leaders tap into people's intercultural potential, they promote creativity, boost performance and enable unity.

This chapter presents coaching across cultures and its four interconnected levels of applications: individual, team and organisational development, which in turn contribute to societal progress by promoting unity in diversity in place of division or uniformity.

It also introduces the cultural orientations framework (COF), which is a roadmap and assessment tool to navigate the cultural terrain.

Coaching across cultures: why and what for?

Traditional coaching and leadership have assumed a worldview that is not universal and is increasingly insufficient to help address the complex challenges in our turbulent, interconnected and global environment. For example, communicating in a direct manner prevents misunderstandings by favouring clarity, but may inadvertently offend your client. Indirect communication, which values sensitivity and harmony, can enrich your communication. By combining the two polarities – for example, by being clear on the content and sensitive in your manner – you can achieve the best of both forms of communication. Your conception of time constitutes another example. If you consider that time is scarce, you are likely to become more productive, but by cramming activities into your agenda and by speeding up, you risk becoming overwhelmed without necessarily spending time on what truly matters. If you view time as plentiful, you are likely to slow down and regain perspective, and may paradoxically better appreciate the scarcity of time. Combining both perspectives will allow you to be efficient (doing things right) as well as effective (doing the right things).

Coaching across cultures has two objectives. As you might expect, it does enable more effective work across cultures (though not only in an international sense). More fundamentally, intercultural coaching is, in essence, a more creative and complete form of coaching (and leadership). The approach challenges cultural assumptions in all situations. It propels you and those you serve beyond previous limitations. It offers new options in the form of alternative ways of thinking, communicating, managing time and engaging in your various activities (Rosinski, 2010: 121-122).

Consequently, if you think coaching across cultures is reserved for those working on international assignments and travelling abroad, or if you view intercultural coaching as a niche market that concerns a minority of professionals (despite the rapid globalisation of our economies), you might want to reconsider.

A dynamic and inclusive view of culture

'A group's culture is the set of unique characteristics that distinguishes its members from another group' (Rosinski, 2003: 20). Our national cultures, which are still the basis for many intercultural comparisons, constitute only one of many groups we belong to, alongside our professional cultures, organisational cultures, generational cultures etc.

Our multiple cultures refer to our 'nurture' (what we have learned along the way, in contact with our families, schools and other social groups) and complement our 'nature' (what we are born with).

Our cultural characteristics are both visible (behaviours, products and artefacts) and invisible (norms, values and basic assumptions or fundamental beliefs). They are not cast in stone: we can unlearn or enrich what we have learned, and develop new characteristics that allow us to more effectively address the challenges we face. By increasing our cultural flexibility and versatility, we can improve our work and relationships with others, as well as our own fulfilment. In sum, coaching across cultures goes hand in hand with a dynamic view of culture.

What is more, coaching across cultures challenges us to think 'and' versus 'or'. Referring to the examples above, the goal is not to replace direct communication with indirect communication, and scarce time with plentiful time, but to synthesise the polarities. Coaching across cultures promotes inclusion in the form of mutual enrichment (true unity) in place of either exclusion or bland uniformity (in which disparities have been eliminated and which constitutes an impoverishment).

A roadmap to navigate the cultural terrain

The COF is 'an integrative framework designed to assess and compare cultures' (Rosinski, 2010: 123). It offers a vocabulary to describe cultural characteristics in the form of cultural orientations (a cultural orientation is an inclination to think, feel or act in a way that is culturally determined, or at least influenced by culture – direct and indirect communications constitute examples).

The COF assessment is a measurement tool that 'facilitates the understanding of salient cultural characteristics for individuals, teams and organizations' (www.COFassessment.com). The tool 'lets users view group cultural profiles in multiple, customizable ways (e.g., team, organization as well as profiles per categories/fields predefined by users, such as division, nationally management level, merging entities, etc.) and allows them to add their own customized cultural dimensions to the 17 standard COF dimensions'. Note that 'intercultural coaching assumes a "multiple realities" view of the world. Culture, from this perspective, is highly contextual, dynamic and fluid. Capturing data through the COF assessment in a particular moment is useful for generating conversations and making sense of change processes, but not so helpful in seeking definitive truths about individuals, groups, or societies' (Rosinski, 2010: 129).

Four interconnecting levels

Intercultural coaching in general and the COF assessment in particular can be applied at four interconnected levels:

1. **Individual**

   If we want to have the expertise and the credibility to help others on their developmental journeys, we need to be prepared to work on ourselves first. The following questions can apply for self-coaching (intrapersonal) as well as one-to-one coaching (interpersonal):

   - What are your cultural orientations?
   - How do these orientations possibly vary depending on the context?
   - How do your cultural orientations impact the way you coach/lead?
   - What cultural orientations do you tend to overuse/underuse?
   - What are your developmental opportunities?

2. **Team**

   Cultural diversity is a double-edged sword. Poorly handled, it becomes a source of polarisation, which drives team performance down. Effectively exploited, it boosts creativity, facilitates synergies, and increases performance and satisfaction (Rosinski, 2019: 132–4). Coaching across cultures allows leverage of cultural diversity in practice: the intercultural team coaching process as well as case studies are described in Rosinski (2010: 134–41 and 2019: 128.59).

3. **Organisations**

Organisations rely on three mechanisms to achieve growth: organic growth, alliances, and mergers and acquisitions. Unfortunately, a high percentage of alliances and mergers and acquisitions break down prematurely, failing to deliver the expected strategic benefits and inflicting financial damage on both partners. 'The main reason for failure is the human factor in general culture in particular' (Rosinski, 2010: 141).

Coaching across cultures allows transformation of the problem into an opportunity. When those in charge are ready to champion the process, synergies can be deployed as exemplified in Rosinski (2010: 141–7). The COF assessment can be used as a cultural audit tool to compare the cultures at play. Cultural gaps, having been identified, can be systematically bridged. Cultural similarities are examined as well to ensure that the alternative polarities, potentially beneficial, are not missed.

4. **Society**

By promoting unity in diversity, coaching across cultures contributes to much-needed societal progress.

Conclusion

More and more attention has been paid to the cultural perspective since the first presentation of this topic (Rosinski's session at Linkage's Coaching & Mentoring Conference – London, 1999). 'Coaching across cultures' is now included in some of the best coaching training programmes (e.g., Henley Business School, University of Cambridge, HEC Paris). However, systematically integrating culture into coaching still represents an untapped opportunity for most coaches as well as a necessity in our intercultural world.

What is more, viewing culture in a dynamic and inclusive fashion is still far from being the norm, and yet is essential for coaches to play their part in promoting unity in diversity in place of detrimental stereotyping and polarisation.

References

Rosinski, P (2003) *Coaching Across Cultures.* London and Yarmouth, ME: Nicholas Brealey Publishing.

Rosinski, P (2010) *Global Coaching.* London and Boston: Nicholas Brealey Publishing.

Rosinski, P (2019) Delivering value through cross-cultural team coaching. In: J Passmore, B Underhill and M Goldsmith (eds) *Mastering Executive Coaching.* Abingdon: Routledge.

Chapter 19:
How do we foster a collaborative coaching relationship?

Elizabeth Crosse

Introduction

'It's all about the relationship.' This seems to be the message when one asks coaches: 'What is the key ingredient that enables your clients to achieve their goals and aspirations?' This is unsurprising as there is virtually unanimous agreement in research on the significance of the relationship in enabling successful outcomes for clients (Boyce *et al*, 2010; Gregory & Levy, 2011; Van Oosten *et al*, 2019). There is also a recognition that the ability to establish, maintain and develop the coaching relationship needs to be a core element of a coach's training and development (Fillery-Travis & Collins, 2017; Gray, 2011; Lane, 2017). In this chapter, we explore what is meant by the coaching relationship and how you can continue to develop this essential capability in practice.

What do we mean by 'the coaching relationship'?

One defining principle of the coaching relationship is that it is a collaborative partnership, based on a sense of mutuality, trust and connection between the coach and the client (Ianiro *et al*, 2013). This stance is endorsed by the ethical standards and professional codes of conduct of the AC, EMCC and ICF. It is also reflected in the competency frameworks of these organisations.

It is tempting to think that enhancing our ability to foster the relationship is all about developing our interpersonal skills. Creating trust and intimacy, presence, active listening and responding to the 'whole person' certainly play important roles in managing the coaching relationship (Boyce *et al*, 2010; Cox, 2012), but this is only part of the story. Studies suggest that it is the 'working alliance', which encompasses three interrelated elements – goals, tasks and bonds, rather than a specific approach or coaching techniques – that underpins success (Gessnitzer & Kauffeld, 2015).

- The term 'working alliance' was first used to describe the therapeutic relationship (Bordin, 1979), and these elements have also been shown to correlate with positive outcomes of the coaching process (Boyatzis *et al, 2015*).
- Goal: Why we are working together – the client's purpose.
- Task: What we are working on to achieve the client's goal(s).
- Bond: How we work together on the task – our interpersonal connection.

What are the implications for enhancing our ability to foster the coaching relationship?

Considering how we manage the coaching relationship more holistically invites us to look at our approach to relationship building through a different lens. In reflecting on how we create the working alliance, we can consider the importance we give to each element and the impact this may have on our relationship-building style.

Managing the working alliance

Establishing the goal:

- Have we got clarity on what the client wants to accomplish?
- Have we got clarity on the client's measures of success?
- Have we explored the client's motivation for what they want to accomplish?
- Have I helped the client define what needs to be addressed or resolved in order to achieve what they want to accomplish?

Managing the task:

- Have I made it clear we are working in partnership?
- Have I supported the client in choosing what happens in the session?
- Have I partnered with the client in ending the session?
- Have I noticed and reflected on the client's progress?

Creating the bond:

- Have I created a sense of connection?
- Have I demonstrated respect for the client and their work in the process?
- Have I encouraged the client to fully express themselves?
- Have I got the right balance of challenging and supporting interventions?

Relationship-building styles

Given the diversity of coaches' backgrounds, training, and the contexts in which they work, it is unsurprising to find there are different views on what is most important in fostering a collaborative coaching relationship (Crosse, 2019). Some coaches place more importance on the process elements, the contribution of the goals and task elements to relationship building. For others, there is a greater focus on the interpersonal elements – the bond.

Differences in the emphasis given to each element of the working alliance is also reflected in coaching models and approaches. The GROW, OSCAR, and a solution-focused approach (Grant *et al*, 2021), imply an emphasis on establishing the goals and give a structure to the task of working toward the desired outcome. In comparison, CLEAR, PPP and Time to Think (Kline, 2004) suggest a greater focus on the bond, highlighting the importance of listening and rapport building skills to create the connection that invites open exploration and dialogue.

Table 19.1: Summary of coaching models

Model	Stages	Author
GROW	Goal, reality, options, will	Whitmore, 2009
OSCAR	Outcome, situation choices and consequences, review	Rogers, 2012
CLEAR	Contract, listen, explore, action, review	Hawking and Smith, 2010
PPP	Perspective, purpose and process	Lane and Corrie, 2006

The relationship styles framework (Figure 19.1) reflect a range of approaches to establishing, maintaining, and developing the coaching relationship. There are four distinct perspectives which represent different ways in which the working alliance is conceptualised. Each style's defining

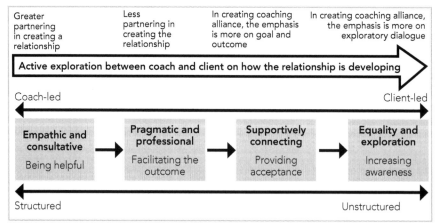

Figure 19.1: Relationship style framework

characteristics are influenced by where they sit on the coach-client led continuum and how much structure the coach creates in the collaborative partnership. The coach-client led continuum encapsulates the amount of shared responsibility for creating the working alliance; the balance of coach-client input in defining and managing how the relationship works. The structured-unstructured continuum indicates whether there is a preference for a focus on structure the way goal and task frame the coaching conversation or creating the interpersonal bond and encouraging exploratory dialogue.

The styles also reflect different viewpoints on the role of the relationship in the coaching process. For some coaches, it informs the way in which they work and their choice of intervention strategies. For others, the relationship sits at the heart of the coaching process (De Haan, 2008) and provides a vehicle that enables the client to achieve their outcomes (Table 19.2).

Table 19.2: Characteristics of relationship styles

Concept	Empathic and consultative	Pragmatic and professional
Main contribution of the working alliance	Goals and tasks	Goals and task
Purpose	To be helpful	To facilitate the client's outcome
Builds the relationship by…	Providing emotional support in a structured framework created by the coach	Ensuring the client achieves their goal in a co-created framework
Characteristics	Highly empathic and goal orientated Willing to share knowledge and gives advice when the client is stuck Uses coaching frameworks and models	Cognitive approach, challenging the client's thinking Focus on exploring conceptual elements of relationship building e.g. expectations, boundaries, ethical code of conduct Wants to be seen as a credible and fair professional who delivers
Role of the relationship	The relationship informs the way in which the coach works	The relationship is necessary to facilitating the process →

Table 19.2: Characteristics of relationship styles

Concept	Supportively connecting	Equality in exploration
Main contribution of the working alliance	Bond	Bond
Purpose	To provide acceptance	To increase awareness
Builds the relationship by...	Creating a mutually accepting relationship in a safe and supportive working environment	Co-developing a trusting relationship that explores the 'who' the client is being and the 'what' they want to achieve
Characteristics	Non-judgemental acceptance Ensure a sense of ease by using more supportive than challenging interventions Importance placed on being 'liked'	Shared responsibility and exploratory focus for relationship building Explicit about the interactions that impact on their relationship Vulnerability from self and client
Role of the relationship	The relationship is essential to facilitating the process	Coaching is the relationship; it is at the heart of the coaching process

The four perspectives in the relationship styles framework reflects different mindsets on how we understand the concept of the coaching relationship. This 'meaning making' underpins how we will respond spontaneously and appropriately in our coaching conversation (Table 19.3).

Table 19.3: Relationship style and coaching mindsets

Empathic and consultative	■ Values a model base approach and provides structure for how the coach builds the relationship with the client ■ Greater focus on the coaching approach and intervention, rather than the relational dynamics ■ Willing to share advice in supporting the client and taking them where the coach thinks they need to go
Pragmatic and professional	■ Focuses on the achieving the client's desired outcome, the solution ■ Engages more cognitively than emotionally ■ Focus on exploring conceptual elements of relationship building, e.g. expectations, boundaries, ethical code of conduct
Supportively connecting	■ Importance is placed on being responsive to the client's needs ■ Exemplifies beliefs in the client's potential and the task element of building the relationship has a developmental focus ■ Uses a facilitative style with an emphasis on contextualising the client issue within their own perspective and enabling the client to do things themselves →

Equality and exploration	■ Responsive to how they are being with the client, placing a great importance on understanding what is going on between themselves and the client and encouraging self-awareness
	■ Willing to sit with uncertainty and allow the issue and solution to emerge
	■ Little reliance on any specific techniques or processes – it's about responding to the client and their context in the moment

The purpose of the relationship styles framework is not to suggest there is a 'right' style to managing the coaching relationship, or that you need to change your approach. It offers a way of exploring your beliefs, assumptions, and feelings about the way you co-create the coaching relationship with clients. The aim is to help you reflect on the fit between your coaching context and how you enhance your ability to meet your client's needs. It is about being curious and asking:

■ How do I define my 'relationship style' approach?

■ Do I have a preferred style?

■ Is the way I create the coaching relationship with my client fit for purpose?

■ What have I learned from my client that suggests what style may work best for them?

■ Where do I want more behavioural flexibility to better meet my client's needs?

It is behavioural flexibility rather than a particular style that helps us manage the coach-client dynamics. If you identify the needs to create a more spontaneous and responsive relationship with your clients, the question is: 'What is the best way for me to address this issue?' One option may be to use supervision as a vehicle for a more holistic approach to developing your relationship building skills. Alternatively, it may be a personal journey of self-discovery, exploring how you manage relationships in the wider contexts, what insights arise as you reflect on how you manage yourself, the process, and interpersonal dynamics in unpredictable situations.

Conclusion

Being successful in fostering collaborative coaching relationships is all about building your capacity to work with complexity, conflict, ambiguity, and holistic understanding. It requires more than assimilating a repertoire of coaching models, skills and competencies to deal with the dynamic and unpredictable nature of interaction between coach and client (Nelson-Jones, 2006). It asks you to consider 'who you are being', as well as 'what you are doing' in managing their client relationships. It encourages you to embrace the concept of self as 'the instrument of practice' (Bachkirova, 2016) and is dependent on your willingness to critically reflect on the way you make sense of their coaching relationship. In this way, we absorb and integrate what we have learned from experience into who we are as a coach.

References

Bachkirova, T (2016) The self of the coach: conceptualization, issues, and opportunities for practitioner development. *Consulting Psychology Journal: Practice and Research*, 68(2), 143-156.

Bordin, E S (1979) The generalizability of the psychoanalytic concept of the working alliance. *Psychotherapy: Theory, Research & Practice* 16 (3) 252-60.

Boyatzis, R E, Smith, M L, Van Oosten, E B, Gessnitzer, S and Kauffeld, S (2015) The working alliance in coaching. *The Journal of Applied Behavioral Science* 51 (2) 177-97.

Boyce, L A, Jackson, R J and Neal, L J (2010) Building successful leadership coaching relationships: examining impact of matching criteria in a leadership coaching programme. *Journal of Management Development* 29 (10) 914-31.

Cox, E (2012) Individual and organizational trust in a reciprocal peer coaching context. *Mentoring & Tutoring: Partnership in Learning* 20 (3) 427-43.

Crosse, E (2019) A Q methodology study: how do coaches foster the coaching relationship?. *International Journal of Evidence Based Coaching and Mentoring* S13 76-93.

De Haan, E (2008) *Relational Coaching: Journeys Towards Mastering One-To-One Learning*. Chichester: John Wiley.

Fillery-Travis, A and Collins, R (2017) Discipline, profession and industry: How our choices shape our future. In: Bachkirova, T, Spence, G & Drake, D (eds.). *The SAGE Handbook of Coaching* (pp729-744). London: SAGE Publications Ltd.

Gessnitzer, S and Kauffeld, S (2015) The working alliance in coaching: why behavior is the key to success. *Journal of Applied Behavioral Science* 51 (2) 177-197.

Grant, A M O'Connor, S. and Studholme, I. (2021) Solution-focused coaching. In: Passmore, J (ed.). *Excellence in Coaching: Theory, Tools and Techniques to achieve outstanding coaching performance* (4th edition) (pp112-140). London: Kogan Page.

Gray, D E (2011) Journeys towards the professionalisation of coaching:

Dilemmas, dialogues and decisions along the global Pathway. *Coaching: An International Journal of Theory, Research and Practice* 4 (1) 4-19.

Hawkins, P and Smith, N, (2010) Transformational coaching. *The Complete Handbook of Coaching* (pp231-244).

Hodge, A (2016) The value of coaching supervision as a development process: Contribution to continued professional and personal wellbeing for executive coaches. *International Journal of Evidence Based Coaching & Mentoring* 14 (2) 87-106.

Ianiro, P M, Schermuly, C C and Kauffeld, S (2013) Why interpersonal dominance and affiliation matter: an interaction analysis of the coach–client relationship. *Coaching: An International Journal of Theory, Research and Practice* 6 (1) 25-46.

Kline, N (2004) *Time to Think: Listening with the Human Mind*. London: Ward Lock.

Lane, D A, and Corrie, S (2006) *The Modern Scientist-Practitioner: A Guide to Practice in Psychology*. Hove: Routledge.

Nelson-Jones, R (2006) *Human Relationship Skills: Coaching and Self-Coaching* (4th edition). London: Routledge.

Rogers, J (2012) *Coaching Skills: A Handbook* (3rd edition). Maidenhead: McGraw-Hill/Open University Press.

Van Oosten, E B, McBride-Walker, S M, and Taylor, S N (2019) Investing in what matters: The impact of emotional and social competency development and executive coaching on leader outcomes. *Consulting Psychology Journal: Practice and Research*, 71 (4) 249-269.

Chapter 20:
How can I help clients to set better goals in coaching?

Ruth E Price

Introduction

Goal setting in coaching is often assumed to follow a singular and linear approach: the goal is identified and agreed early-on; this goal is shaped as a SMART goal; the coaching is centred on the attainment of this goal, with client behaviours adjusted accordingly to meet the goal. However, there is an increasing recognition that goal setting in coaching is much more multi-dimensional and fluid than this. This is not surprising when you consider how the messy, multifaceted context of coaching differs from the top-down, controlled managerial context that has informed this singular, linear approach. How we conceptualise a goal, who our client is, who we are as coach, and the environment in which our client operates, all influence goal setting. There are coaching questions at the end of the chapter to help you broaden your own skill set and mind set in developing a more flexible and nuanced approach to goal setting for the benefit of each individual client.

The classic approach to goal setting in coaching

The classic approach to goal setting in coaching is to start with the client identifying a goal they would like to achieve. Here, goal setting happens early on, and the goal guides the remainder of the coaching session(s). An example of this is the linear application of the GROW model (Alexander & Lanza Tans, 2021; Whitmore, 2017), where:

G a Goal is identified by the client

R the distance they are from that goal and their current Reality is established

O the Options for closing the gap between their current reality and desired goal are explored

W the Way Forward / Wrap-Up / Will to commit to action that leads to this goal success is decided upon and carried out by the client.

To help ensure goal achievement, coaches have encouraged their clients to frame their goals as SMART goals. This is in-line with the goal setting theories and research findings from studies of goal success in organisations. The major theory of goal setting comes from the work of Locke (1968) and Locke & Latham (1990), and their early research is likely to have been the inspiration for this SMART framework (Doran, 1981). The SMART framework states that, for objective setting in organisations to be effective, the objective must fulfil five criteria in Table 20.1

Table 20.1: SMART

S	**Specific** – target a specific area for improvement
M	**Measurable** – quantify, or at least suggest, an indicator of progress
A	**Assignable** – specify who will do it
R	**Realistic** – state what results can realistically be achieved, given available resources
T	**Time related** – specify when the result(s) can be achieved

Suitability and limitations of the classic approach to goal setting in coaching

There are certain coaching issues and coaching contexts where this classic approach – borrowed from an organisational context – is likely to be a good fit. When a client is looking to increase their performance, the route to achieving the goal is relatively straightforward and the client believes they have the competence and self-efficacy to achieve the goal, then this type of goal-setting is likely to lead to goal achievement. In this scenario, clients are likely to desire specific and measurable goals and a goal-focused relationship between coach and client becomes the strongest predictor of goal attainment (Grant, 2013).

However, the coaching context is not the same as an organisational context, which emphasises top-down managerial control. Coaching also encompasses a much broader range of issues than those just described, and so the classic approach may not be the best fit in all circumstances. Studies with practising coaches have found that they utilise different forms of goal setting in their practice, which more closely reflects the multifaceted reality of coaching (David *et al*, 2013). Professional coaching bodies, such as the ICF, are updating the competencies for coach practitioners in order to capture this. Coaching research is beginning to challenge best-practice assumptions on goal setting, with a call for more testing of what we hold to be true.

The complexity of goal setting in coaching

There are four main factors in coaching that result in a unique context for goal setting.

1. The goal

Goals are much more multi-dimensional in their nature than suggested by a SMART goal definition (see Price, 2021, for a comprehensive review). Whereas a SMART goal is highly specific (concrete) in nature, perhaps with a relatively short time frame, other types of goals can be fuzzier (abstract), and have a longer time horizon. Indeed, the most likely starting point for coaching clients is somewhere in the middle of this concrete-abstract range; often, clients come to coaching with a general intention of how they would like things to be (Clutterbuck & Spence, 2017). Even at times when a client does enter coaching with a specific goal, this may be a reactive goal and not the 'best' one for them. By providing time and space for exploration, a new adapted goal may arise that better serves the client's needs (Clutterbuck & David, 2013).

2. The client

Clients differ in their preference for goal setting, with some feeling energised and motivated by the use of specific goals and others feeling under pressure and demotivated by them (McKee, 1991, unpublished PhD dissertation, cited in Clutterbuck & Spence, 2017). Clients also differ in their readiness to move to action – some will seek coaching to think, reflect and learn rather than as a support to enact an immediate change (Prochaska et al, 1994). The type of goal a client may present could be driven by their intrinsic values (an autonomous goal) or by a feeling of what they 'ought' to do (an internally controlled goal) (Deci & Ryan, 2000). Client goals may also be influenced by the involvement of an organisational sponsor prescribing the goal (an externally controlled goal), which may or may not align with the client's goals.

3. The coach

Each coach comes from a philosophy or 'school' of coaching, which will prioritise goal setting to a greater or lesser degree, as well as a general personal preference for or against goal setting. At a group level, research has found a general trend that coaches who have trained for longer are more goal-oriented in their coaching practice (David et al, 2014). From the same study there is also evidence that coaches from the USA are generally more goal-oriented than their European peers, perhaps due to the differences in how coaching has developed in each region. For European coaches only, the more experienced they were, the less their orientation towards using goals. The researchers speculated about whether this is due to training differences (perhaps goal setting is more prominent in recent coach training programmes) or increases in confidence (meaning more experienced coaches rely less on goal setting).

4. The operating environment

Goal setting occurs within a system. SMART goals are likely to work best in an environment that is linear, predictable and slow to change; where the connection between a goal and the action taken to achieve it is clear and stable, and behaviour is adapted to keep on-track for goal achievement. In operating contexts that are messy, complex and fast-paced, a specific goal may quickly become redundant, or the actions needed to achieve it may not be obvious. Here the priority is to adjust the goal itself, rather than adjust the action towards it (Cavanagh, 2006).

Broadening your approach to goal setting

Through understanding and appreciating the variety of factors at play in coaching, we can rethink and reconceptualise what is meant by goal setting – and not be limited to only the classic approach. We can use goal setting in a more flexible way, considering how we work best in the service of each client. You are encouraged you to think not of SMART goals but of goal setting as a skilled and mindful art.

Expanding your skill set to goal setting

■ What do you understand 'a goal' to be? How can you extend your own understanding of what is meant by 'a goal'?

■ What are the factors that you have seen at play and how might these influence your approach to goal setting?

■ To what extent do you currently gain a comprehensive understanding of your clients' preference for using goals, their readiness to set goals, and the factors that may be influencing their goals? How can you develop this?

■ What do your clients mean when they talk about 'goals'? What opportunities are there to expand your clients' own understanding of goals, in terms of their multi-dimensional and dynamic nature?

Expanding your mind set to goal setting

■ A goal can give a sense of direction and, as such, provide security to the coach. How comfortable do you feel working without a goal (in the classic sense)? What would make you more comfortable to try working in a different way?

■ How comfortable do you feel with goals shifting, changing and emerging? How can you feel more comfortable with being open to this change?

■ What would happen if you think of a coaching conversation as one that is based on learning, rather than based on goal setting?

■ How can you best serve your clients' needs? How can you take what you know about the complexity and fluidity of goal setting, and use this most effectively for the benefit of your client?

Conclusion

The singular, linear goal setting approach – that often comes to mind when we think of coaching – is just one of many options available to us as coaches. For clients who enjoy working to specific goals, and have set goals that are achievable, straightforward and performance related, then the principles of goal-setting taken from these management models are likely to work well. For other clients, who may not be ready to set a goal, are not motivated by goals, or have a goal that is fuzzy, a different approach is needed. How can you work flexibly with goals to best serve your individual client?

References

Alexander, G and Lanza Tans F. (2021) Behavioural Coaching – the GROW model, pp105-120. In: J Passmore (Ed.) *Excellence in Coaching –Theory, tools, techniques to achieve outstanding coaching performance (4th ed)* . London: Kogan Page.

Cavanagh, M J (2006) Coaching from a systemic perspective: A complex adaptive conversation. In: DR Stober, and AM Grant (Eds.) *Evidence-based Coaching Practice: Putting Best Practices to Work for Your Clients*. Hoboken: Wiley & Sons.

Clutterbuck, D and David, S A (2013) Goals in Coaching and Mentoring: The Current State of Play. In: S David, D Clutterbuck and D Megginson (Eds.) *Beyond Goals: Effective Strategies for Coaching and Mentoring*. Surrey, England: Gower.

Clutterbuck, D and Spence, G (2017). Working with Goals in Coaching. In T Bachkirova, G Spence and D Drake (Eds.) *The SAGE Handbook of Coaching*. London: Sage.

David, S, Clutterbuck, D and Megginson, D (2013) *Beyond Goals: Effective Strategies for Coaching and Mentoring*. Surrey, England: Gower.

David, S, Clutterbuck, D and Megginson, D (2014) Goal orientation in coaching differs according to region, experience, and education. *International Journal of Evidence Based Coaching and Mentoring* 12 2 134-145.

Deci, E L and Ryan, R M (2000) The "what" and "why" of goal pursuits: Human needs and self-determination behaviour. *Psychological Inquiry* 11 227-68.

Doran, G T (1981) There's a S.M.A.R.T. Way to Write Management's Goals and Objectives. *Management Review* 70 35-36.

Grant, A (2013a) Autonomy support, relationship satisfaction and goal focus in the coach-coachee relationship: Which best predicts coaching success? *Coaching: An International Journal of Theory, Research and Practice* 7 18-38.

Locke, E A (1968) Toward a theory of task motivation and incentives. *Organizational Behavior & Human Performance* 3(2) 157–189.

Locke, E A and Latham, G P (1990) *A theory of goal setting & task performance*. Prentice-Hall, Inc

Price, R (2021) Goal setting in coaching. In J. Passmore (Ed.), *The Coaches Handbook*. Abingdon: Routledge.

Prochaska, J O, Norcross, J C and DiClemente, C C (1994) *Changing for good*. New York: Avon Books.

Whitmore J (2017) *Coaching for Performance* (5th Edition). London: Nicholas Brealey.

SECTION 3:
THE SESSION CORE

Chapter 21:
How can I make better ethical decisions in my coaching practice?

Jonathan Passmore

Introduction

Leaders and coaches face ethical dilemmas every day in their practice – for example, when to respect confidentiality, when to highlight dangerous or unethical practice or when to report illegal practices to regulators. Ethics is about making a choice about what we consider to be right or wrong. It is an essential component of good coaching and good leadership. But how can coaches and leaders manage this tightrope? Ethical codes of conduct may explain what we should do in black-and-white cases, but most situations in the real world are full of ambiguity, half facts and multiple shades of grey. Is it always right to blow the whistle, how should we do it and to whom? In this chapter we try to offer a handy guide to ethical decision making, giving coaches a head start with the aim of improving ethical conduct.

What is ethics?

Ethics, at its most simple, is about deciding between what is right and wrong. But really what we mean is what is 'morally' right or wrong, as opposed to financially, commercially or strategically. Morality itself is concerned with the norms, values and beliefs embedded in society. Such views are often unspoken and can be difficult to name, or at least become more and more unclear the deeper we explore the issue. For example, is it wrong to take someone else's life? What about assisted suicide? Is war always wrong? What about fighting the Nazis? Is it wrong to kill someone? What if this is done in order to save a member of your family? The ethical dilemmas in coaching may be less extreme, but similar ambiguities occur.

What are ethical dilemmas?

Ethical dilemmas are choices that occur when the answer about a future course of action is unclear: 'Should I do A or should I do B?' In coaching, these choices may involve issues about managing or breaking confidentiality: in what circumstances would it be acceptable to whistle-blow on an individual client or client sponsor? It may involve maintaining an appropriate relationship with a sponsor client or individual client: in what circumstances would it be appropriate to go to an organisation's premises or individual client's home? It may involve conflicts between the needs of the individual client and the organisational client who is paying for the coaching: in what circumstances would it be acceptable to protect an individual client who is using their employer's resources to run their own business?

Resolving ethical dilemmas

How can coaches and leaders best resolve ethical dilemmas? One way is to follow the ethical codes offered by professional bodies. Almost all professional bodies have a code of ethics, whether this is in financial services, health or coaching. In coaching some of the main bodies, such as the AC and EMCC, have come together to form a Global Code. While other bodies, such as the British Psychological Society (BPS), American Psychological Association (APA), and ICF have their own codes. Often individual organisations also have codes of conduct that relate to their organisation and sector. However, such codes can be vague, or offer black-and-white solutions in a world of grey, ambiguous complexity.

One way forward is to use a heuristic, a rule of thumb, to help guide our thinking and thus improve the overall decisions we make. One such model is APPEAR (Passmore & Turner, 2018; Passmore & Sinclair, 2020). The APPEAR model offers a step-by-step process, going from encouraging greater ethical awareness to recognising that making ethical choices brings with it consequences that both we and others must live with (see Table 21.1).

Table 21.1: Six stages of the APPEAR model
■ **A**wareness
■ **P**ractice
■ **P**ossibilities
■ **E**xtending the field
■ **A**cting on reflections
■ **R**eflecting on learning

These six stages are non-linear. The first stage of the process is **awareness**. For high-quality ethical decision making, coaches and leaders need to be sensitive to ethical issues. This may involve an awareness of best practice, awareness of one's own values and of cultural and societal norms: what's acceptable and what is unacceptable at this moment in time and in this cultural, national or organisational context.

In considering this we recognise that values are situated within a historical context: what may have been common practice 50 years ago may lead to dismissal in the modern workplace. Ethical practice also varies between countries: what is acceptable in the UK may be very different to practice in the Middle East or Africa. The sector will also have an impact: higher expectations exist of public sector employees than private sector employees, and of regulated sectors than non-regulated sectors. For example, the ethical standards we expect of a cancer nurse are likely to be higher than the ones we expect of a used-car salesperson. Finally, organisations may set different standards for what they consider to be acceptable – whether that's in how they report their profits or the ethical standards they expect of their suppliers.

The second stage is **practice**. While coaches and leaders engage in their roles, regular reflection through supervision, journaling or personal reflection can help develop greater situational and self-awareness.

Stage three of the process (**possibilities**) is the emergence of a dilemma. In some roles this can happen every week, in others every few months, or once a year. This stage involves generating alternative courses of action in response to the emergence of the dilemma. This may start with a dichotomy: 'I can do A, or I can do B', but as reflection deepens, and through conversations with others, multiple options are likely to emerge.

At stage four, **extending the field**, the individual should aim to work through the options to better understand the options available, discounting less attractive options and selecting the more ethical and practical option.

The fifth stage, **acting on reflections**, is about implementing the appropriate course of action. This can take courage and can come with unpleasant consequences. These consequences may not just be for others i.e. those who may have committed an illegal action; whistle-blowing itself can carry its own consequences, which may include the person being ostracised, losing their employment or the contract and damage to reputation, as Edward Snowden, the US whistle-blower, discovered.

The final stage is for the individual to **reflect** on their learning. This reflection should be at two levels: first, a reflection of the process and the various stakeholders, and what they have learned as a coach from thinking through and implementing this ethical action; second, reflection on the issue and themselves. What have they learned about themselves in this process?

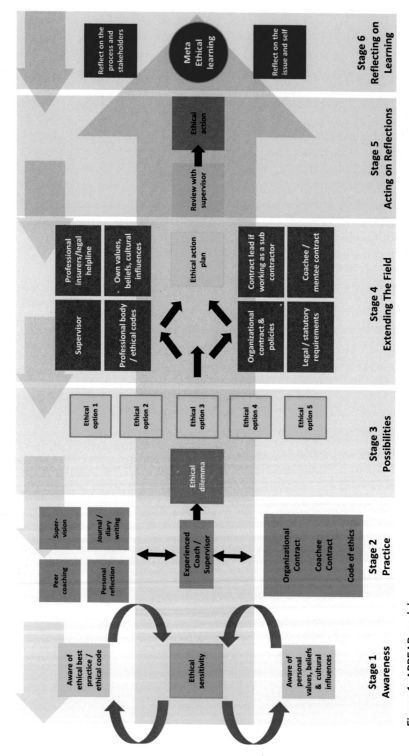

Figure 1: APPEAR model

Conclusion

The APPEAR model is a not a formula that guarantees a successful outcome in all circumstances. However, using a staged approach can be a useful compliment to professional body codes of ethics. The model helps individuals consider more deeply the various factors and make a more informed decision in the complex, multifaceted and ambiguous world in which we now work.

References

ICF (2017) *Code of Ethics* [online]. Available at: https://coachfederation.org/code-of-ethics (Accessed 1 July 2018).

Passmore, J. and Sinclair,T. (2020). *Becoming a coach: The Essential ICF Guide*. Worthing: Pavilion.

Passmore, J and Turner, E (2018) Reflections on integrity: the APPEAR model. *Coaching at Work* 13 (2) 42–46.

Chapter 22:
How can I ask better coaching questions?

David Clutterbuck

Introduction

Great questions make someone think. They derail expected trains of thought, opening up new tracks to follow – typically by taking different perspectives. The task of creating powerful questions is not just the coach's. Very often, the most impactful questions arise from within the client. All the coach does is open a window that lets the light shine in. Generating such questions is a collaborative act between coach and client, built upon intense and compassionate listening. The harder you try to create a powerful question, the less likely you are to succeed. The better you listen, the more naturally the right questions will occur of their own accord.

What makes an impactful question?

In their early training, coaches are taught a number of questions that have the potential to help clients think. In practice, these rapidly lose their impact because:

- the client has already encountered them before, in other contexts, so they lose the surprise factor
- they encourage lazy questioning, where the coach automatically falls back on faithful standbys
- they encourage lazy answering, because the client has developed a formulaic response (which they are often unaware of).

A question is only powerful or impactful if it causes the client to step outside of their normal narrative or self-discourse.

From analysing hundreds of coaching questions, it is possible to identify the core characteristics of an impactful question. These are:

- **Personal:** the client feels that this question is specifically crafted or chosen for them and the situation they are in. Example: *In what ways is this your responsibility alone?*

- **Resonant:** in addition to any rational perspective, it carries a substantial emotional essence. Example: *How do you reward yourself?*

- **Acute and incisive:** it gets right to the point. Example: *What would it be like to care just enough?*

- **Reverberant:** it is not easy to answer once and for all. Any initial response is just a first take, subject to further reflection hours, months or even years later. Example: *What is the contribution you want to make to the world?*

- **Innocent:** it has none of your agendas – overt or hidden – within it. Example: *What is the question you are avoiding asking yourself about this?*

- **Explicit:** it is very simply expressed, as opposed to long and convoluted. Example: *What can you forgive yourself for?*

To help remember these, they make the acronym PRAIRIE.

A consistent observation is that the more the coach focuses on managing the coaching conversation, the fewer really impactful questions they ask.

A good starting point is to build your portfolio of powerful questions. When a question works, note it in your journal and store it for another occasion.

Five motives for questions

We suggest there are five question styles, based upon the reason for asking them.

These are:

1. Questions to demonstrate superiority. Examples are: *Who do you think you are? You don't think that's going to work, do you?*

2. Questions for information sharing – swapping data with someone else. Example*: So, what's different about working in this industry?*

3. Questions for self-curiosity i.e. information you are interested in for your own purposes and in relation to how you make sense of the world. Example: *How does that work?*

4. Questions for other-curiosity – how the other person makes sense of the world. Example: *What values drive how you approach these decisions?*

5. Questions that lead to better questions. This is about recognising that impactful questions are stimulated by great questions, which derive from good questions, which derive from… you get the picture! For obvious reasons there are no example here: it is the gradual emergence that is key.

Should you use *why* questions?

Standard textbooks say no, because *why* can put people on the defensive and because *what, where, who, when, which* and *how* tend to lead to more open responses. Experienced coaches often say yes, but suggest using them sparingly and in context, because defensiveness can't be dealt with unless it is brought out into the open. The more comfortable you feel about challenging your clients, the more useful *why* can be. Just don't overuse it and always consider first other ways of expressing the same thing – so 'What causes you to...?' rather than 'Why do you...?'

Taiichi Ohno (1988) advocated the value of 'five whys' – each probing a little deeper into the client's reasoning and rationalisations. Another way to make questions more challenging is to ask the same question multiple times, with different emphases. Here's an example, sticking with *why*:

■ Why do you care? (no emphasis)

■ Why *do* you care?

■ Why do *you* care?

■ Why do you *care*?

Four perspectives of questioning

Observation of dozens of coaches and mentors a couple of decades ago found that they were constantly shifting perspective. If someone is viewing an issue only from the perspective of their immediate response, they are unlikely to achieve any significant insights until they shift perspective. These shifts can be described on to spectra – rational to emotional, and stepping in (seeing things from your own perspective) to stepping out (seeing things from the perspective of other people).

When a coach realises the client is stuck in one perspective, they first explore that perspective, using questions such as those below, then help them gradually move into another perspective.

Examples of questions in each perspective:

Stepping in/emotional

■ How do you feel?

■ What values are you applying?

■ Did that make you uncomfortable?

■ What would that mean for you?

Stepping in/rational

- What (really) happened?
- What do you want to achieve?
- What's the impact on your job?
- What choices do you have?

Stepping out/emotional

- How do you think the other person felt?
- How might your colleague feel if you handled it this way?
- What could you do to reduce their fears?

Stepping out/rational

- Can you look at it from another perspective?
- How would you advise someone else?
- What prevents you?
- What outcome do you think they would want?

Sometimes the coach also uses bridging questions, such as: '*How do you want to feel about this?*'

You can also shift perspective by using questions that address the client's mood. Laughter and smiling have a strong, positive effect on creativity of thinking. So, questions such as '*What's the most ridiculous part of this situation?*' can redirect their mental energy along more beneficial paths.

With questions, less is more

Observing highly effective and less effective coaches reveals that the former ask far fewer questions than the latter, but the impact of the questions they do ask is much greater. Two practical techniques can help develop the habit of asking fewer but better questions:

- Before you ask any question, count to three. The client will often continue with their own thinking, which you might otherwise have interrupted. As you gain confidence, extend the count to five, seven, ten, or just wait for the client to give you a firm signal they want you to take the lead.
- When you think of a good question, first ask yourself, '*For whose benefit am I asking this?*' If you still think it is useful to ask, hold on to it and encourage the client to continue. Do this at least twice. By the third opportunity to pose the question, either it will have matured and become

more powerful, the client will have come up with the same question on their own, or you will have found a better question.

Dos and don'ts

■ Don't waste time worrying whether you will have a question when it is needed – that will get in the way of your listening.

■ Do trust your intuition to express curiosity. *'I'm curious about what is going on for you at the moment'* doesn't carry a question mark, but it implies a deeply compassionate level of questioning.

■ Avoid 'queggestions': these are suggestions disguised as questions, such as *'Have you considered…?'*

■ When questions you ask do have an impact, reflect upon why.

■ Whenever a question you ask clearly has an impact, **don't** follow it up with another too soon – give the client space (which could be several minutes or longer) to reflect.

■ Remember that you are not the judge of whether a question was impactful or not – experienced coaches frequently find that clients value and are stirred most by apparently ordinary questions, and that 'clever' questions often have little impact at all.

Building your own library of impactful questions

Once you have used an impactful question a few times, it becomes readily available in your memory. To get to that point, reflect on coaching conversations you have and keep a file of the questions that had impact. Compare them to PRAIRIE and see if you can sharpen them up. Refer to them from time to time when you feel that a coaching conversation could have gone better, if you had asked different questions. You can access hundreds of impactful questions, categorised by situation in the book *Powerful questions for coaches and mentors (2018)*.

Conclusion

Questioning is a fundamental skill for a coach. But it is only one of many tools. A simple raised eyebrow is a tool, when used appropriately. A few really strong questions at the right time are worth dozens of standard questions.

References

Clutterbuck, D (2018) *Powerful questions for coaches and mentors*. European Mentoring and Coaching Council.

Ohno, T (1988) *Toyota Production System: Beyond Large-Scale Production*. Portland, Or: Productivity Press.

Chapter 23:
How can I improve my listening?

Karen Foy

Introduction

We all know as coaches that listening is a foundational skill we must learn. Most of us would class ourselves as good listeners. After all, we have had years of experience of listening. But what are we listening for? Is listening more than paying attention to what people say? How can we take our listening skills to the next level, where we understand what our clients are trying to communicate, hearing what they are not saying as much as what they are? This chapter offers some thoughts on the barriers to effective listening and some ideas on how to overcome them.

What are we listening for?

There is a deep human need in all of us – to be heard. As humans, we want to communicate with others: to express our deepest thoughts and feelings and to be understood. Yet few of us experience this level of engagement in our everyday conversations with our families, colleagues or with our boss. Thoreau and Rosenblum (1996) suggested that listening is the 'greatest hospitality' we can offer another. Understanding the purpose of our listening will help us to improve this basic human skill to the level of a 'gift' or as 'hospitality' to the person being heard. Starr (2010) likens this gift to 'basking in sunlight', suggesting we actually grow when being listened to. There are a range of useful discussions about different levels of listening (Covey, 2004; Starr, 2010; Passmore, 2021) to support coaches in developing their listening, but first let's consider what we are listening for.

As coaches, we are seeking to understand rather than be understood (Covey, 2004). We are aiming to view reality as our clients see it, by exploring it in partnership with them and by being curious together.

We are listening for what is being said and, equally importantly, what is not said. We are listening for the subtleties of language and expression, of emotion, values and beliefs that make up the world view of our clients. It is highly unlikely that as coaches we can view the world exactly as our clients view it, but we can develop a deeper, more empathetic understanding by listening deeply for the clues.

Most coaching manuals and competence frameworks recognise listening (see, for example, the ICF, 2019; Passmore and Sinclair, 2020) as a key component of coaching. Active listening is what takes listening from a passive process to active engagement with our clients. Many coaching models and approaches suggest the coach is a passive listener and that the coach should provide the opportunity for clients to fully express themselves. Of course, there is value for the client in this space to speak. But there is so much more we can offer as a listening partner if we become more active in the process. To listen actively we need to draw on the full range of our client's communication. We are drawing information from the energy exuding from the client, their bodily actions and facial expressions. We could refashion the quote often attributed to St Francis of Assisi, 'Preach the Gospel at all times and, if necessary, use words' into 'Listen at all times and, if necessary, use your ears'.

What am I listening for?

Table 23.1 offers a few examples of physical changes you might be 'listening' for that will help to explore the narrative beyond words. We will explore more about this in the next chapter.

Table 23.1: Examples of physical changes

Body	Movements (i.e. foot tapping, comfort stroking of skin, playing with jewellery or hair), muscle changes (i.e. tension)
Voice	Words, pace, tone, pitch
Face	Muscle movement, facial expressions, skin colouration changes
Breathing	Depth and pace
Eyes	Eye contact, pupil dilation, amount of moisture in the eyes, gaze
Lips	Colour changes, tension, expressions

When we do listen for the actual words and expressions, there are a few approaches we can take that make listening more active and, therefore, more powerful in raising awareness for the client. What are the assumptions underlying statements that are offered by the client as facts? What are the beliefs at play that keep the person stuck? Listening actively means that we listen for powerful words in what the client is saying. It can help to be listening out for words that stand out; I like to think of these as portals to a deeper understanding or a greater awareness. Listening with curiosity and with the awareness that we all have subtly different definitions or meanings behind the words we use will mean you explore your client's use of language.

We can go even further in our listening, beyond the words and content to the rhythm of expression. Instead of getting caught up in the story of the other person we can notice the different pace a client uses when they are re-telling a well-known story and when they are thinking beyond their current awareness. The listening we are engaged in as coaches is for the purpose of bearing witness and to offer support to evoke greater awareness in our thinking partner. We don't need the content, or 'story'. If, in the coaching conversation, the pace and rhythm suggest story-telling, or providing information, we need to get active in prompting deeper reflection.

As a listening partner for our clients we want to be fully connected to them and listen effectively. So, what gets in the way of listening actively? One barrier is that our cognitive processes are distracted as we focus on preparing the next question. We can also get distracted by our own thoughts, emotions and internal dialogue, as our mind jumps from focusing on our client to focusing on ourselves.

To help you work through these barriers, here are two suggestions for you to practise building your 'listening muscle': freefall listening and listening to yourself.

Freefall listening

As noted above, when we listen in coaching, we are often using what we hear to build our next question. We can miss so many 'portals' or key words, allusions to beliefs or assumptions, patterns or even deeper clues of what might be going on, of what might be at the heart of the matter for the person we are listening to. To listen in freefall, go back to one of your recordings of a coaching session and listen to the person talking without the need to think of a question or a response. Take the pressure off yourself and give yourself permission to listen for:

- words that seem powerful or curious
- patterns, beliefs or assumptions
- what you think might be underneath it all
- anything you feel is not being said
- anything that helps you understand how the person views the world
- energy shifts, changes in tone or pace of speech.

Make a note of anything that you now hear that you otherwise missed in real time. Practising in this way can help attune you to listening at a deeper level.

Listening to yourself

We have been advised to lose our judgements in coaching. But what if your judgements are just more data in the conversation that might raise the awareness of the person you are listening to? The Association for Coaching (AC) competency framework encourages coaches to use 'self' as a resource for the development of the client's self-awareness and learning by offering here-and-now feedback (2012).

Instead of spending our time trying to push these judgements out of our awareness, what might we learn from attending to them and, instead of censoring them, using the information to inform our listening and questioning? Again, we can experiment with recordings first to get used to listening to ourselves in service of our clients, gauging whether what we are saying to ourselves has the potential to raise the awareness and insight of the client. It takes practice to get comfortable with this dual listening, and part of that process is to trust that if your intention is to support the client, you are less likely to be judging and more likely to be integrating your own reactions.

The quality of our listening is the foundation for the people we work with to grow in the sunlight Starr (2010) refers to. If we can be fully present, listen with our whole self to what is and isn't being said and use our curiosity, we are more likely to be awarded a glimpse into the world viewed by our client, on which we can build our powerful interventions.

Conclusion

Good coaching starts with listening. Listening to what our clients are saying, and not saying, and the rhythm in which they express themselves is, thus, a central skill reflected in all of the global professional body competencies. However, listening is a skill many of us struggle with. By stepping back we can listen both more effectively to what our clients are truly saying, as well as listening more effectively to ourselves.

References

Association for Coaching (2012). Available at: https://cdn.ymaws.com/www.associationforcoaching.com/resource/resmgr/Accreditation/Accred_General/Coaching_Competency_Framewor.pdf (Accessed 28 October 2019).

Covey, S R (2004) *The Seven Habits of Highly Effective People*. New York: Simon and Schuster.

ICF (2019) ICF Core Competencies. Available at: https://coachfederation.org/core-competencies [Accessed 28 October 2019].

Passmore, J (ed.) (2021) *Excellence in Coaching: Theory, tools and techniques to achieve outstanding coaching performance* (4thedition). London: Kogan Page.

Passmore, J. and Sinclair, T. (2020). *Becoming a coach: The essential ICF guide*. Worthing: Pavilion.

Starr, J (2010) *The Coaching Manual: The Definitive Guide to the Process, Principles and Skills of Personal Coaching* (3rd edition). London: FT Press.

Thoreau, H D and Rosenblum, N L (1996) *Thoreau: Political Writings*. Cambridge: Cambridge University Press.

Chapter 24:
How can I use reflections in my coaching?

Jonathan Passmore

Introduction

While much is talked about in coaching about the role of active listening and open questions, the other friends from the communication gang of six are often forgotten or at least neglected: affirmations, summaries, reflections and the role of silence. Yet all six are essential communications for the coach, and from what we call AL-OARSS. In this chapter we will focus on two: summaries and reflections. The terms are often confused and thus we will aim to illustrate what each is and when to use them, as well as explore the different forms of reflection that the coach can use. If a coach is able to master the use of these, alongside the use of active listening and open questions, they are well on their journey towards becoming an effective coach.

Reflections

Offering a reflection, or making reflective listening statements, is a key skill for strengthening key aspects of the relationship. Reflective listening involves saying back to the person something of what they have said, but in a way which deepens their understanding. Many coaches believe that the coach should use the exact words or phrase the client has used. In essence, they claim the coach should not 'put words in the clients' mouth (Dunbar, 2016). But this is not what Carl Rogers recommends, nor is that view supported by research evidence on empathic listening (Rogers, 1962).

Just repeating or mirroring what the client says can be irritating. The coach sounds more like a parrot, resulting in the client responding: 'I just said that'. This approach does not demonstrate deep listening, but simply echoing back and thus requires a lower level of skill to what we are suggesting here. In contrast, the focus of reflective listening is to get inside the meaning of the client's words and to be able to reflect back that meaning. This requires paying attention to the whole communication not just the words being used.

When we listen at an empathetic level, we can accurately capture the meaning of what the client has said, and let them know you are really being understood. Listening at this level enables us to achieve a number of things: check for understanding, encourage the client to reflect on what they have just said and encourage further exploration of the topic. When we follow a reflection with a question, we can then also move the conversation forward.

Reflections come in different shapes including simple and complex reflections. Most of us are used to the simply reflection, but using more complex forms can help clients in subtle ways to more deeply consider their feelings about an issue, topic or person.

Simple reflections

The simple reflection is what most of us would consider to be a reflection. In this case, the coach aims to accurately mirror back what they gave heard, but mirror back in a way that reflects the meaning, as opposed simply to the word used by the client. The coach should aim to stay as close as possible to the client's intended meaning.

For instance:

Client: 'I wasn't really sure about the new role when I started, but I thought I would see how things went.'

Coach: 'You were uncertain about your new role, but you were willing to see how things developed.'

This type of simple reflection usually generates a response from the client, where they talk more about their feeling or situation, explaining their thinking or perspective. In so doing we help the client understand their feelings more deeply.

Complex reflections

The second type of reflection are complex reflections (Miller & Rollnick, 2013). These aim to 'go underneath the surface' of what the person has said. One way to do this is to use a metaphor. This approach encourages the coach to imagine what the client is feeling through a 'guess' in the form of a metaphor.

For instance, using the same client statement:

Client: 'I wasn't really sure about the new role when I started, but I thought I would see how things went.'

Coach: 'You had mixed feelings about the new role, but you were willing to be open minded to see how it developed.'

Other ways of reflecting can be to change one or two words. For instance:

Client: 'I use to really enjoy my role, but since we switched to working mainly at home, I don't enjoy it anymore.'

Coach: 'You used to enjoy your job, but home working is much harder.'

Capture the imagined feeling:

Client: 'I use to really enjoy my role, but since we switched to working mainly at home, I don't anymore.'

Coach: 'This must be frustrating for you.'

Finish the sentence:

Client: 'I used to really enjoy my role, but since we switched to working mainly at home, I don't enjoy it anymore.'

Coach: 'And you're looking forward to returning to work in the office with your colleagues.'

All of these reflections bring a slightly different spin and each will have a slightly different impact on the client. However, in general, a complex reflection is likely to keep the client talking about the topic.

To change the way the client is thinking, the coach can use one of two options – an amplified and a muted reflection.

The former, an amplified reflection, is likely to result in the client dialling down their emotions about a situation, and to explore their feelings with a more critical lens. For example:

Client: 'I used to really enjoy my role, but since we switched to working mainly at home, I don't enjoy it anymore.'

Coach: 'You really hate working from home.'

The effect of this reflection is the client will start to produce some of the benefits of working from home. For example:

Client: 'Well, I would not go that far, it does mean less travel time, plus I do get more done and despite my initial anxieties the technology works really well.'

Coach: 'It sounds as if you can see upsides, as well as downsides to working from home, and it does mean you are more efficient in your job and have more time for your family, as you are not wasting time in commuting.'

This reflection is likely to generate more talk about the benefits of working from home. In this way, the coach can help clients explore both sides of a current situation.

The second is the muted reflection. This, in contrast, downplays the emotion, and is likely to lead to the client correcting the coach in the other way, providing more arguments about why working from home is a negative experience.

Client: 'I used to really enjoy my role, but since we switched to working mainly at home, I don't enjoy it anymore.'

Coach: 'You really enjoy your role, but working from home can sometimes be a bit frustrating.'

This reflection is likely to lead to the client exploring examples of how working for home is more than 'a bit frustrating', but lacks the fulfilment of working in the office.

However, care needs to be taken when using both muted and amplified reflections. If used more than once in a session the coach can be experienced as not listening, and such communications failures will damage the coach-client relationship. They are thus best used sparingly to help clients explore in more depth both sides of an argument or perspective, and are best used as sandwiches between multiple simple reflections.

Roadblocks

Thomas Gordon (1970) describes 12 'roadblocks' that get in the way of reflective listening. These roadblocks act to divert the client away from the continued exploration and elaboration of their train of thought, and can stop forward momentum. These roadblocks are summarised in Table 24.1

Table 24.1: Roadblocks to coaching conversation
1. Ordering, directing, or commanding
2. Warning or threatening
3. Giving advice, making suggestions, providing solutions
4. Persuading with logic, arguing or lecturing
5. Moralising, preaching, or telling clients their duty
6. Judging, citicising, disagreeing, or blaming
7. Agreeing, approving, or praising
8. Shaming, ridiculing, or name calling
9. Interpreting or analysing
10. Reassuring, sympathising or consoling
11. Questioning or probing
12. Withdrawing, distracting, humouring, or changing the subject

(Adapted from Gordon 1970)

Conclusion

Summaries and reflections can be hard to use, and even harder to do well. But the good news is that coaches can get better the more they practise. It is also helpful to cultivate the right mindset and, as we have discussed elsewhere, this includes having a genuine interest in what your client has to say, respecting their views as to what's right for them and having a desire to share the full meaning, not just say the client's words back, to help them deepen their understanding.

References

Dunbar, A (2016) *Clean coaching*. Abingdon: Routledge.

Gordon, T (1970) *Parent Effectiveness Training*. London: McKay: Random House.

Miller, W and Rollnick, S (2013) *Motivational Interviewing*. New York: Guildford Press.

Rogers, C (1961) *On becoming a person: A therapist's view of psychotherapy*. London: Constable.

Chapter 25:
How can I use affirmations in my coaching?

Jonathan Passmore

Introduction

We all like someone to speak well of us, to encourage us and to believe we can succeed. In the coaching relationship, affirmations offer a way for the coach to express their belief in their client – to offer support, encouragement and to help build the client's self-esteem. In this chapter we will review these aspects of the coach's role, and how the coach can act to support their client in making the psychological changes needed to step forward and make the change.

Affirmations

Affirmations are one of the six key communication skills required for coaching, the others being active listening, open questions, reflections, summaries and silence. Together, these form the AL-OARSS model. Blending these elements enables the coach to understand, empathise and help clients develop insight while progressing toward their goals.

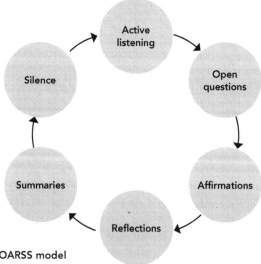

Figure 25.1: AL-OARSS model

What are affirmations?

Affirmation are statements made by the coach about something positive about their client's life, role or their situation. Affirmations may relate to a wide range of aspects about their client including past behaviour, achievements, their display of strengths, resilience, determination or future aspirations.

Before being able to offer genuine affirmations, first the coach needs to develop a relationship with the client where the client values the opinion of the coach. Secondly, the coach needs to understand their client. Thirdly, the coach needs to listen deeply to be able to spot when their client is at their best; what is right about them, not what is wrong with them.

Affirmations can be brief and commonly take the form of a short sentence of recognition or appreciation. They may sound something like:

- 'You've been successful in the past.'
- 'From what you have shared with me, you are the kind of person who cares a lot your team.'
- 'You're someone who in your last role built a good team.'
- 'You are really trying within this new role in marketing, even though you were reluctant to be redeployed from the sales team.'
- 'You're quite a determined person, based on how you succeed in getting the additional help at school for your child.'
- 'You sound to me as if you are the kind of person who cares a lot for other people.'

Affirmations may help to build a client's feeling of self-belief, self-efficacy and hope. They can also significantly strengthen the relationship between the coach and client. They help us to show the client that they have some of the resources, skills and strengths within them that can help them improve, and they can also induce a mild positive emotional experience, which can be important for openness and personal growth (Fredrickson, 2004).

It's important to understand that affirmations are not the same as compliments or praise. The latter usually takes the form of a general statement, such as 'Well done', or, 'You're an excellent manager'. Praise is typically a general statement made with little or no supporting evidence. In contrast, affirmations are specific statements, highlighting a personal attribute, and based on an event or with supporting evidence used in the statement.

Affirmations also have two other important features. The first is they are genuine. If the client thinks the coach is not genuine but just trotting out a commonly used phrased to all clients, it is more likely to have a negative than a positive impact. Secondly, affirmations need to be used sparingly. If the coach uses them every few minutes, the affirmation has a diminishing effect. Used once in the right place during a session it can be powerful; used twice, the effect may be positive; used three, four or five times in a session, the coach begins to sound like a fake cheerleader.

Making affirmations is one of the ways in which the coach can express unconditional positive regard towards a client. Unconditional positive regard was one of the six necessary and sufficient conditions that Carl Rogers argued were the key ingredients for a healing relationship (Rogers, 1957).

How can coaches affirm their client?

Coaches who embody positive regard for their clients will find this easier. When we prize others, we are always looking for ways to 'catch them doing it right', whether it's our first child who has just taken their first step across the living room, or our teenager who has just received their exam results. The coach who prizes their client in the same way will be constantly on the look-out for positives, seeking ways they can encourage and motivate them forward. However, we know with our teenager, if we over-do it, the effect can be negative. Being selective actually helps.

Affirming clients seems to serve a number of functions. It strengthens the client's sense of self or personal agency and belief in their capacity to be engaged in an effective relationship, reinforces engagement in the therapeutic process, and facilitates psychological growth and resilience.

When do affirmations work best?

In addition to offering specific affirmations, the coach should aim to convey a general feeling of positive regard, if affirmations are to land. This is best conveyed through multiple channels, including active listening, establishing eye contact, maintaining positive body language, offering reassuring words, creating positive narratives and speaking in a gentle tone of voice.

This wider repertoire of communications must reflect client need. Coaches will vary in the extent to which they naturally convey positive regard, and clients vary in the extent to which they need, elicit, and benefit from it. The coach needs to monitor how the relationship is proceeding, and how clients respond to affirmations, as well as the feedback they give at the end of each session

Table 25.1: Five steps for affirmation

1. Listen careful to what your client is staying.
2. Occasionally reflect back to demonstrate empathy and understanding, and thereby developing the relationship.
3. Be aware of your own feelings, how are these changing as you listen to your client. →

4. Identify a statement that demonstrates a positive aspect of your client, and which will be a useful asset when moving towards their goal for the session.
5. Reflect this back to them in a short statement, which includes a positive evaluation made by you of the behaviour (or other personal quality) and links this to the event (evidence).

Conclusions

Affirmations are an essential tool in the coach's repertoire. Affirmations sit alongside open questions, active listening, reflections, summaries and silence, as the six core communications skills. In using affirmations, coaches need to ensure they are genuine and used sparingly if building self-regard is to be realised.

References

Rogers, C R (1957) The Necessary and Sufficient Conditions of Therapeutic Personality Change. *Journal of Consulting Psychology* 21 95-103.

Chapter 26:
How can I stop giving advice to my coaching clients?

Karen Foy

Introduction

It has been suggested that coaching is fundamentally about unlocking a person's potential to maximise their own performance (Whitmore, 1995); it is about helping them to learn, rather than teaching them. Yet one of the biggest struggles for a coach is to resist the temptation to give advice. How do we manage this boundary between supporting people to learn and teaching them from our experience? In this chapter, we will explore a few ideas as to how coaches can manage the boundary between support and advice to create more impactful coaching that enables clients to take control.

The boundary between support and advice

Many coaches come to coaching with a desire to help others. We feel we want to 'give back'; we feel we have something to offer. Perhaps we have had a successful career and we want our legacy to be supporting the next generation to succeed. Or maybe, in life we have navigated some rough seas and we want to share what we have learnt to prevent others facing those storms in life. Left unexamined, this drive to help others, well-meaning as it may be, can create pitfalls for us as coaches. These can retard our development to become a transformational force in someone else's life. Elizabeth Gilbert (2016) urges those who write with the motivation of 'helping someone, to save themselves the bother – most people don't want that'. This seems sage advice for coaches, not just budding writers.

If we believe our job is to help others, we risk forming the belief that we are responsible for the success of our clients, and this can lead us to become distracted as we seek solutions to the issues the client brings. Even worse, given that we know that the 'rules' of coaching tell us to avoid directing the client, by taking on the responsibility for their success, we set ourselves up for an internal struggle. There we are: looking for solutions, working through the internal conflict, trying to resist giving advice. The result is often that we seek ways to find a clever question that forces our client to see the world through our eyes and to navigate their way through their world with our compass.

How might we resolve this issue and identify the boundary between supporting our clients fully while avoiding giving advice? Korotov *et al* (2012) explore the need for former consultants, therapists – and we could add executives to this list – to lose their identities and attachments to their former roles. As coaches, we must be clear on our role and our motivations in order to keep the coaching space as a fertile ground for the benefit of the client's growth, and not as one set up to meet our own needs to be helpful. To do this, the first focus for our attention may be to revisit some of the assumptions underpinning coaching.

As coaches, we honour the client as the expert in their own life and work, and believe they are whole, creative and resourceful. Standing on these foundations, as coaches we encourage self-discovery and support client-generated solutions and strategies based on their own goals and aspirations. Could this offer our first compass point to help us to navigate the boundary?

Coaching is a powerful intervention but that does not make it a panacea for every situation. As Korotov *et al* (2012) note, at times, a consulting approach is more appropriate, while at others, therapeutic approaches may be required. In these latter cases, the skilled coach's role is to refer the client to the appropriate helper. We need to be clear that coaching is the appropriate intervention for the person and the presenting issue. This will always lead us back to robust contractual agreements for the relationship and the firm establishment of coaching agreements for each session.

But even assuming that coaching is the correct intervention, this does not necessarily mean we no longer face boundary challenges. It is interesting that we note that clients are 'experts in their own life' – but does that make them experts in everything? This is an area that can cause a great deal of soul-searching for the reflective coach. If the client really doesn't know the answer to a question they seek and the coach does, how ethical is it for the coach to withhold information? How useful is it to dig for answers that are just not there? This can bring us right back to the heart of the 'rules' of coaching: Am I allowed to tell?

As humans, we seek for certainty. Our brains are wired to look for the rules that keep us safe and, as coaches, we want to learn what we should and shouldn't do. But this is one of those areas where, sadly, there is much more ambiguity than certainty. The boundaries of coaching and mentoring can be permeable, such as in the area of advice giving. This is especially true for coaches building their experience, where it is important to learn the rules. As we get more experienced, we may be able to flex a little more, but first we must practise keeping solid boundaries before making a choice to stray from our true north.

Anthony Grant (2019) argues that too rigid an approach in our coaching is in direct opposition to the needs of the individual or the organisation. Instead, the coach needs to adapt and flex to meet the needs of their client. Marson

(2018), too, highlights the coaching continuum, where individuals move from across the spectrum of pull and push interventions, akin to John Heron's six intervention styles (Heron, 1989). Offering advice is at the opposite end – the push end of the continuum; this means it is more closely associated with mentoring. So how do we stay clearly in a coaching framework?

Sir John Harvey Jones, the business leader and TV presenter (BBC, 1990) has suggested that two things happen when we offer advice: the client is happy because they have one fewer problems, and we feel good because we feel smart and clever. However, he suggests two other things happen: we have failed to help them grow and we have solved today's problems with yesterday's thinking. Even more concerning, if we 'help' our clients with our solutions, what does that say about them? Do we make them 'help-less'? There is a danger that we tip the balance of power in the favour of the coach, unintentionally signalling that we do not believe that they have all the resources they require to solve their own dilemmas. As coaches, our first aim must be to allow the clients to sit at the feet of their own experiences to learn and grow (Zachery, 2000).

While accepting that there are no clear steps we can take as coaches to navigate this murky area of supporting clients without leading them with our solutions, there are some areas we can reflect on that could help us to find our own unique way to manage this balance.

(i) Role clarity

We can be clear from the start of the coaching relationship, and at the start of each session, about what our role is in the conversation. We should also ensure that coaching is the most appropriate intervention for the client. We can remind ourselves that coaching is an equal partnership and we can examine our own need to 'help', reasserting our basic assumption that 'I am OK, you're OK' (Harris, 1995). From this foundation we can be clear about who owns the goal, the issue and the solution, liberating ourselves from the need to provide the answer.

(ii) Sharing knowledge and experience mindfully

Part of our role in supporting our clients is to share our knowledge in a way that moves the person forward, especially when they are lost or overwhelmed. This can appear to be in contradiction to all we have learned about coaching, unless we set it in the context of *not* leading with our ideas and solutions. The second criterion is that our 'advice' is limited to facts as opposed to opinions: 'Moscow is the capital of Russia' is a fact. 'Moscow is the most beautiful city in the world' is an opinion. As a general rule, we should try to avoid providing personal opinions and limit our advice to facts, when asked. The key here is 'when asked' and even then, not being too eager at the first invitation.

An exception to this might be when the client asks about your experience. Here it may be best to hold back, saying: 'Can we come back to this in a moment? Let's focus on your thoughts first.' Only after fully exploring a client's ideas should we return to this. And when we return to it, we should avoid giving our opinion, but instead share our experience. For example: 'You asked what I would do. Well, this is a common challenge I have heard from many leaders. I have heard others suggest X, Y and Z as possible ideas they wanted to explore. I wonder how these ideas from other leaders might fit your organisational context, while recognising that every organisation and every leader is different.'

Our approach aims to reduce the impact of our influence as the coach in the relationship, and instead draw on our experience in working with others, while also encouraging the client to adopt a critical perspective of such experience from others, reflecting on their own context and personal style. It is useful here to remember that our job is to support our clients to get a greater awareness of choice and to then make a choice that fits their schema.

(iii) Regular self-reflection and supervision

As there are no guarantees that we will manage this boundary successfully all the time, we need to honesty reflect on our voice and views in each session and on the impact of our need to be helpful.

Jane Austen reminds us in *Mansfield Park*: 'We have all a better guide in ourselves, if we would attend to it, than any other person can be.' Reflection and supervision offer us the opportunity to identify gaps in our approach and continue our personal journey of development. Honest reflection becomes paramount as we can all be skilled at justification to explain away our drift into offering our thoughts and suggestions. How many coaches, I wonder, would be honest enough to reflect on this with a supervisor and be humble enough to admit they were seduced by the offer to become the expert in the relationship? For some coaches this is the area in which they feel they need to prove their worth, show value for money in the relationship and, paradoxically, it is this self-deception that removes the power from the relationship.

If as coaches we can become more concerned with supporting our clients to discover their inner guide, rather than working hard to prove our worth as a coach, we could let go of the responsibility for finding answers and trust our clients to find their own. As Bob Keegan (2014) puts it, we bring our humanity and not our pedigree to coaching.

Conclusion

As coaches, our role is to help clients to become more self-aware and through this to take more personal responsibility for the choices they face in life. When we step in to provide advice as to what we think is best for the client, we deny them their choice. The most effective coach, while sharing feedback and encouraging the development of new insights, leaves the ultimate choice to the client as to the path they wish to follow.

References

Austen, J (1992) *Mansfield Park*. London: Wordsworth Editions. (Originally published 1814.

BBC (1990) *Troubleshooter*. BBC TV.

Gilbert, E (2016) *Big Magic, Creative Living Beyond Fear*. London: Bloomsbury.

Grant, A (2019) Third Generation Workplace Coaching & Evidence-Based Coaching, British Psychological Society Masterclass. London.

Harris, T A (1995) *I'm OK You're OK*. London: Arrow Books.

Heron, J (1989) *Six Intervention categories*. Guildford: University of Surrey.

Keegan, R (2014) *Presentation to BT Global Leaders*. BT Headquarters, London.

Korotov, K, Florent-Treacy, E, Kets De Vries, MFR and Bernhardt, A (2012) *Tricky Coaching, Difficult Case in Leadership Coaching*. London: Palgrave McMillan.

Marson, N (2018) *Leading by Coaching, How to Deliver Impactful Change One Conversation at a Time*. London: Palgrave McMillan.

Zachery, L. (2000). *The Mentor's Guide: Facilitating Effective Learning Relationships*. San Francisco, CA: Jossey-Bass.

Chapter 27:
How can I work with emotions in coaching?

Aboodi Shabi

Introduction

In the early days of coaching, coaches commonly claimed that coaching was about action, not emotions. Part of this narrative derived from an attempt to distinguish – and to distance – coaching from counselling etc, and to promote coaching as a way to change behaviour without having to consider the role of emotions.

This view has been changing as the coaching profession has matured, and emotions are now widely accepted as being a legitimate part of coaching, and even explicitly included in the International Coaching Federation's (ICF) core competency model, which identifies the ability to manage one's emotions to stay present with the client, and demonstrate confidence in working with strong client emotions during the coaching process (see Passmore & Sinclair, 2020).

Emotions reveal something important about the client's inner world, and about their capacity for action, both of which need to be addressed and explored for sustainable change to occur.

Why work with emotions in coaching?

There are many reasons why emotions are both useful and critical in the coaching process. First, emotions are not just about feelings – they predispose us to action. Emotions shape both how we act and what actions are available to us. When I am happy, I will see different actions available to me than when I am sad; when I am resentful, I will perform the same tasks differently than I would if I were feeling grateful or content; a client who is feeling hopeless will experience coaching very differently to one who is enthusiastic. This last is especially relevant; if a client is resigned and doesn't believe they can change, then no coaching goal or idea for action is going to mean much until we address the underlying emotions.

Second, we live in a world where we tend to prioritise the rational over the emotional. We say things like: 'I know I should get over my sadness', or 'I shouldn't be worried about my future'. Often clients don't legitimise (or even notice) their own emotions, never mind listen to them or be curious about them. It's all too easy for a coach, when faced with a client with 'negative' emotions, to ask questions like: 'What would you do if you weren't afraid?', or 'How can you turn that into a positive?', thereby both delegitimising the client's experience of themselves and closing off the possibility of curiosity about what their emotions might be telling them. Furthermore, neuroscience shows us that the limbic (emotional) brain does not respond to commands or instruction – it responds to connection and relationship. So, a client telling themselves to 'get over' a feeling (and a coach going along with that) will not be successful.

When we, as coaches, can work freely and openly with a client's emotions, we give them space to be who they are, and we can help them to work with underlying issues, and increase both their capacity for action and their range of possible actions.

This space also serves to enhance the client's feeling of safety and trust in the coaching process. Coaching is, more than anything else, all about relationship. A coach is not just a neutral or distant observer of the client. As Lewis *et al* noted, the attuned practitioner 'doesn't just hear about a [client's] emotional life – the two of them live it' (Lewis *et al*, 2000). We need to be *intimately* involved in the coaching conversation, immersed in the connection, and, if we are, then we will be impacted on many levels by the client, by what they are saying, and not saying, and by *how* they are being.

Approach

There are two places to look when we start to work with emotions in coaching. First, a coach can be curious about the *client's* emotions. Sometimes emotions are clearly visible and clearly expressed (the client might say, 'I feel very angry about this', or they might cry, for example). Sometimes the clues are in the client's language, and the coach can enquire to uncover underlying emotions. When a client says, for example, 'There's nothing I can do about a work situation', or 'I don't know how to get my manager to listen to me', there will be emotions behind those statements, which careful questioning from the coach can elicit. Or the client's body might reveal emotions – the client's voice shakes when they talk about a difficult relationship at work, or they fidget when they are talking about the deadlines they are struggling to meet.

Second, we as coaches can look at *our own* emotional state, and notice and be curious about any changes that occur during the coaching conversation. We might notice, for example, that we feel sad when a client talks about not achieving their goals, or angry when a client tells us about how their boss is treating them. While it is true that our attention needs to be on the client, we also need to be aware of what might be happening to us emotionally when we are present with our client as a whole person. The coach's very self is involved in the coaching relationship; it is important to acknowledge 'the use of self as our prime asset in achieving the helping relationship. It is not an option but the cornerstone of our work' (Cheung-Judge, 2001). Our reactions might serve the coaching by uncovering things that are not explicit in the client's words. If my emotional state changes when a client is speaking, then I want to at least be curious (but not to believe that I am 'right') about what might be happening with the client that could be causing that change in me.

In both avenues of exploration above, we can be curious about any emotions that are acknowledged by the client. For example, we might explore the following kinds of question:

- What do those emotions tell the client about their issue and any underlying issues?

- What becomes different for them as they pay attention to their emotions?

- How do those emotions shape their capacity for action?

- What might they do differently as they start to listen to and honour their emotions?

Examples

Rahman talks about the pressure on him following a new promotion. He acknowledges that he is very worried about his ability to perform, but also feels that he should be on top of everything: 'I should be able to cope'. As we explore this, he starts to see that this self-talk only increases the pressure on himself, and we then explore how he might listen to his feelings about the challenges ahead, and how to ask for the support he needs. He acknowledges that his manager has offered him support, but he had refused all offers until now because of his unwillingness to legitimise his worries and fears.

Eva talks about leaving her job as a teacher. Initially, she says that her mind is made up and that she'll be 'only too glad to see the back of those kids'. As she talks about this, I notice that I feel sad, and I share that with her, asking her if that means anything to her. She pauses and thinks for a while, and then responds that it's not that she doesn't care about the kids, but that her work has become very demanding, and that she has very little time for herself and is 'exhausted all the time'. She acknowledges her own sadness, now, and this opens up a new path in our coaching about how she can take some time for her own self-care and to reconnect to what she really cares about.

Reflections for the coach

For us to work more with our client's emotions requires more than just an understanding of the importance of emotions in coaching: it requires ongoing emotional work on ourselves (Shabi, 2020). If we find a particular emotion in a client difficult, then we are likely to be managing ourselves (or closing down the emotion in the client for our own comfort). To develop our ability to be able to support the client and be present with them, we need to work on that emotion in our personal work. This is at the heart of the development of the coach and can help us to discover who we truly are.

With that in mind, you might want to reflect on the following questions as you work (and in your post-coaching reflections, or in supervision):

- What happens to you emotionally when a client is speaking?
- What emotions do you open to? Which do you close to?
- Which emotions do you find difficult to own in yourself?
- How does that shape your listening?

Conclusion

There is much to be gained from working with emotions in coaching – for the client, but also for the coach. The developmental challenge for coaches is to do our own ongoing personal work – the more comfortable we are with our own emotional world, the more present we can be with our clients. We can then accompany them on a deeper exploration of their inner world, and support them in discovering new learnings and insights for more sustainable behavioural change.

References

Cheung-Judge, M.-Y. (2001). 'The self as an instrument'. *OD Practitioners*, 33(3), pp. 11–16.

Cheung-Judge, M.-Y (2001) The self as an instrument. *OD Practitioners* 33 (3) 11–16.

Passmore, J. and Sinclair, T. (2020). Becoming a coach: The essential ICF guide. Worthing; Pavilion.

International Coaching Federation (2019) *Core competencies* [online]. Available at: https://coachfederation.org/core-competencies (accessed 7 July 2020).

Lewis, T, Amini, F and Lannon, R (2001) *A General Theory of Love*. New York: Vintage.

Shabi, A (2021) Using Emotions in Coaching, pp141-151. In J. Passmore, J. (ed) *The Coaches Handbook*. Abingdon: Routledge.

Chapter 28:
How can I work with the body in coaching?

Aboodi Shabi

Introduction

We might think of coaching as a *talking* profession: the client talks about an issue, and the coach listens and asks questions. But we are not disembodied voices – there is a body doing the talking, a body doing the listening and a body asking questions. And, outside the coaching session, the client's body (in addition to their words) affects how they show up in life. Focusing the client on their body, and what it reveals, will help them to explore and understand their coaching issues more deeply, and increase awareness of how they impact on others.

Why bring the body into coaching?

We live in a world where we prioritise the rational, and most of us are often disconnected from our bodies – as James Joyce described Mr Duffy in *Dubliners*: '[He] lived at a little distance from his body.' And yet, we are not disembodied beings. Our bodies reveal who we are, sometimes contrary to our words. We notice this when, for example, we are talking to someone who says they are listening, but their bodies give a very different message. Also, when we are in our heads, we might be focused on all the things we have to do, and thinking only about those. Listening to the body might remind us that we need to rest or take a break, and therefore tell us more than simply that we just need to work harder. Such data are really important in coaching – so that we coach the whole person and help the client listen to the whole person that they are.

Somatic coaching brings the client's attention to their bodies – by both observing and enquiring about how the client shows up somatically during the session, and also by supporting the client in developing new practices to help them embody a new learning goal. The body holds our embodied habits and our history – a history that is pre-linguistic; working at this level will produce change that is more powerful and more effective than working with language alone. For example, it's one thing to know that we have the right to say 'no', but we all know that people can say no with their words, while their bodies (including the voice) communicate a lack of commitment to holding that no. Delivering a no is both a linguistic act and an embodied act.

The path of becoming a somatic coach might be a long one that requires learning and practice on the part of the coach (we are just as much in our heads as everyone else!), but a key way of bringing this into your coaching is to notice the client's body and your own body's reactions to your clients – how what they are saying impacts on you – and to be curious about what you notice. In a very real sense, you and your reactions are instruments of coaching.

Approach

You can introduce this work into your coaching by following a six-step approach:

1. **Scan:** Before the coaching session, do a quick scan on where you are: What is going on in your body, how 'centred' are you? What tensions etc are you aware of? What do you notice about your energy? How is your breathing? It's important to notice your own state before the session, so that you can be more aware of any changes that occur once you connect with the client.

2. **Tune in:** When the client arrives at the session, start to tune in to them and their energy. What do you notice about the client as they come into the room or on to the call? What changes in your own body or energy etc. as you start to engage with the client?

3. **Notice:** During the conversation, in addition to paying attention to the client's goal and what they are saying, keep noticing what is going on in your body and what you observe in the client's body – gestures, breathing, tone, speaking pace etc.

4. **Share/enquire:** Share your observations with your client and be curious about them, especially if you notice changes in your client's body – or your own – as they talk about a specific person or issue. Ask your client to reflect on what their body might have to say about their coaching issue.

5. **Reshape/sculpt/move:** Invite your client to change how they sit or stand while they speak about a specific issue. Loop back to noticing and enquiring about what is different when the same issue is spoken about from a different body position, or a different pace etc.

6. **Practice:** To build on the learning and insights that come from a coaching session, work with your client to explore practices that will help them to embody the new learning.

Example

Marek has recently been internally promoted to manage the sales team he has been a part of for several years. He comes to coaching to work on the transition from being a peer in this team to becoming the team leader.

As he turns up to the coaching session, I notice that he is smiling and moves in a warm way that invites connection, and I feel myself relaxing in his company. As he starts the session, he speaks about the difficulties he has in asking his team to perform tasks and in being taken seriously. As he talks, I observe that he continues to smile, even when talking about his challenges, and that he giggles when he talks about making requests of his team. I also notice that this produces a reaction in me of not wanting to take him seriously. I enquire about this – sharing that I notice his smiling and giggling while he is talking about wanting to be taken more seriously. His first response is that he wasn't aware of this; I go on to ask whether he smiles/ giggles when he makes his requests. He acknowledges that he does, and I share my observation of my own reactions. As we talk about this, he shares that he is uncomfortable with having to manage people who were previously his peers; he wants to be 'part of the gang' and to be liked by everyone, so he smiles and is friendly all the time, to the detriment of his leadership role. I invite him to think about how he might deliver a request if he wanted to be taken seriously, and to pay attention to how he stands and his facial expressions. He practices doing so, working to resist the temptation to break into a smile. We explore this for a while and then talk about what embodied practices he might adopt to develop this more serious disposition so that it becomes more available to him. He suggests that rock climbing or ballroom dancing both require a certain seriousness and focus, and agrees to try both and see what difference those practices will bring.

Developing somatic awareness

To develop your own somatic awareness as a coach, in addition to taking part in a somatic coaching course, there are also some simple things you can do to sharpen your awareness. You can observe your own reactions to people, for example when watching a film or during a meeting. How do you react to what someone is saying? What do you notice about the way they are speaking – gestures, voice, pace etc – that produces that reaction in you? What does it tell you about them? Or you can 'people-watch' at a café or in an airport, for example, and just be curious about the people you see. Would this person be a leader whom you would trust? Would that person be someone who could say 'no' convincingly? What is it about the way they move that produces that reaction in you? Note that this is not about being right: it's about developing your curiosity and sharpening your awareness about human beings and the way they move – and about how they impact on your own body.

Finally, in addition to the reading material below, you could also watch the movie *The King's Speech* (an excellent example of somatic work) or Tim Roth's TV series *Lie to Me* (where Roth plays a private investigator who assists criminal investigations through his observations of people's body and facial gestures).

Conclusion

Working with the body in coaching is by no means an exact science with precise techniques to master, rather it is a relational approach that requires ongoing work on the part of the coach. That said, simply by being curious about what they observe and notice in their own and their client's bodies, coaches can begin to develop their somatic coaching capabilities, and to bring a rich and deep source of insight and change to their clients.

References

Aquilina, E and Strozzi-Heckler, R (2019) Somatic coaching. In: S Palmer & A Whybrow (eds) *Handbook of Coaching Psychology: A Guide for Practitioners* (2nd edition). London: Routledge.

Cheung-Judge, M-Y (2001) The Self as Instrument: A Cornerstone for the Future of OD. *OD Practitioner* 33 (3) 11–16.

Shabi, A and Whybrow, A (2019) Ontological coaching. In S. Palmer and A. Whybrow, eds., *Handbook of coaching psychology: A guide for practitioners* (pp219–228). London: Routledge.

Silsbee, D (2008) *Presence-Based Coaching: Cultivating Self-Generative Leaders Through Mind, Body, and Heart*. New Jersey: Jossey-Bass.

Strozzi-Heckler, R (1993) *The Anatomy of Change: A Way to Move through Life's Transitions*. Berkeley: North Atlantic Books.

Chapter 29:
How can I be more courageous in my coaching?

Karen Foy

Introduction

Have you ever considered the need to add courage to your coaching? Do courage and coaching seem strange bedfellows? Have you ever noticed something about your client, or sensed something that you think may be a blind spot for them, but never quite found the words to draw it to their attention? Coaches need to be both courageous and compassionate to help their clients discover the insights for transformation. In this chapter, we explore how coaches may develop a more courageous approach to their work in service of their clients.

Courageous coaching

Marjorie Brody defines courageous coaching as 'saying the right thing and asking the right questions at the right time to the right people in the right manner', even when it isn't easy (Brody, 2017).

In his foreword to *Challenging Coaching* (Blakey & Day, 2012), Sir John Whitmore reflected on the potential for executive coaches to be more courageous. He advocated coaches needed to 'do more to warn about, help or even avert the challenges faced by their clients'.

For new coaches, coaching can increasingly stray towards the supportive, as the coach focuses on the relationship and increasingly colludes with the client. Blakey & Day (2012) introduced the idea of coaches 'speaking their truth' and 'holding the tension' with clients to keep them accountable to themselves and their goals. However, to achieve this style the coach needs to call on their courage, to bring an independent perspective to the conversation.

Barriers to courageous coaching

One of the often-cited reasons for not being more challenging in conversations is the fear that drawing the client's attention to something that the coach notices could be construed as 'leading the client', therefore breaking a golden rule of coaching. This is a genuine concern in some instances, but there are ways to manage this. When we do inappropriately lead the client we do so by asking questions that have a hidden agenda to get the client in our line of thinking, or choosing where the conversation will go, what the goal is, or how to get there. The subtle difference in a courageous approach is that we are authentically noticing and sharing our observations to support the client to consider data that may be currently out of their immediate awareness. Some may fear that this is 'not allowed' in coaching, just as they assume it is 'not allowed' to interrupt a client when they are in full flow. The easiest way to be more courageous in your coaching is to debunk these myths and accept that, as a coach, the way you will add value is to develop a mindset to serve your client.

Many coaches are supportive in nature. Some may even slip into 'rescuer' styles. A supportive mindset helps us to build the trust and intimacy we need to create a safe working relationship. It can also help clients to build confidence and self-belief. However, when overused it can act as a barrier. The coach sometimes needs to dial up the level of challenge and offer clients a glimpse into their dark places.

One helpful metaphor (Passmore, 2018) is for the coach to see themselves as their client's torturer: holding their client's feet to the fire and asking questions that no one else has the privilege to ask. A more biblical take may be to think of the coach's role as less of a comfort to the afflicted, but rather to afflict the comfortable. I find a more useful metaphor comes from the work of Brené Brown when she talks of the need to 'sit in the dark' with someone.

> 'No one reaches out to you for compassion or empathy so you can teach them how to behave better. They reach out to us because they believe in our capacity to know our darkness well enough to sit in the dark with them.' (Brown, 2013)

Supportive coaches able to tap into this kind of compassion can sit alongside their clients until their self-exploration yields its work. Coaches less comfortable with this darkness are tempted to 'turn the light on', moving on too quickly, changing the subject or offering platitudes. Sometimes the self-exploration can be aided by a coach sharing what they notice or sense about the client or the situation that has the potential to support the client to move forward. Again, Brown helps us to recognise that clarity is key when offering feedback in order to help our clients grow in her book *Dare to Lead* (2018). She argues that most of us avoid the difficult conversations believing we are being kind, inadvertently becoming unkind and unfair, and this is the same for coaches as people generally. In fact, she has said:

> 'Feeding people half-truths or bullshit to make them feel better (which is almost always about making ourselves feel more comfortable) is unkind.'

As coaches, we need to call upon our courage in order to be fair and kind to our clients. We need to be able to speak our truth with compassion and with the intention of helping our clients find their own light switch.

If we are bringing this courage into our coaching, and speaking from our hearts in service of our clients and their goals, how can we also stay true to coaching? One key to this is to keep in mind our intention; another is to recognise we hold 'our truth' but that does not mean it is 'the truth'; and a third is to remember the person you are working with has every right to reject your truth, which means you must have the courage to be wrong. As Jonathan Passmore notes, the line between appropriate and inappropriate challenge is a fine one. The coach needs to ensure they balance high challenge with high support; working to maintain the relationship through 'keeping their client in a comfy chair', while at the same time 'holding them in a place of discomfort' (Passmore, 2018).

As for breaking the rules of coaching, Whitmore agrees with Blakey and Day (2012), suggesting there are times for the 'golden rule' of staying with the coach's agenda to be broken to benefit not only the client, but also the organisational sponsor and wider society. In order to introduce the thoughts and observations of the coach without leading, we need to work in close partnership with our clients, allowing them to lead the 'dance in the moment' (Kimsey-House *et al*, 2011), while offering a view from the balcony. The partnership begins at the first meeting and is redefined at every coaching session, agreeing what will create a safe space for exploration and discovery based on compassion and clarity.

Setting the foundations for courageous coaching

As most coach supervisors will tell you, when a coach feels they have got into difficulty with a client it can often be traced back to the coaching agreement or contract. When we are discussing how we will work together, in partnership, with our clients we are really considering 'What will we do if…?'

At the beginning of every relationship and session we are agreeing how we will work in service of the client's aspirations; we are seeking clarity and permission. A key aspect of this is the role the coach will play in that process. This is the foundation for courageous coaching. The coach must secure the client's permission to share observations, offer thoughts and bring challenge into the conversation.

One way of doing this would be for the coach to contract on the level of challenge that the client feels comfortable with. 'On a scale of one to 10, how challenging would you like me to be during this session?' is one possible question to ask a client at the start of the conversation. Another is to start from the foundation of a partnership: 'How will we do this work together?' 'What can I do to support your learning?' 'How can I help you to dig deep?' 'How will I know I have gone too far?'

Setting these foundations means both partners are signed up to deeper exploration and challenge, adding value and power to the conversation that goes beyond what could be expected from a friendly chat.

Practical steps to courageous coaching

As a coach, there are a few simple steps you can take to increase your courage in the coaching conversation and reframe your mindset. We have summarised these in Table 29.1

Table 29.1: Practical steps

1. Create the conditions for exploration and challenge in the conversation by contracting to draw on all of the data in the session, including your observations, thoughts and feelings.
2. Allow your curiosity a voice in the conversation; if something seems incongruent, share that as an observation or gift with the intention of supporting the client's forward movement.
3. Before you intervene, always ask yourself: Is this about me, or is this in service of the client?
4. Resist the temptation to rescue the client when you start to feel uncomfortable; notice your reaction, reflect on it and trust the client to find their own insight.

The reframe comes from recognising that 'holding the tension' or sitting alongside of them in the dark serves them in a much more powerful way than keeping them comfortable.

Conclusion

As a coach, our role is to encourage our client to think differently. To challenge their own habituated patterns of behaviour and thinking and consider new opportunities for being and doing. As Sir John Whitmore asserts, 'building awareness and responsibility is the essence of good coaching' (Whitmore, 2004). We cannot bring that essence into our work without having the courage to shine a light into the darkness.

References

Blakey, J and Day, I (2012) *Challenging Coaching: Going Beyond Traditional Coaching to Face the FACTS*. London: Nicholas Brealey Publishing.

Brown, B (2013) *The Power of Vulnerability: Teachings on Authenticity, Connection and Courage.*

Brown, B (2018) *Dare to Lead: Brave Work. Tough Conversations. Whole Hearts*. Vermilion Publishing.

Brody, M (2017) Trends: a holistic approach to management development. *TD Magazine*, 71 (11) 70.

Kimsey-House, H, Kimsey-House, K, Sandahl, P & Whitworth, L (2011) *Co-Active Coaching: Changing Business, Transforming Lives* (3rd edition). London: Nicholas Brealey Publishing.

Passmore, J (2018) *Coaching: No one expects the Spanish inquisition*. Deutscher Bundesverband Coaching Conference, Germany, 2 November.

Passmore, J (2018) How can I make better use of contracting in my coaching? *Insight Guide #18.* Henley Business School.

Whitmore, J (2004) *Coaching for Performance: GROWing People, Performance and Purpose* (3rd edition). London: Nicholas Brealey Publishing.

Chapter 30:
How can I use ecopsychology in my coaching practice?

Anna-Marie Watson

Introduction

Have you gone for a walk in the countryside and come back feeling rejuvenated? Do you sometimes look at the sunset or watch the clouds move across the sky and feel the wonder of nature? There is something about nature that seems to connect with us as humans – maybe it's the scale of the mountains or the beauty of the forest. When nature is combined with an outdoor walk, run or swim, it seems to have a transformative effect. In this chapter, we explore the potential of ecopsychology to transform the coaching experience.

What is ecopsychology?

Ecopsychology blends concepts and methodologies from ecology (the study of relationships between organisms and their physical surroundings) and psychology (the study of the mind). It focuses on the nature–human connection and offers an alternate lens to examine our psyche, behaviour, values and deeper self. The relational, enquiry-based learning and discovery approach mirrors fundamental concepts that underpin coaching practice. The three key strands of ecopsychology are:

1. the emerging synthesis of ecology and psychology

2. the skilful application of ecological insights to the practice of psychotherapy

3. the discovery of our emotional bond with the planet (Roszak, 1994).

The current underpinning dominant cultural and societal approach focuses on the importance of the individual within primarily hierarchical and pyramidal power structures. This is an egocentric and anthropocentric (Rust, 2020) construct that illustrates the 'psychiatry of the modern western society that has split the "inner life" from the "outside world" – as if what was inside of us was not also inside the universe, something real, consequential, and inseparable from our study of the natural world' (Roszak, 1992).

Ecopsychology offers an alternate perspective where humans are located in a wider networked ecosystem, which creates a more connected, holistic, sustainable and eco-centric methodology. This builds on the notion of synergetic interplay between personal and planetary well-being, and adds an ethical and systemic dimension, which moves the work of the coaching profession beyond service to an individual or organisation and into the wider living ecosystem.

Emergence of ecopsychology

Ecopsychology is an interdisciplinary subject that draws from environmental ethics, human geography, transpersonal ecology, deep ecology, biophilia and psycho-ecology. Notable influencers include the cultural historian Theodore Roszak, who coined the term 'ecopsychology' in his book *The Voice of the Earth*, in which he addresses industrial culture's longstanding historical gulf between psychological and ecological constructs (Roszak, 1992).

Howard Gardner (1983), known for his multiple intelligences model, added an eighth intelligence to his model: 'naturalist intelligence'. This, alongside the original seven (linguistic, logical-mathematical, musical, spatial, kinaesthetic, interpersonal and intrapersonal), presented an alternate awareness of nature. More recently, the Austrian biologist Clemens added to somatics the concept of 'ecopsychosomatics' (Clemens, 2018). This offers a framework to focus on movement and embodied presence, such as mindful walking, within nature.

Benefits of ecopsychology

The benefits of integrating ecopsychology into coaching cover a range of physical, mental, emotional and spiritual factors. The American author, Richard Louv, succinctly describes a dose of Vitamin N (N for nature) as a 'deceptively simple treatment for improving physical and mental health, for stimulating learning, creativity and a sense of feeling fully alive' (Louv, 2016). This sentiment has been supported with evidence from neuroscience, psychology, physiology, biology and evolutionary studies.

The integration of ecopsychology positively supports coaching through:

- deeper ability to contemplate and reflect
- immersion in different space; removed from day-to-day environment
- greater awareness of individual behaviour, emotions, values and beliefs
- stronger connections to self, others and the environment
- expanded sense of identity beyond the ego and development of the ecological self

- increased cognitive control. Directed attention is replenished as involuntary attention is captured through soft fascination at nature. This is known as attention restoration therapy (ART).

- connection to a deeper intuitive compatibility based on the concept of biophilia, which describes human being's genetic predisposition to the natural world; our innate yearning for connection with nature.

- improved well-being and mood through exposure to blue spaces. Research indicates short walks in blue spaces offers positive psychological benefits (Vert *et al*, 2020).

Techniques to bring ecopsychology into coaching

There is a variety of techniques to integrate ecopsychology into existing coaching practice to complement existing coaching methodologies, theories and styles. The key is to organically interweave each technique within a dynamic environment. The extent to which ecopsychology is openly acknowledged can range from nature unconsciously forming the backdrop to actively inviting nature to co-create the coaching process.

Ecological self: Drawn from the school of deep ecology, the process of self-actualisation transpires when an individual transcends the 'egoic' to ecological self. This theory focuses on ethical and moral responsibilities to ourselves, others and the environment. Deeper questions can be framed to explore connections and disconnections with nature (and within ourselves) against the wider natural environment.

Systemic approach: The natural ecosystem offers a framework to view the world based on a client's connection and/or disconnection within the wider social system. Networks of relationships and perceptions of gestalts can be explored to encourage self-examination and self-confrontation of personal responsibility to the wider system. The hierarchical pyramidal system can also be used to contrast thoughts, feelings, values and beliefs.

Evolution: Evolutionary theory can be drawn into conversations on change. The nature versus nurture debate could be introduced as a metaphor to explore fixed versus growth mindset.

Deeper questions: These provoke how clients think, feel or believe differently about information within a frame of reference as opposed to simply eliciting more information. Deeper questions challenge assumptions and norms to generate alternatives and possibilities; then they create change.

Metaphors: These are a rich area for exploration and can link to visual, linguistic, auditory and physical. Visual metaphors observed in the natural environment can be used to externalise and explore ideas e.g. path junctions, or seasonal cycles (see above). Linguistic metaphors that reference nature can be explored e.g. 'black sheep in the family', 'she's the shining star in the business'. Auditory metaphors stem from the natural soundscape with different noises from wildlife, water, wind and other sources. These can range from soothing and gentle to ear-splitting shrieks, and can invoke a variety of feelings, physical sensations and cognitive associations. Physical metaphors from touch can be connected to past experiences and support future aspirations – for example, the sensation of wind blowing across bare skin can inspire feelings of freedom.

Seasonal cycles: Observations from the annual seasonal cycles (winter, spring, summer and autumn) can be linked to other cyclical themes that emerge during coaching e.g. life, career, self-development or a specific project. Timelines (or circles) can be created to identify interrelated elements, connections, opportunities and possibilities (this links to nature play, which is discussed below).

Nature play: This creative approach uses natural resources (stones, leaves, moss, bark, flowers etc) to symbolise and externalise a situation e.g. timelines and relationships (particularly on 'stuck-ness'). This experiential element allows different perceptions and emotions to emerge and shift.

Sit spot: Identify a quiet and restorative location near home or work. Make the commitment to visit regularly e.g. for 20 minutes, three times a week over four months. Use a journal to record observations related to changes in the environment and personal thoughts/feelings.

Mindfulness: There are different approaches to being fully immersed in the present moment to acknowledge and accept feelings, thoughts and bodily sensations e.g. body scan, loving kindness, observer etc. See below for further details. The "sit spot" mindfulness practice can be introduced by identifying a quiet and restorative location near home or work and making the commitment to visit regularly e.g. 20 minutes, three times a week over a four-month period. The client can record observations in a journal related to changes in the environment and personal thoughts/feelings.

Nature retreats or pilgrimages: These are generally longer than an individual coaching session and a variety of coaching approaches can be integrated. Nature retreats usually focus on a holistic lifestyle approach, whereas pilgrimages are a prolonged journey with a possible moral or spiritual component; often to a specific destination of significance.

Table 30.1: Still or walking mindfulness

- **Appreciate** your body, surroundings and ability to move.
- **Reflect** on the ways we're interwoven to our surroundings.
- **Ground** yourself to the earth. Physically connect with each toe, base of foot and heel. Walk in the moment.
- **Activate** your senses: listen, breathe, smell and notice.
- **Mantra:** recite a phrase e.g. 'be here now', or simply 'breathe'.

(Adapted from Hanh, 2015)

Practical steps

The following areas should be considered in advance:

Dynamic environment: Stepping outdoors involves an element of risk, from physical safety to more discrete psychological safety and emotional containment. The multi-sensory environment might involve unforeseeable situations that trigger emotional responses, disrupt rapport or raise negative thoughts. Be prepared to embrace an organic and fluid mindset into your practice, and to work with a supervisor who has experience within this coaching niche.

Location, location, location: Think about the venue (near nature versus wilderness) and route in relation to terrain, distance, accessibility, session timings, fitness levels, confidentiality and medical issues.

Wet-weather plan: Some clients are content to don waterproof jackets, boots and huddle under an umbrella, although some might prefer a more comfortable, dry option.

Health and safety at work: A risk assessment is a systematic method of analysing factors that influence eco-coaching, consider possible challenges and identify suitable control measures. Information related to accessibility, route, terrain, other users and local amenities should be recorded in a generic or location-specific document. Make sure the necessary first aid, public liability, professional insurance, outdoor qualifications and land access are covered. Carry a suitable first aid kit for the location.

Client medical disclosure: Clarify any physical or psychological medical conditions relevant to walking outdoors that might not usually arise.

Personal safety: Consider your personal safety, especially meeting a new client for the first time – for example, inform a friend of the route and expected time of return, and ensure the client knows in advance you will do this.

Client comfort: Not everyone enjoys spending time outside. Co-create the entire outdoor element with your client and reference in the coaching contract.

Experiment: Trial the concept in advance with your peers or willing clients. Select an accessible local park or open space to test, then adjust and learn from the experience.

Conclusion

Ecopsychology offers an alternate narrative to base our coaching practice upon and supports our clients to reap the benefits from the wider outdoor environment. The ecopsychology coaching tools and technique offer the ability to align our inner and outer worlds as part of a larger interconnected web through connection to nature. There is enormous scope for coaches to embrace the emerging niche of ecopsychology so 'eco-coaching' becomes a widely accepted part of the coaching profession in the near future.

References

Clemens, A (2018) *The Healing Code of Nature: Discovering the New Science of Eco-psychosomatics.* Germany: Riemann Verlag.

Gardner, H (1983) *Frames of Mind.* New York: Basic Books.

Hanh, T N (2015) *How to Walk.* Ypsilanti, MI: Parallax Press.

Louv, R (2016) *Vitamin N: The Essential Guide to a Nature-Rich Life.* London: Atlantic Books.

Roszak, T (1992) *The Voice of the Earth.* New York: Simon & Schuster.

Roszak, T (1994) Definition of ecopsychology. *The Ecopsychology Newsletter* 1, Spring, 8

Rust, M (2020) *Towards an Ecopsychotherapy.* London. Confer Books.

Vert, C, Gascon, M, and Ranzani, O T (2020). Physical and mental health effects of repeated short walks in a blue space environment: A randomised crossover study. *Environmental Research*, 188

Chapter 31:
How can I use psychometrics in my coaching?

Jonathan Passmore

Introduction

'She is such a people person', or 'He's a big picture person'. We often hear these types of phrases used to describe others at work, and sometimes among our friends, who have had the fortune, or misfortune, to have completed a personality questionnaire. However, these phrases often hide a greater complexity, not only within the instrument, but also in understanding the true richness and diversity of what it is to be human. In this chapter, we look at what is personality and how psychologists have tried over the past one hundred or more years to categorise it, and we consider the implications of different personalities for coaching.

What is personality?

The word 'personality' derives from the Latin word 'persona', meaning the mask worn by actors or performers as a disguise or to project a specific role in a play. A wide range of definitions has been offered over the decades; here are just a couple:

> 'That which permits a prediction of what a person will do in a given situation.' (Cattell, 1950)

> 'Although no single definition is acceptable to all personality theorists, we can say that personality is a pattern of relatively permanent traits and unique characteristics that give both consistency and individuality to a person's behaviour.' (Feist & Feist, 2009)

In summary, a person's personality may be defined as being made up of the characteristic patterns of thoughts, feelings and behaviours that make the person who they are. This personality arises from a mixture of our given traits, contained within our genetic code, and our environment, where we were born, brought up and live now.

Different ways to think about personality

Coaches have an expanding range of psychological assessment tools from which they can draw to help clients build the self-awareness that is necessary to identify new career and life goals, and to enhance their performance at work. The burgeoning psychological testing industry has produced a myriad of measures enabling coaches to support clients to better understand their behaviour, their preferences and their capabilities, as they relate to work and life. Personality tests, aptitude tests and questionnaires assessing values, interests, leadership and motivational needs represent some of the kinds of tests currently available on the market internationally. Many of these psychological tests have made a positive contribution to coaching and have been rigorously tested to ensure their reliability and validity.

There is an abundance of personality questionnaires on the market, each measuring a broad or narrow domain of individual behaviour and personal preferences. Four commonly used kinds of personality measures (see Passmore, 2012) used in work-related coaching are:

1. Trait-based questionnaires such as NEO-PI-R, 16PF, Saville Wave and OPQ32
2. Type questionnaires such as MBTI® and 16Personalities
3. Competence-based tools such as ILM72 and TLQ
4. Specialist questionnaires such as MTQ48, VIA or MSCEIT

Trait-based questionnaires ask us to consider how much of a specific trait or behaviour we have. They compare our score with others to give us a comparative score. These instruments are often based on the Big Five personality factor model, originally developed during the 1970s, but which is now widely accepted as a result of cumulative research into personality over the past five decades.

Table 31.1: The five-factor model of personality

Big Five Factor	Description
Conscientiousness	Careful, reliable, hard-working, well organised, punctual, disciplined, ambitious
Extroversion	Sociable, fun-loving, affectionate, friendly, talkative, warm
Agreeableness	Courteous, selfless, sympathetic, trusting, generous, acquiescent, lenient, forgiving, flexible
Openness to experience	Original, imaginative, creative, broad interests, curious, daring, liberal, independent, prefer variety
Neuroticism (emotional stability)	Worrying, emotional, high-strung, temperamental, insecure, self-pitying, vulnerable (emotional stability: calm, at ease, relaxed, even-tempered, secure, hardy)

Adapted from McCrae and Costa, 1987

A second common example is the type-based instrument. MBTI® is one example, but others are 16Personalities, TDI and Insights. These are often used by coaches to help clients reflect on their working styles and how they relate to others. The approach is based on Jungian psychology that believed personality was both innate and fixed – that is, it did not change significantly over time.

Also widely used are competence questionnaires. These are often developed by the organisation or by a professional body, and aim to capture the key behaviours that lead to successful outcomes in a role or the organisation. Individuals may rate themselves or the questionnaire can be used as a 360-degree tool with self- and peer-ratings. The 360-degree model has become very popular. It offers the opportunity for clients to reflect on their own behaviours, but also to consider how others see them. In many cases this scoring is supported by confidential, qualitative feedback that can provide a richness, and personal examples, to drive deeper reflection by the client.

Using 16Personalities and type-based questionnaires in coaching

Some instruments, such as MBTI®, require a licence. However, in recent years new instruments have been developed and are free to use online – examples include 16Personalities. This has revolutionised psychometrics and means that more clients can complete the questionnaire themselves and watch online explanations before having their coaching session.

For coaches too, such questionnaires offer benefits, helping us to reflect on our innate preferences and being more aware of how such preferences may impact on our coaching work. Table 31.2 gives a brief summary of how different personality preferences may impact on our coaching. Other guides (Rogers, 1997; 2017) provide more detail on preferences and how they can influence our wider behaviour at work.

Table 31.2: Potential impacts of personality preferences

	Likely strengths	Likely areas for development
Extraversion (E)	Helping clients explore a wide range of issues. Establishing the coaching partnership. Thinking on feet.	Using silence. Helping clients explore issues in depth. Reaching the 'way forward' stage.
Introversion (I)	Helping clients explore issues in depth. Reflecting on strategies. Using silence.	Helping clients move to action. Helping clients explore all relevant issues. Establishing the coaching partnership.

	Likely strengths	Likely areas for development
Sensing (S)	Observing details. Using the 'reality' stage. Helping clients decide on practical steps at the 'way forward' stage.	Taking the big picture into account. Generating ideas at the 'options' stage. Using intuition.
Intuition (N)	Seeing the big picture. Using intuition. Generating ideas at the 'options' stage.	Being specific. Testing out intuition. Helping clients decide on practical steps at the 'way forward' stage.
Thinking (T)	Being objective. Challenging.	Picking up client's feelings. Being empathetic. Challenging in a supportive way at the right time.
Feeling (F)	Being warm. Being empathetic.	Taking thoughts into account as well as feelings. Challenging the client. Being more objective.
Judging (J)	Being organised. Being decisive.	Helping clients make decisions in a timely way. Being flexible.
Perceiving (P)	Being spontaneous. Being flexible.	Being organised. Helping clients make decisions.

(Adapted from Passmore *et al*, 2006)

A word of caution

Personality questionnaires have become increasingly popular. They are often used by organisations to help with recruitment and selection in development centres and many coaches use them with their clients. However, it's important to keep in mind that the questionnaire results are only based on our responses. As living beings, we change and develop over time, and thus many people think that our scores may also change over time. Secondly, questionnaires only ask us about certain aspects of our personality. The reality is that humans are highly complex animals and our behaviour is multifaceted. We can't simply be reduced to a series of scores from a questionnaire to explain all of our behaviour. Thirdly, many people believe that our behaviour is situational, and thus how we report our behaviour in one situation or circumstances will be different to how we may behave in a different situation. Finally, many questionnaires require the coach to be formally trained or licensed to use the tool. Before embarking on using an instrument, check out what training is required so you can use the tool ethically. Training can often be very expensive. It's therefore also worth considering the likely return on your investment. How many times will you use the tool and what can you charge clients? How many sessions over a year or two years will you need to undertake to recoup your investment?

Conclusion

Psychometrics can be a useful tool to help us better understand ourselves and also a useful tool to use with clients. However, there is a wide range of tools available and we need to be selective in what we choose. Tools are not the answer to any question by themselves. They are simply a useful starting point for a conversation. They give us a language to talk about behaviours, or leadership, with clients. From this, combined with a coaching approach, they can help clients to develop new insights into who they are and how they behave. Combined with good coaching, we can help clients to become more choiceful about how they may develop their best self.

References

Cattell, R B (1950) *Personality: A Systematic Theoretical and Factual Study*. New York, NY: McGraw-Hill.

Feist, G and Feist, J (2009) *Theories of Personality*. New York, NY: McGraw-Hill.

McCrae, R R and Costa, P T (1987) Validation of the five-factor model of personality across instruments and observers. *Journal of Personality and Social Psychology* 52 81–90.

Passmore, J, Rawle-Cope, M, Gibbes, C and Holloway, M (2006) MBTI types and executive coaching. *The Coaching Psychologist*, 2 (3) 6–16.

Passmore, J. (2012) *Psychometrics in Coaching: Using Psychological and Psychometric Tools for Development (2nd ed)*. London:Kogan Page

Rogers, J (1997) *Sixteen Personality Types at Work in Organisations*. London: Management Futures Ltd.

Rogers, J (2017) *Coaching with Personality Type: What Works*. Maidenhead: McGraw-Hill Education.

Chapter 32:
What should I do if my client cries during a coaching session?

Jonathan Passmore

Introduction

Emotions play a central role in coaching, as they do in all human interactions. For many coaches, managing strong emotional responses feels a daunting challenging at the start of coach training. Many feel they are ill-equipped to cope with a client who cries, shouts or does not engage. In this chapter, we will explore the role of intense emotional reactions and how the coach can work with clients during these moments of deeper emotional expression.

The role of emotions in coaching

Emotions play a central role in what it is to be human. Emotions not only keep us from danger (fear and disgust), bring us closer to others (joy and happiness), help us defend what's important to us (anger) but they also help us to choose what we want for lunch or whether we should follow Plan A or Plan B (Kahneman, 2012). It is thus not surprising that emotions are a feature of most coaching conversations: '*I hate my job...*', '*I love having the freedom to...*' or, '*I am frightened about the new role*'. Some believe emotions should not be part of a coaching conversation. However, the reality is that emotions are an integral part of every coaching conversation, whether they are expressed, discussed or hidden beneath the surface of rational thoughts.

The coach's role is to help clients to explore this emotional life, helping them make the connection between their emotions and their decision-making. The coach can help clients bring the emotional aspects of their life from the shadow into the light. In this way, the coach can help their clients to become more emotionally literate, and better able to be aware of, and manage, their emotions. However, what happens when the emotions move from the spoken word, to being expressed? These expressions of intense emotion may be through raised voices or tears.

It is in these moments when the greatest benefits of coaching can be realised. Coaching offers a safe space to explore emotions. A relationship, and a physical space, where the client is not judged but accepted, not rushed but allowed to dwell, and where the coach can offer the opportunity for the client to gain new insights about themselves as well as their situation. Coaching offers the opportunity to step beyond action, into understanding.

What shall I do if my client cries?

A crying client is one of the most frequently expressed fears from coaches. However, tears, or intense emotions, are not a situation to be feared by the coach. Tears, shouting and silence may express joy, as well as sorrow, frustration or anger. Whichever it is, the coach needs to maintain a calm and collected presence, demonstrating to the client they are as comfortable with tears as they are with laughter, and that both provide opportunities for the coach to demonstrate empathy and for the client to develop insight.

What should the coach do when a client starts to cry? Firstly, the coach should avoid looking concerned, or ask immediately if the client wants to stop the session. Equally, they should avoid rushing to hug or touch the client, as if in 'rescuer mode', seeking to sooth the tears away. Instead, the coach should acknowledge the emotion. This may be through a slight nodding of the head, while maintaining silence. Or a gentle, 'It's OK'. It's also OK for the coach to experience a slight increase in moisture in their own eyes. This empathic response is natural, and is a sign of responding to the client's sadness or pain.

If the crying persists, the coach may wish to draw the client's attention to tissues, or ask if they would like some water. Again, ensuring the client does not feel rushed, pressured or that their emotional response is inappropriate. In some cases, the client may ask to take a break to gather their thoughts. However, as the client returns it's important for the coach not to lose the moment, or be directed away from the topic. Instead, the emotional expression provides valuable material with which to work.

Working with emotions

This may involve exploring why the client feels as they do: the assumption, beliefs and values that may underpin their response, as well as helping them explore the situation from different perspectives, and the systemic roles they and others may be playing out.

By exploring these factors, the coach can help their clients to understand themselves and how they are part of a wider system (Oshry, 1990). In fact, it may be argued that is it these adversities in life that make us who we are. By acknowledging, exploring and understanding our reactions, and those of others, we can develop a greater level of emotional maturity and, ultimately, become more emotionally resilient. As many writers over the millennia have noted, it is the fiercest storms that shape the mountain.

Emotions and diversity

While there is little published research on coaching and emotional expression, gender, age and cultural differences may influence how individual clients express, or feel they are able to express, their emotions. The coach needs to be sensitive to this diversity, and recognise the systemic and structural forces in play, as well as the individual personality factors. For example, research into national differences suggests that Japanese and northern European countries have traditionally been less emotionally expressive than Latin cultures (Hofstede, 2001). This data does not mean Japanese people experience fewer emotions, it's just the coach may witness less behavioural express of the behaviours, and thus needs to be more observant for small signals. In contrast, a Latino client may raise their voice, cry and laugh, all in the space of a one-hour session. Of course, care needs to be taken with such generalisations. Humans are immensely diverse, and caution is needed to avoid generalising from a national cultural trait to all individuals from that national group.

A further factor to consider is the gender interaction between the coach and client. The rise of the #MeToo movement has highlighted how gender, age and power have been used inappropriately over decades. These factors are often unspoken and unconscious, but can impact on the coaching relationship, and thus an awareness of these factors and a higher level of sensitivity needs to be recognised by the coach, and managed appropriately.

Conclusion

The coach needs to keep in mind their intention, which is to remain wholly in service of their client: helping their client move towards their goals and, while doing so, to help them deepen their self-awareness and personal responsibility. Emotions are a powerful factor in our thinking and our decision-making as humans. Thus, to be of best service, the coach needs to help clients to explore and better understand their emotional lives, and how the client can use this new understanding to move closer to fulfilling their dreams.

References

Hofstede, G (2001) *Culture's Consequences: comparing values, behaviors, institutions, and organizations across nations* (2nd edition). Thousand Oaks, CA: Sage.

Kahneman, D (2012) *Thinking Fast and Slow*. London: Penguin.

Oshry, B (2007) *Seeing systems* (2nd edition). Oaklands, CA: Berrett-Koehler Publishers.

Chapter 33:
How can I develop a coaching mindset?

Tracy Sinclair

Coaching at its best is a partnership between coach and client that results in the client tapping into their resourcefulness and reaching their fullest their potential. It is this partnership and the quality of the relationship that underpins and forms a key part of this outcome. Therefore, it means that coaching is not just about what the coach does or indeed what they know about coaching, it is also significantly about how the coach is *being*.

How the coach is being with their client will be influenced by the coach's mindset. In this way, coaching is not just about the client, it is about the coach too, as an equal partner in the work they will do together. This need for an optimal coaching mindset is considered crucial to the coaching engagement. It's for this reason that professional bodies such as the ICF have included this in their coaching competency (ICF, 2019; Passmore & Sinclair, 2020).

What is a coaching mindset?

Holding a coaching mindset focuses on how a coach conducts themselves, not only when coaching, but in all professional interactions with parties related to the coaching process. A coaching mindset therefore aims to describe some of the who of the coach; who the coach is 'being', as opposed to the 'what' of coaching or the 'doing' of the coach in that process.

The intention is that this mindset underpins the professionalism and integrity that is expected from professional coaches, and provides a foundation upon which other competencies can sit. Good coaching not only involves demonstrating a skill set, it is also about the coach's approach. It is this mindset that informs how we work generally in our coaching practice.

How can we embody a coaching mindset?

An optimal coaching mindset is when we are being open, curious, flexible and client centred. The key then is what we do in order to access and maintain that state of mind.

Life-long learner

One of the terms often heard about coaches is that they are 'life-long' learners. When we make a commitment to study and subsequently practice as a professional coach, we are also making a commitment to keeping our own skills up to date over time. This is to ensure that we are fit for practice and are not applying 'rusty' skills that we learned 10 years ago, which are now peppered with bad habits. This commitment therefore comes with an expectation that we will stay up to date in our knowledge, skills and attitudes, reflecting new research, emerging models and evolving attitudes. As such, we extend our learning beyond our initial training so that our competence is deepened and enhanced through a broader understanding of coaching and complementary areas of study, as we navigate our path from being a novice practitioner to one who is more experienced and matured over time.

Reflective practice

Of the range of continuing professional development activities we might undertake, reflective practice has been identified as being of significance, and is considered core to the development of the coach and their professional practice. Reflective practice can take many forms, including:

■ coaching supervision

■ peer-group reflection

■ journaling

■ mentor coaching

■ observed coaching practice followed by debrief and feedback

■ listening to recordings of client work.

The key to good reflective practice is that it is ongoing and regular, as opposed to a random, ad-hoc activity.

Conscious awareness

Core to the process of coaching is that the client's thinking about their topic expands beyond the limitations of their habitual thinking patterns and habits. We all have patterns and strategies that help us to decide how we will approach situations. However, those patterns can also get in the way of new thinking. Contextual and/or cultural assumptions, beliefs and biases are examples of what shape our thinking and as coaches we need to challenge these in our clients and in ourselves for us both to maintain a mindset that is open, curious and flexible. The coach might actively check their own assumptions and those of their client. For example, by saying *"I realise I am making an assumption here; however, I am wondering if..."* or, *"What assumptions might you be making about this situation?"*

In this way, the coach is consciously aware of what is going on in the moment and has not succumbed to the seduction of that automated place of habitual thinking, assumptions and biases.

Intuitive coach

What we describe as 'intuition' can be a very powerful tool for the experienced coach. The evidence suggests that while many coaches say they trusted to their intuition, accurate intuition is related to experience (Giannini, 1984). The more experience of coaching or working one-to-one a coach has, the more accurate their intuitive judgements. Care thus needs to be taken in drawing on what we think is intuition, unless there is deep experience underpinning this intuitive feeling.

As already noted, a good coaching mindset is client-centred so any intuition shared should always be in service of the client. In this way, the coach uses intuition with careful judgement, good sense and a lack of attachment or sense of knowing. An example of how this might be displayed is if the coach says something like: 'I'm feeling a strong sense of (XYZ): what do you think or feel about that?'

Self-regulation

Self-regulation is key to being able to remain open, curious, flexible and client-centered. Regulating our own emotions is one of the ways we stay out of the client's way in the coaching process, so that we can remain fully available and present for them. Part of our ongoing learning and development may therefore include our *personal* development as well as our *professional* development. Increased self-awareness enables the ability to self-regulate and self-manage so that we can strike the elegant balance between drawing upon our intuition and, at the same time, not bring in too much of ourselves.

An example of when we might need to regulate our emotions could be: *Your client shares that they are getting divorced and you have just recently experienced a painful and acrimonious divorce yourself. How will you make sure that your own emotional experience does not creep into your coaching practice?*

Being prepared

This aspect begins to pull the various elements of a good coaching mindset together as our mental and emotional preparation will undoubtedly be informed and enhanced by what we have covered so far. Our preparation is ongoing as well as session specific. Our 'pre-session' preparation may take on various forms, based on personal preference, such as taking a walk, doing some exercise, meditating, sitting quietly etc. It is also useful to draw upon our self-awareness to consider when and how we access our optimal coaching mindset. Are there times of the day when we are 'at our best'? How can we be as fresh and as present for our last client of the day as we were for the first client of the day? How many clients, therefore, can we engage with in one day and maintain our ability to fully embody our coaching mindset? All of these questions, and more, are a very valuable part of our reflective practice.

Seeking help

So far, the elements of this competency have taken a proactive perspective on how we develop and maintain a mindset that is open, curious, flexible and client-centred. However, we are also human, life happens and there may – probably will, in fact – be times when our mindset becomes impaired in a way that is not helpful to our clients. This reinforces the need for ongoing reflective practice so that our self-awareness signals to us that we need to do some work on ourselves in order to be of service to our clients. Coaching supervision is a very useful source of support for this and also for our ongoing learning and development as a coach.

Client-centred

Last but not least, let's look at the being client-centred aspect of our coaching mindset. In fact, one might argue that developing and maintaining a good coaching mindset is directly in service of us being client-centred, which is at the very heart of effective coaching practice. This concept shows up in many areas of coaching competence and is intended to give the client choice about every aspect of the coaching engagement. For example, part of our ethical practice is that we demonstrate personal integrity and honesty in interactions with clients. All elements of establishing the coaching contract and agreements (both for the overarching coaching package as well as session by session) are done in partnership with the client. We seek to fully understand our client, demonstrate respect for them, acknowledge them and their work in the coaching process, show empathy and support and encourage their full expression of thoughts and feelings. We demonstrate curiosity, evoke awareness through challenge and powerful questioning, remain focused, observant and responsive. Finally, we partner with the client to integrate new awareness and insight into actions and behaviours that lead them towards their goals and their potential.

Being so consistently client-centred calls upon the art, as well as the science, of coaching. That art is in the *being* of the coach and how they continuously work on themselves to develop, maintain and embody a coaching mindset.

References

International Coaching Federation (2019) ICF Core Competency Model. Available at: https://coachfederation.org/core-competencies (accessed 19th April 2020).

Giannini, A J, Barringer, M, Giannini, M and Loiselle, R (1984) Lack of relationship between handedness and intuitive and intellectual (rationalistic) modes of information processing. *Journal of General Psychology* 111 31-37.

Passmore, J and Sinclair, T (2020). *Becoming a coach: The essential ICF guide.* Worthing: Pavilion

Chapter 34:
How can I use tools and techniques in my coaching practice?

Sarah Leach

Introduction

The draw of new tools and techniques that coaches can add to their repertoire is compelling, particularly for coaches looking to expand their range. Tools and techniques can be incredibly helpful and being able to use a wide variety of tools is a strength for any coach. However, it is important to recognise that using a tool to address a client's problem is not the solution in itself. In this chapter, we offer some thoughts regarding the benefits of using tools and techniques, what to look out for and some simple tips on integrating them into your coaching practice.

What are tools and techniques?

Coaching tools and techniques are a mechanism by which coaches may support their clients using a tried-and-tested process. They are often practical, tangible interventions that can be used during the process of coaching to move the client forwards in their thinking. They can be used in isolation, in their purest form, or adapted and blended with others to support the coach's style and/or specialism, or the needs of the client.

> *"Some of these tools are universally relevant in a wide range of situations whilst others work best when addressing specific issues such as decisions and problem solving..."*
> (Bossons *et al*, 2012)

The terminology used to describe different tools and techniques gets used interchangeably. However, as a guide the following might be useful:

- Perspective – describes the theory or source upon which a coaching tool or technique is based e.g. behavioural psychology.
- Approach or method – describes the application of a perspective e.g. cognitive behavioural therapy.

- Model or framework – describes a structure to enable a client's thinking, which is often easy to use and remember e.g. GROW model.

- Toolkit – describes the collection of tools the coach draws upon.

- Tool – describes the individual exercises that form part of a toolkit e.g. the ABC client sheet is a tool used to capture thinking having applied the ABCDE framework.

- Technique – like a tool, but describes something less formal or structured e.g. mirroring.

How can tools and techniques help in coaching?

If used correctly, tools and techniques can bring creativity, clarity and insight to the coaching relationship and, ultimately, a successful outcome. Tools can be used to great effect to help clients move away from their normal thought patterns and consider a new perspective on a challenge. When used well, they become a seamless and integral part of the coaching, almost unnoticed by the client.

Often clients present multiple and complex issues, and the use of tools and techniques can help both the coach and the client to maintain a degree of focus (Scoular, 2011). This is also helpful when working at speed or under pressure, to help structure the client's thinking.

In a very practical sense, tools and techniques often help to build credibility with the client, and can be used specifically as a marketing tool in highlighting a coaching specialism or describing a coaching niche that a client can more readily connect with depending on their coaching need.

Table 34.1: Benefits of using tools and techniques	
For the coach	■ Increases confidence in having a range of interventions to work with ■ Helps to remain objective and detached from the issue ■ Helps to maintain focus when dealing with complex issues ■ Provides structure to the coaching session ■ Presents an opportunity for creativity, depending on when or how it is used ■ Provides a tried and tested process, increasing the likelihood of a successful outcome
For the client	■ Builds confidence in the process and provides a degree of structure, particularly useful for those new to coaching ■ Helps to maintain focus on the issue ■ Encourages thinking beyond the obvious →

For the client (continued)	■ Prompts additional insights from a new perspective
	■ Enables creative thinking
	■ Enables wider reflection

What are the risks of using tools and techniques in coaching?

"You have to know all the techniques yet restrain yourself from using them except when they are totally appropriate." (Rogers, 2016)

There is a distinction between *doing* coaching and *being* a coach. If you focus too hard on the *doing*, in other words the process of coaching, using all the tools and techniques in your toolkit, there is a risk you forget about *being* a coach. You can become stuck or start working too hard. Coaching is easier and more fluid when you trust the process. Using too many tools and techniques can potentially interfere with the natural process of coaching. At an extreme, the coach can stop listening as they direct all their attention to the process and the next question or tool they can use.

Table 34.2: The risks of overusing tools and techniques

- ■ An overly formulaic approach to coaching
- ■ Coaching becomes clunky as tools are not fully integrated
- ■ Coaching is less spontaneous
- ■ Client's thinking becomes limited
- ■ Tools are 'forced' on a client whatever their preference or issue
- ■ The tool becomes a 'test' for the client, rather than an 'enabler'
- ■ Coach shifts towards a more directive style of coaching
- ■ Coach becomes trapped into using their favourite tools

Things to remember when using coaching tools and techniques

During the course of a normal coaching conversation, tools and techniques can be used to draw out specific learning points and actions. An experienced coach will be able to introduce, very naturally, a new tool into the conversation that is well matched to the presenting issue. With lots of practise this can feel utterly seamless, adjusting and adapting the tool to suit the situation. It's important not to become trapped by the tool and/or assume every technique is suitable for every coach. As confidence builds, the coach will 'destructure the concept' (Whitmore, 2009) as it becomes their own.

If you are drawn towards tools, it's a good idea to develop a broad range of tools that you are able to use. If you have 30 to 40 different tools, you will be able to make the best use of the right one on the right occasion. There are a variety of books available offering multiple tools, techniques and experiences (see for example Passmore *et al*, 2021)

By reading widely and testing out different tools and techniques, the coach can gradually extend their repertoire much like reading and practicing recipes from a cook book. The difference being each type the tool is used it needs to be adapted and flexed to meet the individual client who the coach is working with.

Table 34.3: Five top tips in using tools and techniques

1. Ensure fit for purpose: use tools and techniques that are aligned and appropriate to the presenting client issue.
2. Build a core set of tools: develop a set of tools that you are skilled at using and know will work in a given situation, but don't get too attached!
3. Practise and experiment: keep it fresh, keep practising and don't be afraid to introduce something new to your repertoire.
4. Push the boundaries: be prepared to adapt, blend or even deconstruct the tools and techniques you use to suit the situation.
5. Contract for their use: be open with the client about the use of tools and techniques from the start, including the possibility of experimenting with new or adapted approaches.

Conclusion

Tools can be a useful element that, when used well, can enhance our coaching. They can help clients to enhance their creative thinking (for example, VIP), they can help us understand other perspectives (for example, empty chair), they can help us structure the start of a session (for example STOKERS), close a session (for example DOUSE) and they can help us consider the potential risks of ignoring wider stakeholders (for example, 13th Fairy). However, in selecting a tool and using it with a client, we need to be clear why we are using this particular tool, and avoid slipping into the trap of using the same five or 10 tools with every client, and thus becoming mechanistic in our practice.

References

Bossons, P, Kourdi, J and Sartain, D (2012) *Coaching Essentials: Practical proven techniques for world-class executive coaching* (2nd edition). London: Bloomsbury.

Passmore, J., Day, C., Flower, J. Grieve, M. and Moon, J. (2021) *WeCoach: The complete handbook of tools, techniques, experiments and frameworks for personal and team development*. London: Libri Press.

Rogers, J (2016) *Coaching Skills: The definitive guide to being a coach* (4th edition). Maidenhead: Open University Press.

Scoular, A (2011) *Business Coaching*. Harlow: Pearson Education Ltd.

Whitmore, J (2009) *Coaching for Performance: GROWing Human Potential and Purpose.* The principles and practise of coaching and leadership (4th edition). London: Nicholas Brealey Publications.

Chapter 35:
How can I use the Primary Colours approach to support leadership development in coaching?

David Pendleton and Jennifer King

Introduction

Most of the current ideas about leadership were created in the 19th and 20th centuries when the world was a very different place. The Primary Colours approach to leadership was created in and for the 21st century: its organisations and their leaders. It is based on four propositions, all of which can be used in coaching to help leaders develop. In this chapter, we will look at the model, how it fits with coaching approaches and how we can apply the approach to help leaders develop.

What is the Primary Colours approach to Leadership?

Leaders have to contribute effectively in three domains: strategic, operational and interpersonal and these domains describe the territory of leadership. This is the Primary Colours model of leadership and is illustrated in Figure 35.1.

Figure 35.1: The Primary Colours model of leadership

The Primary Colours model also defines seven tasks that leaders need to achieve, and these provide a common language and a set of criteria for assessing and developing leadership at all levels: individual, team and organisation. Its focus on tasks is designed to make it easy to translate business challenges into leadership challenges. Because the model focuses on domains and tasks, it can be overlaid on existing competency models to provide an over-arching framework for leadership and a core curriculum for leadership and team development programmes. We think of it as a map of the territory of leadership.

Because the underlying structure of the model is consistent with the psychological factors that are most influential in shaping an individual's leadership strengths and weaknesses, it supports a leadership assessment that reflects enduring differences between people. Thus, it helps to clarify

The Primary Colours Model™ of Leadership

Strategic Domain

Setting strategic direction

Planning and organisation

Planning and organisation

Leading

Delivering results

Team working

Building and sustaining relationships

Operational Domain

Interpersonal Domain

Source: Pendleton, D and Furnham, A (2012, 2016) *Leadership: All you need to know.* London, Palgrave Macmillan

™The Primary Colours Model of Leadership is registered trademark of the Edgecumbe Consulting Group Ltd

the kinds of leadership role for which an individual is fundamentally well-suited, and those in which they are unlikely to thrive. Finally, because it is based on broad leadership tasks rather than detailed competencies whose importance depends on context, it enables benchmarking of leaders across functions, organisations and industries.

The Four Propositions and their use in coaching

1. The first proposition concerns the territory of leadership and what leaders are expected to achieve in it. This is the Primary Colours model, *which can be explored in the coaching,* and specifically the extent to which this formulation of leadership, its domains and tasks, provides a helpful structure within which to identify the key leadership issues for the client.

2. The second asserts that most leaders are incomplete so that it is extremely unlikely that any individual leader will become excellent in all aspects of leadership – *clients can identify where their current contributions are strongest and can potentially come to recognise and accept that they do not need to strive for excellence in all aspects.*

LIMITATION	STRENGTH	
Potential Strengths	Natural Strengths	**PERSONALITY HELPS**
Resistant Limitations	Fragile Strengths	**PERSONALITY HINDERS**

Source: Pendleton, D and Furnham, A (2012, 2016) *Leadership: All you need to know.* London, Palgrave Macmillan

Figure 35.2: Different kinds of strengths and limitations

3. The third describes two different kinds of strengths and limitations so that any leader wanting to develop needs to choose carefully and realistically where development effort is most likely to yield results: *coaching can enable leaders to identify and then focus on their natural and potential strengths, manage their fragile strengths and call on others in their team(s) to lead in areas in which their limitations are resistant to significant change.* These are frequently aspects of leadership that have been tackled in the past but with little success.

4. The fourth proposition suggests that leaders need to work in teams made up of colleagues whose differences are complementary to his or her own: *coaching can help leaders reflect on where those differences exist, what strengths exist in their team, and how best to harness them for the benefit of the whole team and/or organisation.* This aspect sometimes seems relatively straightforward but it is not. It means learning to work effectively with others who are significantly different from oneself and that can be challenging, especially when under pressure.

Compatibility with other approaches

GROW: The Primary Colours model is a helpful organising framework for the client to set 'goals' in the relevant domains or tasks of the model, identify and work with or around the 'reality' of their context and situation based on what they now understand about their own strengths; explore 'options' that make the most of their natural and potential strengths; and agree on which of those options they will pursue, individually or with their team(s).

Strengths-based coaching: the Primary Colours approach is particularly well suited to a strengths-based approach (MacKie, 2016). Clients can be helped to identify, build, expand and apply their existing strengths to be the best leader they can be, rather than over-investing in their weaker areas where they may struggle indefinitely and under-achieve as a consequence. Appreciative enquiry can be used to ask about skills, successes or strengths, help the client acknowledge achievements and existing good practice, tap into enthusiasm and engender feelings of hope, even in some pretty challenging situations.

The Primary Colours approach to coaching: The Primary Colours approach includes a piece on 'enablers' of leading, each defined by a single verb. These are: inspire, focus, enable, reinforce and learn. These help leaders especially in creating alignment, facilitating team working and planning and organising (Pendleton *et al*, 2016).

They can also function as a coaching model. 'Inspire' encourages a discussion of the specific improvement a leader wishes to make in his or her leadership: what will it be like if the change is made? How will she or he feel about that and how will it help in his or her leadership? Next, we have to 'focus' on specific changes that might be required to bring about the changes envisaged. 'Enable' encourages practice, working out exactly how the client will attempt to bring about the changes discussed. 'Reinforce' reminds coach and client to identify and celebrate success in the practice opportunities created. 'Learn' suggests reflection and drawing together of the lessons learned as well as identifying the next change we want to work on. It is a cycle as shown in Figure 35.3.

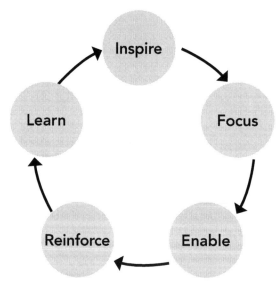

Source: Pendleton, D and Furnham, A (2012, 2016) *Leadership: All you need to know.* London, Palgrave Macmillan

Figure 35.3: A Primary Colours coaching model

Avoiding pitfalls and maintaining best practice

If you are considering introducing the Primary Colours model into your coaching, as with any model, it's important to contract explicitly and carefully with the client. Throughout, remain in coaching mode, and avoid making suggestions (directly or indirectly) or being prescriptive about where or how the model should be applied. Providing information about the model is a legitimate coaching activity; backed up with exploring, supporting, confronting and challenging. Questions might include:

■ How much do you know about the model?

■ Would it be relevant or helpful for you to explore it here?

■ How do these domains and tasks resonate with your experience?

■ Which domains or tasks do you find yourself most drawn towards?

■ Within this framework, what do you consider to be your strengths? And what do you find more difficult? What do you do at those times?

■ As I listen to you talking, your strengths in the interpersonal domain are coming to the fore – how can you make more of these?

■ How might this model serve you best?

■ Which areas come most naturally to you? What more could you do to build on these?

■ How might your team members complement your strengths?

Conclusion

Leadership means many different things to different people. It is helpful to agree between coach and client how we are going to understand such a broad field in order to work on it most productively. The Primary Colours model provides a helpful framework, which is not prescriptive but describes the territory of leadership so that it can be explored. It can be used in the context of most coaching models but it also contains a framework that can itself provide a coaching structure and thereby deepen the client's understanding of how to enable effective leadership.

References

MacKie, D (2016). *Strengths-based leadership in organizations*. London: Kogan Page.

Pendleton, D, Furnham, A and Cowell, J (2021) *Leadership: no more heroes* (3rd edition). London: Palgrave Macmillan.

Chapter 36:
How can I help clients find their place in the system they work in?

John Whittington

Introduction

Organisational systems are alive with hidden dynamics. Some limit, others resource the flow of leadership and organisational vitality. If you really want to help your client understand the system they belong in, you'll need an approach that illuminates both. You'll need a methodology, to bring alongside all that you already do, to reveal the hidden architecture, the geology under the geography.

This is important because all coaches will work with clients who are somehow caught up in the undercurrents of the system in which they work. It's inevitable. So, to be effective as a coach you need to be able to facilitate respectful access to the system in which your clients belong. Once managers and leaders can see the system and their place in it, they can find their authority and are open to benefit from the many developmental gifts that coaching offers.

To understand a system, you need to be able to see it

To understand what's going on in a system – the invisible loyalties and dynamics, the repeating patterns and the hidden source of conflict – you have to be able to see it. To really see and understand a system, you need a map.

Once you have a map, you can begin to find the best place within the system from which to lead. Then all your talent, experience and skill can be brought to bear and you can have influence.

The self-distancing that a map provides is a gift to give your executive coaching clients as it reveals fresh information and ensures that they are deeply connected to their developmental material and journey. It's for this reason that many coaches report that this way of working not only feels liberating for their clients, but also for them.

Walking in the field

Every group of human beings that gathers around a common cause generates a field of information that we call culture, or 'how we do things around here'. This field is full of unspoken, unwritten rules on belonging – codes of behaviour and patterns of belonging that are deeply felt, even though rarely articulated.

A physical representative spatial relationship map, that shows the relative place and size of each member of the system, opens that field.

One of the advantages of representative maps and the facilitated process called a constellation is that they liberate the client and the coach to move beyond the story and simply work with what is. This is in itself a great gift to offer a coaching client as it disentangles them – and their coach – from all the stories, judgements and ideas about how this 'should be'.

The inner attitude, the stance, of the coach who offers mapping of the kind described here is central. Working beyond the stories and judgements and simply offering access to the field of information that coaching clients live and work within. In this way you can walk through the field of information with your client and see the truth of the system and what is needed for a step to better.

System awareness

When we really become aware of what is, just as it is, we can see the larger patterns, the sources of the difficulties and a fresh range of potential resources and resolutions.

In psychological-based coaching you might say that we are bringing what is out of awareness into the client's awareness. In systemic coaching we are enabling clients to go a step further, to actually see what is out of awareness, to make it visible. Once you can see what's unconscious – in you and the system you are a part of – you can bring the insights and resolutions back into conscious awareness. This informs fresh actions and the flow of leadership and organisational health.

Mapping the system

The first stage of every constellation is the creation of a map of what is, just as in the case study briefly described here.

Mapping gives clients immediate access to the system-level information and enables them to see and understand their place in the system. It allows them to see themselves in the living system they are trying to manage and step out of it with useful distance so they can see the people and the parts.

Visual mapping of this nature is the language of the unconscious. It facilitates the embodied knowledge in the client and the system and enables the tacit information in both to surface. This in turn illuminates the hidden architecture, the geology under the geography of the organisational system.

The process allows what's beyond words to be articulated, the truths of the system to be expressed and quickly uncovers new information. It goes a step further with practice and invites client and coach to test options and alternative paths to resolution.

Box 36.1 Looking for authority

The coach sat down with her new coaching client, the divisional head of an international pharmaceutical company. It was clear from the briefing that he was a talented and experienced senior executive with a long track record of success in similar positions in competitor organisations.

However, it was also clear that he was struggling to find his authority in this role, in a way that was unfamiliar to him and didn't quite make sense to him or the CEO and HRD who appointed him.

So the coach invited him to create a physical representation of the relationship dynamics – to map his team, direct reports and key objectives. He did this and the sense of inertia was palpable. Then the coach asked questions about the hidden dynamics in the system. Firstly, "Who occupied this role before you and how did they leave?"

Representing the former occupant of the role in the map created a key shift in the client and he started to share with the coach how this person had apparently been ousted quickly as a result of some issues that were hard to define and not talked about openly. As a result, the coach was able to offer some resonant systemic language that she co-created with her client. Words that honoured the contributions of the previous role-holder and invited an acknowledgment of the difficult, incomplete ending.

These were informed by the first principle of health in an organisational system – the importance of honouring who and what came first. Who has belonged and in what order, rather than the stories of whether their performance was 'good' or 'bad'. Just this simple intervention followed by some sense-making created a shift in the client, and the coach was able to then look at the second entanglement in the system around their client. This was created by the fact that two of the people who were now supposed to be reporting into him had applied for the post themselves.

Again, the inclusion of them in the physical map, combined with some respectful language acknowledging both length of service and belonging, allowed the client to make a significant inner shift in the stance and language when talking with his two colleagues.

Six months later, the client said he felt 'much more relaxed and confident in my role and people are willingly following my lead'. This change came about through systemic perception and intervention, which is what is required when there are hidden dynamics holding the system back in organisational life.

From mapping to constellations

Mapping is just the first step of a fuller process known as a 'systemic constellation'. Constellations originated in healing work with family system dynamics. Developed in workshops, it is an embodied process, even when facilitated on the tabletop that allows unique access to fields information.

A constellation is a facilitated process that enables coach and client to work with the dynamics held in the system and, through a combination of words and movements, enable change and fresh solutions that serve not just the client but the wider system in which they live or work.

What our body knows

We all carry around within us, just out of conscious awareness, an inner image of every relationship we have been in, including the most formative patterns of our childhood and every educational, personal and professional relationship system since. Respectfully accessing these patterns is the gift of spatial relationship maps, of business constellations. 3D mapping and constellations allow the system to reveal itself to itself, as well as illuminate the deep patterns and directions within the hidden architecture of the system.

It's easy to assume, or hope, that the rational mind can resolve everything, but this can result in us undervaluing the wisdom of our somatic self, our embodied mind. Contemporary understanding through the extraordinary advances in neuroscience and psychobiology is starting to give us a far greater insight into the intelligence held in our bodies. Mapping gives us access to our embodied mind and can offer us a fresh perspective of the fields of information in which we are held.

> *'I hear and I forget. I see and I remember.*
> *I do and I understand.'*
> Confucius

Conclusion

If you can support your coaching clients to really see the systems in which they work and then find their place in those systems, you will have given them a precious gift.

And that is something you might like to do yourself, because the way we engage with our clients, in particular whether we have really understood the systems we have belonged to and left, makes a significant difference to the way we can walk alongside our clients.

Can you see the deep patterns held in you and the system in which you have belonged? Try mapping your place in each and you will have begun the inner journey that's required to offer the approach to others.

References

Whittington, J (2020) *Systemic Coaching & Constellations* (3rd edition). London: Kogan Page

Chapter 37:
How can I best use digital platforms to deliver online coaching?

Jonathan Passmore

Introduction

Increasing globalisation combined with the impact of the global pandemic during 2020 have led to an increasing use of online platforms to deliver coaching. But given so few coaching courses explore the differences between online to physically present coaching, how can coaches adapt their practices to these new ways of working? How can they develop their online presence? How can they make the most of technology? Which platforms should they select and what implications does this have for working practices? In this chapter we will review these questions and offer some insights on how coaches can make the best of online coaching.

The impact of globalisation

The past few years have seen a continued growth in online platforms such as Microsoft Teams, Zoom and Google Hangouts. These platforms enable individuals and teams to come together online. Many managers are now using these platforms daily and are highly familiar with the technology and the benefits in terms of reduced travel time and cost. Many coaches have responded by going online. But how much thought have they given to adapting their practice for the online world? How much training have they received in digital coaching? Do you know what research tells us what works and what to avoid? For many coaches, the answer to all these questions is 'no'.

How do I get going online?

You may have already selected your preferred platform, but, if not, it's worth reviewing the market. While Zoom is a popular choice, there are other providers too. A key consideration when making a choice is to ensure that the provider offers a stable and secure connection. Table 37.1 provides a checklist of points to consider.

Table 37.1: Coaching online checklist

- The best advice is to connect directly to the internet via an ethernet cable or to plug into your home hub. This will offer the fastest connection to the network.

- When connecting, you also want to ensure your connection is via a private, not a public network. The use of a VPN is highly recommended, especially if the data is commercially sensitive.

- Put your mobile phone on plane mode and switch off or limit any other connected devices in the home, all of which can otherwise reduce the bandwidth available for your call.

- It's helpful to close down other communication software that may be running on your machine, such as email or social media programmes, in order to reduce interruptions.

- Consider using a separate, high-quality microphone and camera if those on your machine are of low quality.

- Consider using a LED ring-light to light your face.

- You may wish to use headphones, especially if you need to ensure confidentiality or if there is any risk of background noise, such as from members of your household.

- Be aware that a full headset can make you look like a call centre operator; a more discreet earbud can work well, without distracting clients.

Setting the scene

The next step is to consider the space you are working in. If you have an office, consider what appears behind you: Is it a tidy bookcase or a jumble of items you've been meaning to sort out for months. A second option is to use the greenscreen function in your software platform. This works best when you have a flat surface like a blank wall behind you. Think carefully about the image you select: Are you seeking to create a formal, professional or playful space? How will clients react to a greenscreen versus a pleasant and well-ordered, real world book case or world map?

Also consider the position of your device to avoid having a light source, such as a window, directly behind you. Otherwise you may be in danger of appearing silhouetted against the light from the window. Try and make sure your face is adequately lit, either through natural light or using an LED ring-light. You can buy a ring light for as little as £30 and this will significantly improve the lighting and can help you change the mood of the session by changing the setting from bright to warm light reflecting the type of conversation. Next think about your positioning from the camera. Around an arm's length works best, with you sitting-up straight facing the camera. In combination, this all adds to the creation of a professional telepresence.

Most coaches now use a laptop. If that's the case it important to also consider the angle of the screen. Most are designed when we are working on a spreadsheet or a Word document to be angled slightly backwards. When coaching, angle your screen more upright. It may help to reposition your laptop on a stand or box, which brings the camera level with your eyes. Finally, try to ensure you and your client can see one another's hands, arms and shoulders as well as face, this helps with non-verbal communications.

Documentation

Before launching in to providing sessions, think about creating the appropriate documentation for your practice, such as policies and forms. Most coaches use a written agreement with individual clients. How does this need to be amended to reflect your revised practice? For example, you may want to reduce the length of each session, given that concentration spans are more limited online. You may wish to advise clients that sessions are not recorded – or if they are, to provide them with information on who will have access to the recording and how long it will be kept. Recorded sessions are a really useful source of data; they can be used in coach supervision as well as in mentor coaching sessions. As such, it is strongly encouraged that you record at least some of your sessions to use for your on-going development. However, as with face-to-face sessions, ensure that clients formally agree to being recorded. As the recorded session begins, briefly reiterate the information given in your documentation on how the recordings will be kept, for what purposes they will be used and how they will be disposed of.

It can be helpful to provide an information sheet to clients on how to set up their screen and equipment, as what might work well in a team meeting may be different for a one-to-one coaching session. The information sheet should also include the meeting ID, password and link, as well as instructions about what happens if the technology should fail during a call. It is suggested that you include a clause offering a full, free replacement session, should such issues arise.

For personal clients who may have less experience of such platforms a summary sheet detailing the pros and cons of online coaching, such as lower travel costs and greater choice of session times versus the downsides of less body-language communication, the stark impact of silence and the challenges of technology may help clients be more choiceful. The information sheet should also include your standard terms on confidentiality and limits thereof, logistics, record keeping, the code of ethics and complaints, as well as a few new considerations such as the circumstances in which clients can email or call between sessions and how quickly you will respond.

The coaching relationship

One of the key concerns for many is how the technology may impact the coaching relationship and coaching outcome. There is almost no research into online coaching, although much has been written about its potential over the past few years (Berninger-Schäfer & Meyer, 2018; Kanatouri, 2020; Ribbers & Waringa, 2017). There is a similar dearth of studies on outcomes, but the evidence suggest the outcomes between face to face and online coaching are similar (Berry *et al*, 2011).

In the parallel discipline of counselling, more research has been undertaken and, as might be expected, there are conflicting perspectives. However, the evidence suggests that on balance, for most relationships, the working alliance is as strong online as it is in face-to-face sessions. Indeed, for some interactions, particularly sessions that are emotionally charged, the 'disinhibition effect' can make clients more likely to be open in their verbal communication and display of emotions.

However, to achieve similar outcomes, coaches need to pay attention to some of the small details in their set up. The following are particularly important considerations:

- Contracting – being clear about how they will work, and acknowledging they will allow more pauses than in normal conversation to ensure their client has finished speaking

- Eye contact – maximise eye contact between you and your client by positioning their image directly beneath your camera. By doing this it will appear to them that, when you are seated at an arm's length from the camera, you are looking directly into their eyes.

- Silence – be mindful of the impact of silence online, which can sometimes be misinterpreted as a fault with the technology or as an adverse reaction to what they have said.

- Movement – Also be mindful of movement, particularly when using a green screen. Excessive or exaggerated movement can be distracting, while no movement may make it appear as if the screen has frozen.

Using online tools

Many platforms have embedded features such as mute, record, screen share, white boards and breakout rooms (for team coaching). These can be useful features to use, although it's best to practise before your first session, to get a feel for how they work.

We have already talked about the benefits of recording. In a similar vein, the whiteboard tool can be particularly useful as a replacement for the flipchart, allowing you to collaborate with clients, to capture their plan from the session or to jointly work on idea generation. For those who prefer more sophisticated tools, collaborative whiteboard platforms, such as Miro, Mural or Jamboard, offer a series of templates that can be particularly useful for coaching around project planning and brainstorming.

Conclusion

The future of coaching will be increasingly online. This offers the potential to act more as global as well as local coaches, reduce the environmental impact of our work, while making coaching more accessible to all. However, to achieve these gains coaches need to understand the subtle differences of working online, develop the skills in online tools and ensure their processes and practices reflect the demands of this new world.

References

Berninger-Schäfer, E and Meyer, P (2018) *Online Coaching.* Berlin: Springer.

Berry, R M, Ashby, J S Gnilka, P B and Matheny, K B (2011) A comparison of face-to-face and distance coaching practice: Coaches' perceptions of the role of the working alliance in problem resolution. *Consulting Psychology Journal: Practice and Research* 63 (4) 243-253.

Kanatouri, S (2020) *The Digital Coach.* Abingdon: Routledge.

Ribbers, A and Waringa, A (2015) *e-Coaching: Theory and Practice for a New Online Approach to Coaching.* Abingdon: Routledge.

SECTION 4:
CLOSING THE SESSION

Chapter 38:
How should I close a coaching session?

Karen Foy and Suzanne Hayes-Jones

Introduction

It is always exciting as a coach to learn a new model or technique to use within sessions, something we can take into our next conversation to dazzle and inspire our clients. In our striving for new ways to tease out change and motivation, we can forget about some of the powerful, more process leaning, approaches to transformational coaching – for example, the 'bookends' of a coaching session, the beginning and the end. Claire Pedrick (2020) offered the first bookend for the beginning of a coaching session, STOKeRS, which we have adapted to STOKERS (Foy, 2021). Now we would like to offer the other side of the structure, the DOUSE model to ensure all of your coaching conversations are held securely in a safe container. Once you have a beginning and an end to each session you have the basis for powerful work between.

Closing a session in partnership

How do you close a session with a client? Do you work towards a gentle and considered close or do you come crashing to the final few minutes, or seconds, and rush to close down the conversation and sometimes just extend the time to fit? In our experience, mentoring and supervising many coaches the crash landing or extension of time is the most common answer. Not because coaches don't care but usually because they have invested so much time into listening and applying tools and techniques to create insights that they, like their clients, get caught out by how quickly the time has gone.

Often coaches talk about the anxiety they feel trying to manage time effectively without seeming rude or too process driven, but we would suggest a considered and structured approach to ending a coaching conversation can provide the container that holds in the learning and insight you have worked so hard to encourage. To achieve this safe container, we need to place as much emphasis on the process at the end as the beginning and the work in between.

Our view is that all coaching is about learning; learning about ourselves and about the situation or topic we choose to explore. If we have worked to set up our first bookend at the beginning of a session, we will have supported out clients to have a clear view of what a successful outcome will be. Throughout the session, we aim to help the client discover insights about the topic and themselves through evoking awareness. We aim to keep moving them forwards towards the goal they set for themselves and sometimes new insights will suggest new goals.

If you imagine at the beginning of the session all of the work you do together on setting the goal identifies a 'golden thread' for discussion. You as a coach are holding on to that thread as a guide, checking in as the learning unfolds how every insight relates to that thread and the ultimate goal. As you draw closer to the end of the discussion you will want to hand that golden thread back, perhaps with more strands added from the learning, but handed back in a way that means your client can hold the strengthened thread and go forward from the session to their next phase. What will ensure that thread is ready for the next phase?

If we have done our work well as a coach, our clients will know something different at the end of the session that they may not have been fully aware of at the beginning. It may be a new option; it may be something about themselves; it may be an action – but whatever it is, we want to make sure the bookend of ending the session allows them to hold on to that learning and use it effectively going forward. This is where DOUSE can help.

When Claire Pedrick created the STOKeRS model, she used the metaphor of the person on the back of a tandem bicycle, the stoker. When we were thinking about a complementary model for the end of a session, we re-framed a stoker as the person stoking a fire on a train or ship, which led us to think of dousing a fire. Like the stoker, the coach is not the engine driver, but instead creates the right conditions, the process, for the driver to move the train from where it is now towards its destination. At the end of the journey the fire can be safely quelled.

To move forward from the coaching session we want our clients to achieve the goal they set for themselves and plan their forward movement, identifying barriers, and drawing on support. We also want them to consolidate what they have learned about themselves and their situation and be able to apply that in their life generally as well as specifically in this situation. We will want to acknowledge their part in the coaching process and help them to own the strengths they have uncovered and finally close the session that leaves them ready to take the next step confidently.

DOUSE

DOUSE offers a reminder of all of the areas for consideration when drawing the coaching conversation to a close. The questions offered in the table are not prescriptive, merely examples, and of course the ending will be less formulaic and more fluid than a list of questions would suggest.

Table 38.1: DOUSE

Double check the contract/goal against the proposed actions	'Where are we in relation to our contract/the goal for the session?' 'What will you do now?'
Obst(A)cles	'What might get in the way?' 'How will you be **accountable** to yourself?'
Uncovered	'What have you uncovered/learned about yourself that will support your continued progress?' 'How will you apply that learning going forward?'
Support	'What support do you need?' 'How can you get that?'
Ending	'How would you like to close the session?' (Acknowledge the work done during the session)

Applying the DOUSE approach to the end of your coaching will not automatically make your ending graceful and smooth. You still need to plan for a timely finish. In fact, in our opinion, throughout the session you need to be preparing to hand over the golden thread, so staying mindful of what will get you to this point.

If the golden thread is your goal at each insight or learning point you can be checking in with your client to identify what the learning means for the goal, and where they would then like to focus their attention, given the time left. This is a partnership and sharing the management of time is part of that work together.

If we mix our metaphors and think of the coaching conversation as a short internal flight, we can think of the beginning as the checks that take place before a plane is ready to depart, it might take ten minutes before the flight is ready to take off and get to the flying altitude. Staying with this metaphor, as a flight starts to descend the pilot will start to signal that we are descending, asking us to take our seats, instructing the cabin crew to do the checks, informing us of the local time and temperature at our destination and how long it will be until landing, finally wishing us a good onward journey. This is a template for what we need to do with our endings in the coaching conversation.

In managing the process, we signal to our clients that we are coming to the last 10 minutes of the session time we agreed at the beginning. We check in that they have got to the destination they aimed for in that time and through DOUSE help them to understand the learning and actions they can take into their onward journey.

One area of concern we hear in our mentoring is that coaches fear hearing something really important or profound towards the end of the session and so they choose to ignore key insights or offer to pick them up on the next session. If we stay with our flight, it could be related to lost baggage that we are told will be sent on in a day or two and we are left on holiday with just the clothes we stand in. If we think that each coaching session, like each flight, should be self-contained and complete, we can relax and rely on our partnership approach. For example, a client having a sudden insight towards the end of our session can be managed by, for example: 'That sounds like a useful insight, given we have five minutes left how do you want to use that?' It is the same with emotion and coaches wanting to ensure a client leaves feeling OK – we can check in: 'That has obviously had an impact. What do you need to be able to finish the session well?'

Conclusion

As a final nod to the 'ending', we as coaches can acknowledge the work that has been done by the client during the session, in a bid to highlight their progress and, perhaps more importantly, support them to continue their onward journey independently of you as the coach – until the next time.

References

Foy, K (2021) Contracting in Coaching. In J Passmore (ed.) *The Coaches Handbook*. Abingdon: Routledge.

Pedrick, C (2020) *Simplifying Coaching*, Maidenhead: McGraw-Hill-Open University Press.

Chapter 39:
How can I manage time within a coaching session?

Jonathan Passmore

Introduction

'*I know you said we will be winding up soon, but I just wanted to tell you about the most important issue that happened this week*'. Some clients seem to want to save their key issue almost to the last minute. Others seem to go on and on about trivial items and time disappears without the coach realising. Managing time within a coaching session can be a challenge for new coaches, as it can be with experienced coaching. But how should the coach deal with these situations? How should they manage time so they make the most of each session? In this chapter, we will explore how the coach can help clients ensure they make the best use of time during the session.

How long should a session be?

There is some debate in coaching as to how long a coaching session should be. Some coaches use the model developed and commonly used within therapy of the 50-minute hour. Other coaches work to a 60-minute session, while others plan on a two-hour session, or even, in some cases, a three-hour session.

In truth, there is no standard or best time for a session. Personally, I find a 30-minute session too short, while anything more than two hours requires a break. For most of my own coaching assignments, I plan on either a 60-minute session when working online, or a two-hour session when working face-to-face with clients.

For personal coaching, which is funded by the client and takes place locally (i.e. there is practically zero travel time), I offer one-hour sessions. I find this is long enough for a focused conversation and enables the fees for the session to be broadly comparable with local therapy rates. I offer the same arrangement for online, video conference call sessions, where maintaining focus for more than an hour is more challenging than face to face.

However, if I have to travel a distance to meet the client, possibly at their office or at a city centre location, I tend to suggest the client allows

120-minutes appointment in their diary. This allows for a 90- to 110-minute discussion, without clients feeling distracted by a concern the session will overrun and thus impact on their next meeting.

How can the coach keep to time?

One way of managing the time in an individual session is chunking the session into three or four parts. The first part of the conversation is the 'casual conversation', helping the client settle, maybe arranging coffee and checking on basic arrangements, such as if there is anything going on I need to be aware of, if the individual needs to leave their phone on, or that we may be disturbed by colleagues, fire bell testing etc. I allow five minutes for these pleasantries.

The second chunk is formal contracting and session planning. In a two-hour session the coach should allow about 10 to 15 minutes for this section. The aim being to either set out or remind clients of the key elements of the contract: roles, confidentially and time, as well as what the client wants to get from the session.

The third chunk is the session content. The coach should plan for about an hour, as this will allow time to explore the topic in depth and from multiple perspectives. How much progress one makes is in part dependent on the client's style; some clients are short and to the point, others rambling and detailed. In early sessions where relationship building is paramount, it may be more helpful to provide time and space for the client to feel heard. In later sessions, the coach might choose to introduce more pace. However, all of this depends on the client and their style.

The final chunk is the planning and review section. Again, about 15 minutes in a two-hour session allows enough time to explore a plan, think about insights and plan when and where to meet again.

Time management

Managing time for the benefit of your client is one of your responsibilities as a coach. It helps to have a clear beginning, middle and end for each session. At the start of each session, remind the client how long the session will last. Signal to the client about halfway through and, depending on the length of the session, signal in the later half, about 15 minutes before the end of the session, to allow time to move towards a conclusion.

Clients often come to coaching with an idea of what they want to discuss. However, it can take time to build up the relationship to a point where the client feels able to disclose the real or a deeper issue. By signally the timing this gives the client the opportunity to control how they manage the time and if or when they move towards this other issue.

Managing the beginning

It is important to keep in mind that the session begins the moment you and your client start to talk. In the informal conversation as you walk to the meeting room, or the initial chat at the start of the online call. For example, when arriving for a coaching session the client may make a statement that appears to be meaningless, such as about the weather or trouble with the trains on their way to the session. However, being sensitive to these passing remarks can prove helpful as the session continues, giving a possible insight to the client's mood, state of mind or focus. However, as with all single sources of data, be careful. A single rain drop does not make a shower. Keep your mind open to other pieces of information as the session continues.

Managing the middle

If you have contracted well, and agreed a clear goal at the beginning, the conversation has a direction and focus. It is clearly important to set a manageable goal for the time you have. This might involve breaking the goal down into a series of elements, and agreeing to focus on different elements in different sessions.

As the session continues, its handy to have a clock positioned above and behind the client's seat, where you can casually keep check of the time without checking your watch. The latter sends a signal you are not interested or distracted. As you become more experienced, the need for a clock disappears and your internal clock will guide you as to where you are in the session.

Clients often lose their sense of time in sessions, so it can be helpful to signal at about the mid-point, or after two thirds, how the session is progressing, and take a moment to structure the rest of the session.

Managing the ending

Endings are as important as beginnings. Time and again a coaching session is coming towards an end and the client will begin to speak about difficult thoughts or feelings. This door-handle moment is a well-known phenomenon.

This may happen as the client knows there is no time to explore the issue, and wants you to consider it for next time, or maybe the client feels rushed, which they had brought up earlier, but time has passed without their awareness. Depending on the nature of the issue, it is usually best to acknowledge the issue and agree with the client to deal with it in the next session, while concluding the current topic.

In managing the end, it is also helpful to clients to signal the last 10 or 15 minutes before the end: 'The session is coming towards an end, let's just take stock of where we are'. This signals a move towards drawing the threads of the conversation together, taking a look at the pattern and making a plan, or thinking about what new insights have emerged through questions such as: 'As you look back over the session today, what new insight has emerged for you about the topic?' Or, 'What have you learned from our conversation that you can take away and apply to a similar challenge at work?'

Conclusion

Time management is an important skill for all coaches, both in running their coaching business, but also in working with clients: helping clients to make the most of the time together. By planning the session and the wider coaching assignment collaboratively with clients, the coach can ensure the individual session and the wider assignment serves the client's needs and delivers what has been promised during contracting.

Chapter 40:
How can I give and receive high-quality feedback?

Jonathan Passmore

Introduction

As coaches, we are expected to give feedback to others, but we can also learn a lot by gathering our own feedback about our work and our style. However, many coaches find it difficult to give feedback, fearing hurting the feelings of others or damaging the relationship, while also being anxious about how they can elicit genuine feedback from clients that goes beyond the platitude of 'excellent job'. In this chapter, we will explore how coaches can give constructive feedback that is both challenging and supportive, and how they can elicit genuine feedback from clients that will help them develop a new understanding about how others experience them, and ways they can adapt and grow as a coach and leader.

What is feedback?

Feedback may be defined as the transmission of evaluative or corrective information about an action, event, or process to another individual, with the expectation the communication will lead to an adjustment, correction in developmental feedback or a repeat of the action in positive feedback.

In coaching, we are likely to both want to give feedback as a way to enhance our client's insights, as well as to solicit feedback as a way to development and improve our coaching practice.

How can I elicit learning from feedback?

There are few better ways to improve your coaching, or your leadership, than through securing feedback from clients. One useful way to think about feedback is as help. When delivered with empathy, understanding and encouragement, it can be a powerful tool to help you on your journey of continual improvement.

Many coaches use feedback forms to gather feedback. While these may be helpful during the early stages of training, they never replace engaging a client in a genuine discussion about their experience of you and your coaching.

Since almost all coaching is completed in private, it can be easy after the first 50 or 100 clients to start to become complacent. Coaches, and leaders, start to believe the generic feedback from their clients: 'That was great', 'That was really useful', 'Thank you'. It's rare for coaches to be as active in soliciting feedback from their 500th client as from their fifth. Yet, in my view, that's what we should do. Eliciting feedback should be part of our script at the end of each session and, at the end of each assignment, just as contracting is part of our script at the start.

In Table 40.1, we suggest possible scripts for four points in the coaching replacement where feedback can be helpful: mid-session review; end-of-session feedback; a mid-coaching assignment review; and end-of-coaching-assignment feedback. The aim of these questions is to help your client move from the platitudes expected by society conventions on to useful development information that can help you adapt for the next time you meet this client, or start to gather information in search of patterns about your overall style of engagement and coaching.

Table 40.1: Eliciting feedback

When	What	Comments
Mid-session review	'I wonder if it would be useful to take a few minutes to review where we are and plan what's going to be of most use for the remaining part of the session?' 'How would you like us to work together over the coming 30 to 60 minutes?'	This type of question helps in both agenda planning and focus, and also provides an opportunity for informal feedback.
End-of-session feedback	'As we draw the session to a close, how was today's session for you?' 'Specifically, what did you find most useful?' 'If there was one thing that I could do differently next time that would make the session even more helpful for you, what would that be?'	This starting question is more a signal that you are moving into the feedback part. The second question provides the opportunity for specific behaviour-based positive feedback, while the third question provides a socially acceptable way to provide developmental feedback.
Mid-coaching assignment review	'We are at the midpoint in our coaching relationship. Many of my previous clients have found it useful to take stock and review how far we have come, consider what still needs to be achieved and reflect on the working relationship. Would you be happy to spend five minutes reviewing your perceptions?'	The question again at this stage is general and the client should always be allowed to take it in whatever ways they wish. It serves as both a review of content as well as style, if used with specific follow-up questions.

When	What	Comments
End-of-coaching-assignment feedback	'This is our last session. It would be really helpful if you can share with me your reflections on our time together.' 'What did you find most useful during our work together?' 'I always value feedback, as this is the way I can improve my coaching. What's one piece of advice you would give me that might be helpful for my work with other clients?'	These questions encourage clients to see providing feedback as a favour. One key point to remember is not to enter into any discussion. At the end of the advice, just offer thanks and close that part of the conversation.

Remember that any feedback you receive is not the truth, it's just a perception. That's how that person experiences you. For me, what's most helpful is to look for patterns. I capture the feedback, word for word if I can, and quarterly review these feedback comments. Is there a pattern? If there is, I might review the past six months of feedback. This is where supervision can come in useful in providing a safe developmental space to take this feedback and explore it with someone else. What does it mean about you, what strengths or watch-outs are signalled? What development or changes in behaviour does it invite?

How can I give better feedback?

Giving feedback to clients can also be a useful skill – for managers as well as for coaches. Yet over my career I can think of more managers who would duck giving feedback, preferring to say that everything was OK for fear of damaging their relationship with the team member. However, constructive, challenging development feedback can be as useful to give as it is to receive.

However, to do it well, follow a few golden rules:

1. Ask permission to explore the topic.

2. Invite the person to review the situation, their behaviour from their own perspective and then from an independent view.

3. Ask permission to give your feedback and make it clear this is a viewpoint.

4. Focus on behaviours, as opposed to the individual.

5. Use specific evidence, such as evidence you have observed (never third-hand information) or feedback from a 360 or psychometric test.

6. Provide the opportunity for multiple interpretations, while acknowledging that this person believes (or you believe) this is an issue to reflect on.

7. Encourage the person to commit to some action – gather further evidence, reflect or develop a plan of action (Gregory et al, 2008).

As coaches, we rarely have the power to make people change, but we do have the opportunity to help people have a safe space to hold up a mirror to their behaviour, reflect and plan to make changes. We also have all the tools to build a relationship, to empathise and to help clients develop the intrinsic motivation to make change.

How can I feed forward?

Marshall Goldsmith, a leading executive coach, prefers to use the term 'feedforward' (Goldsmith, 2015). He argues that we don't need to think about what we did less well yesterday or an hour ago, instead we need to focus on what we can do better tomorrow. This future-focused developmental conversation can be incredibly powerful. It shifts the focus from what we did wrong towards what we can learn to do right; a shift in thinking from a static mindset to a growth mindset (Dweck, 2016).

A simple question can start this process: 'If there is one thing that I could do to be a better coach, what's the one piece of help you would give me?' We can explore this through further questions, but what is critical is that the answer we always give to whatever comments we receive is 'thank you'. All feedforward help is a gift. Whatever they say, positive or negative, never argue, never justify, never defend your behaviour. Simply offer thanks, and take the gift away to reflect, consider and possibly explore the feedforward with your supervisor.

Conclusion

Feedback is a gift. When offered to our clients with the right intent, it can help them to deepen their self-awareness. It is also a gift, which we can encourage our clients to give to us, helping us to improve our coaching practice. To secure such valuable feedback, we need to be both open and encouraging of our clients to share their genuine views as to what was most helpful for them and what we could have done differently. The best coaches are the best learners, and view their 5,000th client the same as the 50th, as a valuable source of learning. We can only do this when we retain the beginner mind.

References

Dweck, C (2016) *Mindset: The New Psychology of Success*. New York: Random House.

Goldsmith, M (2015) Feedforward. *In*: J Passmore (ed) *Leadership Coaching: Working with Leaders to Develop Elite Performance* (2nd edition) (pp167–74). London: Kogan Page.

Gregory, J B, Levy, P E and Jeffers, M (2008) Development of a model of the feedback process within executive coaching. *Consulting Psychology Journal: Practice and Research*, 60 (1), 42–56.

London, M and Smither, J W (2002) Feedback orientation, feedback culture, and the longitudinal performance management process. *Human Resource Management Review* 12 (1) 81–100.

McDowall, A (2008) Feedback in coaching. *In*: J Passmore (ed) *Psychometrics in Coaching* pp26–40. London: Kogan Page.

Peterson, D B and Millier, J (2005) The alchemy of coaching: 'You're good, Jennifer, but you could be *really* good.' *Consulting Psychology Journal: Practice and Research* 57 (1) 14–40.

Chapter 41: How should I use notes in my coaching?

Jonathan Passmore

Introduction

'They look like great notes – can you type those up and share them with me?', a client once asked. If that has ever happened to you, what should you do? Should coaches make detailed notes during a session? Should they share them with their clients? Should they share them with the sponsor? What is the role of the notes in coaching practice? What information should coaching notes contain? In this chapter, we aim to help you answer these questions and be better prepared for each session as a result.

Should you take notes?

There is little specific guidance or advice from professional bodies or thought leaders on whether or what to make notes about in a coaching session or afterwards. The topic is not discussed in competency frameworks (AC, 2012; EMCC, 2015; ICF, 2019). There are few definitive right and wrong answers.

Most coaches take notes during a session, with a preference for keeping notes light so the coach can focus on what the client is saying. This reflects the difference between coaching and a job interview. In coaching, the aim is to facilitate insights for the client. In an interview, the aim is to gather evidence of the suitability of a candidate for a specific job vacancy. As a result, in an average session, my notes may run to no more than 20 to 60 words, while in an interview there are likely to be a page of notes for each interview question.

In reality, coaching practice varies widely. Some coaches take detailed notes that run to several pages. Other coaches take notes that they share with the client or the sponsor as part of their contract with the organisation or the individual.

PIPS framework is a useful framework, which can guide note taking in coaching.

Table 41.1: PIPS framework

- **P**ersonal
- **I**deas
- **P**lans
- **S**uggestions

'Personal' issues are non-sensitive, personal details. For example, if the client mentions the name of her husband, Tony, I will make a note. Or if the client is excited about her daughter, Jemima, who is looking forward to playing in a football tournament the following week, I will make a note. In this way I will be able to ask about these aspects during the initial relationship chat before the session formally begins. As an example, my notes might simply read: 'Daughter – Jemima – January football tournament'. At the next meeting, in reviewing the notes before the session, I will recall the conversation from this trigger and may ask during the initial chat as we walk to the meeting room: 'How did Jemima get on in the football tournament?'

The second area is 'ideas'. These may be passing remarks that are worth capturing and may be worthy of exploration at a later time. For example, when focusing on one issue, a client may talk about the challenge of balancing work–home priorities. My notes may simply record: 'Future topic? Balancing work–home priorities'. In this area I would ensure I was careful not to use shorthand or clinical labels to describe client behaviours, such as 'workaholic' or 'autistic'. This is for several reasons: am I qualified? Do I have evidence? Is it my role to offer a diagnosis? What would be the implications if the client asked to see my notes?

The third area for notes is 'plans'. At the end of a session, I will typically ask the client to summarise their plans for action and to make a note of these for review after the session. It can be helpful for the coach to be able to recall at the start of the next meeting the actions the client had agreed to explore and use these as the starting point for the conversation.

The fourth and final area is 'suggestions'. These may be comments, feedback or ideas from the client for the coach to action. There may have been a request for a book suggestion, website or other material to help the client explore their topic in more depth. It may be feedback, behaviours to continue doing or things to change for the next session. It might also include referrals or actions that the coach needs to implement, such as contacting the client's organisation or sponsor, or connecting the client with someone else in their network, such as referral to a therapist or another coach.

What notes should you make after a session?

This depends on your personal style. The journey to improvement requires reflection and a personal learning journal can help in this respect, gathering material for supervision as well as to look back on to identify and reflect on patterns over the weeks and months. This journal may be short or long, running to 100 words for a session or 1,000 words, depending on your style and the issues the session provoked.

The 'Henley8' can be a useful framework to keep in mind (Passmore, 2021). This invites the coach to consider eight questions about the critical incident that is the centre of their reflection.

Table 41.2: Henley8 questions

What did I notice?
How did I respond?
What does this say about me?
What does this say about me as a coach?
What strengths does this offer?
What watch-outs do I need to be aware of?
What did I learn?
What will I do differently next time?

What should you do if your client or sponsor asks for your notes?

This issue is best managed before it arises through the contract with the organisation and the individual client. As a general rule, using tripartite contracting can reduce the risk of a sponsor asking for a feedback report. Feedback can instead be managed through the tripartite meeting with the sponsor and client present. In terms of individual clients, the issue is covered by the General Data Protection Regulation (GDPR). All clients have a legal right to access their personal data, which includes their coach's notes. This is a good reason to keep them short, helpful to you, without including judgment or opinions that you would not wish to share with your client.

When should I dispose of my notes?

Recording keeping is a separate topic we discuss in Chapter 42 but essentially, I keep my notes from a session for about a year after completing the assignment. Using an A5 note book to record my notes from coaching means I typically get through one a year and, when full, I set this aside to the end of the calendar year, before the cover is removed and the item placed in the shedder pile with bank statements and other personal data.

Five tips on note-taking and management

As a guide, I keep five points in mind when taking notes and managing the notes I have taken:

1. The coach's role is one of facilitator, helping their clients to become more self-aware and to take greater personal responsibility. Thus, clients should be encouraged to take notes that are going to be helpful to them. It is not the coach's role to take notes for them or for the sponsor.

2. Any information collected is covered by GDPR. This means coaches need a policy describing the personal data they will hold, how long they will hold it and how and when they will destroy it.

3. Any notes collected by the coach might be seen by the client and could potentially be accessed by a court, such as an employment tribunal.

4. Notes should be as minimal as possible to facilitate the next conversation, while avoiding diagnosis, labelling or excessive detail.

5. Personally or commercially sensitive information should be kept to a minimum in case notes are lost or stolen.

Conclusion

In this chapter we have offered a few insights to how the coach can best manage the challenge of note taking, collecting a few useful insights without creating an administrative burden of making notes for their personal or organisational clients.

References

Association for Coaching (2012) *AC Competency Framework*. Available at: https://cdn.ymaws.com/www.associationforcoaching.com/resource/resmgr/Accreditation/Accred_General/Coaching_Competency_Framewor.pdf (accessed 6 August 2020).

European Mentoring and Coaching Council (2015) *Coach Competences*. Available at: https://www.emccglobal.org/quality/supervision/competences/ (accessed 6 August 2020).

ICF (2019) *ICF Coach Competencies*. Available at: https://coachfederation.org/core-competencies (accessed 6 August 2020).

Passmore, J (2021) *The Coaches' Handbook*. Abingdon: Routledge.

SECTION 5: POST SESSION

Chapter 42:
How can coaches and leaders better manage personal data?

Jonathan Passmore

Introduction

Coaches setting up a coaching business often focus most on the coaching process, upgrading their skills or obtaining coach accreditation. But business considerations are just as important. These include deciding which coaching niche to focus on, arranging professional indemnity insurance and addressing basic business management issues, such as regulatory and legislative compliance. In this guide, we focus on one such issue: managing personal data. Specifically, we will focus on the EU regulations and General Data Protection Regulation (GDPR).

Data protection

Most coaches hold significant quantities of private data about their clients. This may include names, addresses and emails, but in coaching it also extends to personal details about behaviours, emotions, thoughts and beliefs. The data is usually both digital, including details in an address book to coaching contacts and meeting dates and times, and paper files containing the details of coaching conversations.

Yet despite this deeply intimate data, alongside general commercial information for marketing and contract management, few coaches have data management policies or have conducted impact assessments. Research that we have undertaken at Henley Business School suggests that only about 11 % of independent practising coaches are registered with the relevant bodies in their country (Passmore & Rogers, 2018).

The reason for this low level of compliance is likely to be due to a combination of factors. Some researchers have highlighted the burden of regulation on small- and medium-sized enterprises (SMEs) and noted that this can mean that they struggle with compliance (Kitching, 2006). Others may wish to avoid the costs associated with annual registration, which they feel offers them no clear benefit individually. However, the GDPR places a stronger emphasis on compliance, with severe penalties for those who fail to comply.

The GDPR extends the scope of the EU data protection law to all foreign companies processing data relating to EU residents and aims to harmonise the data protection regulations that exist throughout the EU. 'Processing' has a very wide definition and includes almost any action relating to data. To ensure compliance, the EU also introduced a severe regime of fines: up to four per cent of worldwide turnover or €20 million for serious breaches, and up to two per cent of turnover or €10 million for organisations and individuals holding data who have failed to conduct an impact assessment against the six core principles. Perhaps crucially for coaches, the liability for breaches of the GDPR extends beyond data controllers and companies on to individual data processors themselves. These factors make compliance essential for all businesses.

What should coaches do?

The answer to this question depends on the size of the business. We have suggested 10 steps that might be helpful to consider, depending on the scale, scope and activities of your business. Which steps you take will depend on the outcome of your own impact assessment, making a judgment about what's right for your business.

Data protection officers

Most large organisations will need to appoint a data protection officer. For smaller organisations, this will be the owner-manager who will be responsible for planning and managing the organisation's data. In larger organisations, this individual will also need to liaise with the board and other employees in order to create systems to ensure compliance with the directive. Whoever fulfils this role should be knowledgeable about GDPR, which is likely to require some training or further reading.

Staff training in compliance

The actions of employees and contractors are one of the biggest risks faced by an organisation. You may need to train your administrative staff, associates and other employees so that they understand the organisation's responsibilities, and to show that you have taken action to reduce the chances of them unwittingly doing something that will result in a data breach. Writing a data privacy statement for the organisation, and training all employees and associates in the policy will help improve compliance, as will evidence of the dates and times when training was undertaken.

Fair processing and privacy notifications to your customers

Do you have a contract that you use with organisational and individual clients? Does this contain information about the data you may hold on them and how you will process this data? Do you have a website that allows individuals to join your mailing list? If this is the case you will probably need to update your fair processing and privacy notifications to your customers. The same may apply to employees, such as administrative staff and associates, whom you may use from time to time. As part of these changes, you will need to ensure that you have a process for regularly reviewing the data you hold.

Seeking permission to hold personal data

A key feature of the regulation is informed consent. You will need to gain consent from individuals to hold data about them, if consent is the grounds on which you are processing data. Such consent needs to be opt-in, as opposed to an opt-out, and the consent needs to be based on genuine choice, knowingly made. Individuals also have the right to withdraw their consent at any time, which will require an active process of managing the data you hold. There are exceptions, such as holding data for legal compliance – for example, to comply with HM Revenue & Customs regulations (UK), but most exceptions only apply to statutory or public bodies.

Managing high-risk data

For most coaches, the organisations and individual clients they work with, and the data they hold, will not be considered high risk, but for some coaches or organisations this may be the case. Privacy impact assessments (PIAs) can help determine whether data is high risk or not. In addition, coaches need to be aware of provisions on data security breaches and the requirement to notify of the breach within 72 hours if the breach is likely to result in a risk to people's rights and freedoms. This might happen, for example, if your computer is hacked and yours and other emails addresses are stolen.

The right to be forgotten

The right to be forgotten has significant implications for some organisations, such as Google. But it also has implications for small businesses too. This may simply require the ability to delete individuals and their records from your files. This might be easy for digital files, but does require some thought about back-ups, as well as for paper records, such as those contained in a note book, supervision notes or personal journals. The importance of reviewing and updating agreements

You may have agreements in place to share data with associates or others. These agreements should reflect the requirements in the GDPR and, as a general rule, data should only be shared with the individual's agreement.

Putting in place IT security

As a data processor, you need to securely hold the data and prevent others from accessing this information. This is likely to mean ensuring that you run anti-virus software on your computer to block malicious programmes accessing your files, and install appropriate firewalls to prevent hackers breaking into your network. It may also mean ensuring that the password protection of computers is robust and that passwords are kept secure.

Managing the security of manual data

We often neglect manual data but this needs the same treatment as digital data. It needs to be securely held, stored and destroyed after a specific period. This means using locked filing cabinets, locking your office and keeping notebooks with client details, client files, reflective journals and supervision notes in a secure location, perhaps in a safe. It also means taking appropriate care of these records when out of the office.

Deleting data

When it comes to destroying data, care is also needed. You need to establish policies when data will be deleted from your computer, as well as when coaching notes will be destroyed. If the quantities of these are large you may need to consider employing professional data services to do this for you, cleaning computer hard drives and back-up devices, and shredding paper files. However, even as a sole practitioner, ensuring the hard drive is deleted before you dispose of your computer is essential.

Conclusions

Data management is one aspect that even experienced coaches can improve their practice. As coaches, we are in a privileged position having access to our client's intimate and commercially sensitive data. We need to respect that position by managing their data with the same care and concern shown by our organisational clients, securing permission to hold data, manging it securely and within agreed and published policy parameters, and destroying it from our digital and paper records at the appropriate times to avoid holding such data unnecessarily.

References

Kitching, J (2006) A burden on business? Reviewing the evidence base on regulation and small business performance. *Environment and Planning C* 24 (6) 799–814.

Passmore, J and Rogers, K (2018) Are you GDPR ready? *Coaching at Work* 13 (4) 30-33.

Chapter 43:
Why should I reflect on my practice?

Elizabeth Houldsworth

Introduction

Learning to reflect in order to improve one's own practice is increasingly important across a range of professions, from teaching to counselling, and from management to clinical work. Knowing and managing the self are surely key skills for coaches and leaders to develop, in order to manage their own performance and encourage reflection among those they coach and develop.

Why reflective practice is important

The accelerating pace of change and rise of technological developments means that no one individual can possess a set of knowledge that can be future-proofed. Educationalists have instead pointed to the need for strategies that support lifelong learning. Indeed, once the years of compulsory education are completed, the vast majority of learning across the lifespan is emergent, experiential and unplanned. According to Boud, Keogh and Walker (1985), the key is to develop skills in order to reflect on these experiences, thus converting them into learning events. Certainly, reflection supports learning objectives on knowledge acquisition (*being able to articulate what I now know*) and the transfer of this to practice (*how I have used this or will use it in the future*). For some learners, there are also deeper personal learning outcomes (heightened self-knowledge and self-identity) evidencing that transformational learning has taken place.

For areas of higher professional practice, such as education, coaching or leadership, the notion of becoming a 'reflective practitioner' along the lines outlined by Schön (1983) has become increasingly prominent with critical reflection being identified as an important meta-skill (Stead & Elliott, 2012). Although the use of reflective writing in support of professional development commentators such as Moon (2007) have pointed out that reflection is not a clearly defined and enacted concept, and a number of different definitions exist (Roberts, 2012). For example, some commentators describe reflection as a form of problem solving (Dewey, 1933; Schön, 1983) – others see it as a means to reach levels of personal emancipation (Habermas, 1987; Mezirow,

1991) and Kolb's (1984) well-known learning cycle suggests a different view, with reflection being positioned as the opposite of action.

Writing about management learning, Cunliffe (2016) advocates developing critical reflexivity in order to go beyond a focus on self within an activity and incorporate an awareness of one's own tacit assumptions. This development of a self-reflexive dialogue requires a rethinking of our notions of learning (Cunliffe, 2016) and is likely to have been emphasised in your coach training. However, the skills acquired in training are just the starting point and once you commence supervision, action learning sets or even a personal learning log as a regular part of your practice, you will have the opportunity to bring reflection into your practice as a regular feature.

How to develop reflective practice

Moon (2007) has highlighted that when reflective writing is incorporated into educational programmes, it can be challenging for students to fully understand what is required of them, suggesting that the requirements might only become fully evident to the candidate at the assessment stage, when the differentiation between reflective writing vs simple description becomes apparent.

In this section, we seek to support your understanding about levels of reflection so that you can build on this to improve your own reflective skills. We will do this by suggesting a series of critical questions, which make it possible to identify a hierarchy of levels from description at the lowest level to deep reflection at the highest.

A number of previous authors have sought to conceptualise and categorise the different levels of reflection that may occur in reflective writing. For example, Bain, Ballantyne, Packer and Mills (1999) identify five levels starting with reporting and then moving through to responding, relating, reasoning and reconstructing. Schön's (1983) approach was to advance three key stages as detailed below:

1. Response to 'puzzlement in new situation'
   ■ What the hell just happened? Or, what the hell *is* happening?

2. Contrast to what I know
   ■ So how have I really been doing this until now?

3. Opportunity to experiment
   ■ What can I gain/learn/get/know from this?

Moon (2004) uses similar terminology and refers to four levels. Usefully, her model is supported with examples (see Moon, 2004; 2007).

The framework below is based upon Moon's work, which distinguishes between description and reflection:

■ Level 0: **Description** of what happened (reporting).

- Level 1: **Descriptive writing** with some reflective potential. Reference to impact of events and indication of points where reflection could occur.

- Level 2: **Reflective writing (1)** Reference to the value of exploring motives or reasons for behaviour. Some self-awareness/criticism or possibly reflection on motives of others. This stage is sometimes described as relating or reasoning.

- Level 3: **Reflective writing (2)** There is clear evidence here of the learner standing back from an event, of mulling it over and holding an internal dialogue. There is awareness of the learning involved and how it will be used in the future direction. This phase is sometimes described as reconstructing.

The Henley8 model for self-reflection

At Henley, we build on these earlier contributions and encourage our coaches and leaders to use eight practical questions (Passmore & Sinclair, 2021). These eight questions are a handrail to guide the reflective process. They provide one way to structure our thinking (see Box 43.1).

> ## Box 43.1: Henley's eight-question guide to reflective practice
>
> 1. What did I observe?
> 2. What was my response?
> 3. What does this tell me about me?
> 4. What does this tell me about myself as a coach or leader?
> 5. What strengths does this offer?
> 6. What are the potential pitfalls?
> 7. What did I learn?
> 8. What might I do differently next time?

The starting point is to notice: *what did I observe?* This requires situation awareness, being fully present and noticing changes in events around us. The observation may be a change in the situation – for example, a fire bell rings during the team meeting. It may be observing a behaviour of an individual, our programme member or a client, or their emotional response to the situation.

For example:

> I noticed that Kate was late for the meeting. She came in and apologised.

The second step is to identify our response: *what was my response?* This may be behavioural, but is likely to also be cognitive (*what was I thinking and why?*) and also: *what was I feeling?* Our thoughts and feelings often drive our behaviour and recognising the relationship between these is helpful, and how these are associated with the trigger event (what we have observed).

For example:

> I observed that I had been clicking my pen while I was waiting and that my heart rate had risen. I was conscious that I was irritated by her lateness.

Behind these initial feelings and thoughts are likely to be beliefs and values. Being conscious of these, and bringing these core beliefs to mind, will help us make more sense of our own response.

For example:

> My values are that time-keeping is very important and a commitment is a commitment, and that her lateness was rude.

The third and fourth aspects of reflection involve considering what these behaviours, thoughts, feelings, and possibly our beliefs and values say about us as an individual, and what they say about us as a leader or a coach within the context in which we are working. Meaning can vary widely depending on the organisational and national culture, and taking these into account needs to be part of our reflection.

For example:

> This tells me that I can be intolerant to others in certain circumstances and that breaking these unwritten rules leads me to be judgmental.

The fifth and sixth questions explore the pros and cons of these beliefs. How do these beliefs or attitudes help or hinder us in our role? Do they make us more effective? Do they contribute to our happiness and well-being? Do they contribute positively to our team or others? What do we need to be aware of in terms of how we can build on these positives and what we should guard against?

For example:

> As a coach, it tells me that certain behaviours can lead me to starting sessions in a judgmental mind-frame.

The seventh and eighth questions are what we learn and may take away from the reflection. They set the stage for future development. Reflection without action is meaningless. The purpose of reflection is to understand ourselves and others more deeply and, through this, to learn and adapt in the future to enhance our own effectiveness and that of others.

For example:

> One of the strengths of my values is that I am never likely to be late for a meeting. The pitfall is that if others are late, this can be a significant hurdle to recovering the relationship.
>
> What I learned about myself was that it would be helpful to change my belief: this is their time and thus how they choose to use it is their responsibility, not mine; I will still finish at the agreed time.

Conclusion

In this chapter we have considered self-reflection and explained its importance in the context of post-experience professional development – whether this is via a formal programme of study or ongoing professional development. For business coaches it is particularly relevant in order to continually improve coaching outcomes for clients and the requirement to be in supervision. This chapter has briefly explained the contribution of earlier commentators such as Schon (1983) and Moon (2004), and introduces the Henley8 model for self-reflection. This framework provides a useful handrail to guide your reflective journey in such a way that the outputs can be captured in a personal learning journal or shared in discussion with your coach supervisor.

References

Bain, J D, Ballantyne, R, Packer, J and Mills, C (1999) Using journal writing to enhance student teachers' reflectivity during field experience placements. *Teachers and Teaching* 5 (1) 51–73.

Boud, D, Keogh, R and Walker, D (1985) *Reflection: Turning Experience into Learning*. London: Kogan Page.

Cunliffe A L (2016) Reflexive Dialogical Practice in Management Learning. *Management Learning* 33 35-61.

Dewey, J (1933) *How We Think: A Restatement of the Relation of Reflective Thinking to the Educative Process*. Boston, MA: Heath.

Habermas, J (1987) *Knowledge and Human Interests*. Cambridge: Polity Press.

Kolb, D A (1984) *Experiential Learning: Experience as the Source of Learning and Development*. London: Prentice-Hall.

Mezirow, J (1991) *Transformative Dimensions of Adult Learning* (1st edition). San Francisco: Jossey-Bass.

Moon, J (2004) *The Handbook of Reflective and Experiential Learning*. London: Routledge Falmer.

Moon, J (2007) Getting the measure of reflection: Considering matters of definition and depth. *Journal of Radiotherapy in Practice* 6 191–200.

Passmore J and Sinclair, T (2021). *The Coaches Handbook*. Abingdon: Routledge

Roberts, A (2012) Classifying the nature of reflective writing during periods of professional experience. *Journal for Education in the Built Environment* 7 (1) 56–72

Schön, D A (1983) *The Reflective Practitioner: How Professionals Think in Action*. London: Temple Smith

Stead V and Elliott C (2012) Women's leadership learning: A reflexive review of representations and leadership teaching. *Management Learning* 44 373-394.

Chapter 44:
Why should I engage in supervision?

Ann James

Introduction

Supervision is an important element of any professional's practice, development and self-care. In relationship with a coaching supervisor, the coach can explore all aspects of their work and keep themselves fit for purpose. In a field that is unregulated, supervision also has a role to play in maintaining the highest ethical standards of practice, and furthering the efficacy of the coaching profession as a whole. This chapter will give you some insights into the key functions of supervision. It will also explore the main ways in which you can participate in supervision, and offer some pointers for establishing and reviewing a supervision arrangement that works for you.

What is supervision or 'super-vision'?

While there is a wide variety of definitions of supervision, the following definition may provide a useful handrail:

> 'Coaching supervision is the interaction that occurs when a coach periodically brings his or her coaching work experience to a coaching supervisor in order to engage in reflective dialogue and collaborative learning for the development and benefit of the coach and his or her clients.' (International Coaching Federation)

While some writers use the term 'supervision', others have argued a better way to see the process is 'super-vision' (Passmore & McGoldrick, 2009). This change in emphasis recognises that the aim is not hierarchical but a collaborative process designed to enhance insight and understanding. By engaging in supervision, coaches are making a commitment that will support them, their clients, the organisations they work for, and the wider system that is impacted by their work.

Through their work, coaches engage in challenging and intimate conversations that take place within complex networks. While doing this, they are managing personal and professional boundaries, noticing the interpersonal dynamics in the relationship between them and their clients, managing themselves in the moment and being alert to the need for best practice and an ethically sound stance.

Beyond that one-to-one relationship, they need to stay mindful of the bigger picture – the broader context of the client's circumstances, as well as information and perspectives that might be important yet outside of their awareness.

Time spent in supervision gives them some breathing space. It is an opportunity to reflect on the things that affected them in a coaching exchange, other options that might have been explored, things that left them puzzled, where they felt at their most or least resourceful, and how their strengths and vulnerabilities might help and hinder them (Hawkins *et al*, 2019).

Coaching supervisors

Coaching supervisors will usually be experienced coaches who have undergone additional training to gain a qualification in supervision skills. Many continue to practise as coaches alongside their supervision work, and will have supervisors of their own.

Like coaches, supervisors will vary in their style, stance, and the approaches they bring to their work. As with coaching, there are many models and frameworks available in the field of supervision (see Passmore, 2011). Some supervisors will work with preferred approaches; others will adopt a more eclectic stance, drawing from a range of thinking and sources.

Types of supervision

Supervision will typically be offered either one-to-one, or within a group.

The **one-to-one** arrangement is in many ways similar to individual coaching: a supervisor will be identified, perhaps based on recommendation and an exploratory conversation, and a contract will be put in place covering the commercial, practical and ethical conditions for the work.

A **group** might be 'closed' and made up of a specified number of regular members who participate at each session. An 'open' group, by contrast, would accommodate a potentially different mix of attendees each time, while still having a limited number on each occasion. The contract for group work will acknowledge these variations and differences.

There are other ways of bringing supervision into coaching practice, which are perhaps best regarded as supplementary to, or even by-products of, the more formal options outlined already.

Peer supervision is a process whereby coaches supervise each other, without any one of them needing to have a supervisor's qualification. This can be a vibrant, cost-effective and readily accessible option, making it possible for coaches to work collaboratively one-to-one or in groups, offering mutual support, insights and shared experience.

For the purposes of meeting the supervision requirements of an organisational client, or accreditation bodies, this would generally be seen as a useful supplement to – not a substitute for – work with a qualified supervisor.

Finally, **self-supervision** – or the development of the internal supervisor – is an asset that all coaches seek to nurture as an integral part of their growth and attention to ethical practice. It is the capacity to bring a level of self-awareness and monitoring of oneself as a coach into the moment when working with clients, grounded in a habit of regular, private reflection.

Supervision role in organisations

It is important to acknowledge here the role of supervision within organisations where coaching is delivered by trained, internal coaches. This can present particular challenges – for example, around confidentiality and boundaries. There is much to be said for the contribution of an external supervisor, who can bring a useful awareness of the business and the system, while remaining outside of it in service of the coaches and their work.

Choosing a supervisor

Choosing the right coaching supervisor or supervisors is in some ways similar to the process that clients might go through when selecting a coach.

It is important that the coach knows what they want from supervision, and what specific experience and skills they would want their supervisor to demonstrate.

They may want to explore a blend of one-to-one and group supervision, perhaps with two or more supervisors who may be particularly well suited to different aspects of their work, their needs, and the contexts in which they are coaching.

Here are some generic, important considerations to keep in mind when selecting a supervisor:

- The supervisor's qualifications, accreditations and experience.
- The scope of the supervisor's practice and their understanding of the contexts in which the coach works.
- Their range of experience as a coach, and whether they continue to practise.

- Their own supervision arrangements for their work as a supervisor.
- Their approach to contracting.
- The ethical code to which they adhere.

Conclusion

Supervision is an important and valuable component in any coach's practice. It's a place of learning to develop capability; a space for exploring the conundrums that come with the work; a restorative sanctuary for the coach to recharge and take care of their own needs. We would advocate all coaches should actively engage in regular supervision, as one of the ways to reflect on their practice and to safeguard their clients.

References

Hawkins, P, Turner, E and Passmore, J (2019) *The Manifesto for Supervision*. Henley-on-Thames: Henley Business School. ISBN: 978-1-912473-24-3.

Passmore, J (2011) *Supervision in Coaching*. London: Kogan Page.

Passmore, J and McGoldrick, S (2009) Super-vision, extra-vision or blind faith. A grounded theory study of the efficacy of coaching supervision. *International Coaching Psychology Review* 4 145–61.

Chapter 45:
How should I select a coaching supervisor?

Ann James

Introduction

Whether you are a newly qualified coach about to launch your practice or an experienced, accredited coach, your coaching supervisor(s) will be at the heart of your ongoing learning, development and well-being. As such, it is important that you choose your supervisor well. In this chapter, we provide a few pointers to guide you in selecting the right supervisor for you.

Why do I need a supervisor?

Coaching supervision is an important element of any professional coach's practice, development and self-care (Passmore, 2011). Within their relationship with their coaching supervisor, the individual coach can explore all aspects of their work and keep themselves 'fit for purpose'.

Hawkins, Turner and Passmore (2019) suggest that supervision '*provides a disciplined space in which the supervisee can reflect on particular work and client situations and relationships, and on the reactivity and patterns they evoke in the mind*'. But supervision is not just a process for the learning and development of the individual coach, it can also be 'the learning lungs of the profession', where the craft of coaching is constantly refreshing itself (Hawkins & Shohet, 2012). Supervision thus hopefully benefits the supervisee (coach), the client, but also the organisation and the wider profession.

How is supervision different from talking to a coach about my work?

During your training it is very likely you will have had helpful conversations with fellow coaches about aspects of your work. These conversations will likely have led to new insights and fresh perspectives on topics that may have been puzzling or bothering to you.

This kind of exchange is to be nurtured and is often described as 'peer supervision'. Formal coaching supervision takes this to another level.

Coaches and coach supervisors share many skills in common; supervisors are usually practising coaches, and most continue to work as coaches alongside their supervision work (Clutterbuck *et al*, 2016).

A key distinction with formal supervision is that the supervisor will have extended their training to acquire knowledge and skills that enable them to adopt a subtly different stance in your conversations. This equips them to assume a 'meta-position' that enables you to explore your coaching through a wider lens, taking account of such things as organisational context and current developments in coaching, as well as thinking through ethical and contractual considerations.

What should I be looking for?

When you are choosing a supervisor, you will probably be asking yourself many of the same questions that coaching clients ask when selecting a coach.

Here are a few questions to keep in mind:

1. What supervision qualifications do they hold?
As with coaching, it's important that anyone working in the field of supervision can demonstrate that they have completed a formal qualification with a reputable provider of supervisor training. Like coach training, supervision training comes in all shapes and sizes. Some providers offer attendance-based courses, while others offer formal qualifications. One good measure is to check whether the training provider is approved – or accredited – by one of the professional bodies.

2. What accreditation do they hold?
Like coaching, most of the professional coaching bodies also accredit supervisors. You can check if your supervisor is accredited by visiting the website of the relevant professional body, as most bodies hold a public register of their accredited members. If your supervisor is to be found on such a register, this also means they operate within a professional code of ethics, so they can be held to account for their conduct.

3. Are they a practising coach?
Most supervisors continue to work as coaches in tandem with their supervision practice. While a supervisor does not need to be an expert, you may like the idea that they have current, hands-on coaching experience in your area of practice – such as health coaching, organisational coaching or coaching in education. This experience can equip them with an understanding of some of the wider cultural and systemic factors that impact on you and your client.

4. Will you get along?

A relationship in which you will be confiding, reflecting and exploring at a deeply personal and professional level needs to feel right. You are going to be entrusting your supervisor with your challenges, your vulnerabilities, your blind spots and, indirectly, your clients' stories. You'll want to know you're in good hands. Once you have covered the 'must haves', such as qualifications and experience, invest some time in experiencing the relationship. You do not necessarily always want to feel comfortable, but you do need to feel safe. Seek out an alliance that will support you in tolerating the discomfort and level of challenge that are necessary and rewarding components of robust supervision.

5. Do they have a supervisor, too?

Supervisors, like coaches, benefit from supervision of their supervision work. They are often required to demonstrate that they have this in place as a condition of attaining accredited status or membership of a professional body. The fields of coaching and supervision are currently unregulated, so it's important to know you are held within a wider system that encourages learning, awareness and accountability for everyone.

6. What's their approach to supervision?

Reputable supervisors are likely to share much in common at the levels of training, qualification and experience. What will distinguish one from another will be the nuances of how they apply these assets in practice. As with coaching, there is an array of tools, models and frameworks available to supervisors, so you may want to explore whether they favour certain ones or adopt a more generalist approach. This will give you some insight into their style, stance and philosophy around supervision, so notice how these sit with your own values and perspectives. As a coach, you will understand the importance of clear contracting; expect the same of your supervisor, and ask all the questions you would expect a potential coaching client to ask you about the scope, practicalities, purpose and ambitions of the work you will be doing together.

Where do I start?

In truth, there are many excellent supervisors out there, and no doubt many that you could work with safely and with confidence. The challenge can be to know where to start, and then to narrow your search until you find the one who's right for you.

Talk to other coaches who already have experience of being supervised; ask them about how their supervisors have worked with them, what approaches they have experienced, what benefits they have gained and how their practice has been supported.

Some might also share some tips and cautionary advice that they have picked up along the way. Remember that this relationship is as personal and unique as that between a coach and their client: a great fit for one coach, might not be a great fit for you.

Conclusion

Supervision is a useful tool to help coaches reflect on their practice, providing support and advice when needed, to reduce the blind spots that affect us all. There is no rule that says you should have only one supervisor, and no rule that says you cannot change your supervision arrangements as your practice evolves. Take some time to explore and experiment with supervision formats and options until you find the 'fit' and blend that works best for you and the work that you do, and review it often. In this chapter, we have offered you some insights into how you can do this with confidence.

References

Clutterbuck, D, Whitaker, C and Lucas, M (2016) *Coaching Supervision: A Practical Guide for Supervisees*. London: Routledge.

Hawkins, P and Shohet, R (2012) *Supervision in the Helping Professions* (4th edition). Maidenhead: Open University Press/McGraw-Hill.

Hawkins, P, Turner, E and Passmore, J (2019) *The Manifesto for Supervision*. Henley-on-Thames: Henley Business School.

Passmore, J (2011) *Supervision in Coaching*. London: Kogan Page.

Chapter 46:
How can I become a more self-reflective as a coach?

Julia Carden

Introduction

Self-awareness is a key part to being effective as a coach, because the coach is the 'main instrument' of the coaching (Bachkirova, 2016; Hardingham, 2004). Alongside this, without spending time and effort really understanding ourselves at a deep level, we cannot expect to take our clients to a deeper level, as we can only take them as far as we have taken ourselves (Laske, 1999). Coach self-awareness enables the coach to work with clients at a level of insight and change (see Figure 46.1). It is a capability that can be developed, but it requires ongoing, continual effort and focus (Carden *et al*, 2021). There are many components of self-awareness that need identification, reflection on and then development. Carl Jung (1957) believed that the most important part of adult development was integrating the different parts of self; self-awareness is about developing the self-knowledge of these different parts.

Figure 46.1: Impact of coach self-awareness

What is meant by the term 'self-awareness'?

There are a multitude of perspectives and definitions of what self-awareness is. When the concept is discussed in relation to coaching it is best explored from both an intra and interpersonal perspective. The intrapersonal aspect focuses on an awareness of one's internal resources, including values and beliefs, cognitions/thoughts, feelings and body sensations, behaviours, personality traits and motivations; and the interpersonal focuses on one's impact and interactions with others, including an awareness of physiological responses and the perceptions of others. Therefore, self-awareness can be defined as: '...a capability, which can be developed through focus, evaluation and feedback, which provides an individual with a self-knowledge of their internal state (emotions, cognitions, physiological responses), what drives their behaviours (beliefs, values and motivations) and an awareness of how this impacts and influences others' (Carden, 2019). To develop self-awareness, it is important to really understand what it means to you, how you would define it, and then be clear on all the components.

How can self-awareness be of benefit in interpersonal relationships for coaches?

Self-awareness is a significant element of emotional intelligence (Goleman, 1996), and many prominent leadership writers (Collins, 2001; Goffee & Jones, 2006; Goleman, 1996) cite the importance of emotional intelligence for outstanding leadership.

Other benefits of self-awareness include:

- Individuals with high levels of self-awareness tend to have more stable self-esteem, because there is an element of self-acceptance of who they are. This then enables the coach to develop a deeper human connection with their clients, where meaningful work can be done (see Figure 46.2).

- This in turn can assist the coach in being more flexible with their clients.

- It enables the coach to minimise their own impact and influence on the coaching outcome.

- Relationships and conflict are managed more effectively as self-aware individuals are aware of their impact on others.

- Self-aware individuals are aware of their 'triggers' and reactions, so they are better placed to manage themselves in challenging situations. This means they are less likely to react aggressively or defensively to others.

The importance of self-awareness can be summed up as follows: 'Without self-awareness, it would be difficult for people to take the perspectives of other people, exercise self-control, produce creative accomplishments, and experience pride and high self-esteem' (Silvia & O'Brien, 2004).

Developing self-awareness

Developing self-awareness as a coach is an ongoing, organic process – it is not something that can be done once but will need ongoing work. The stages of developing it are summarised below:

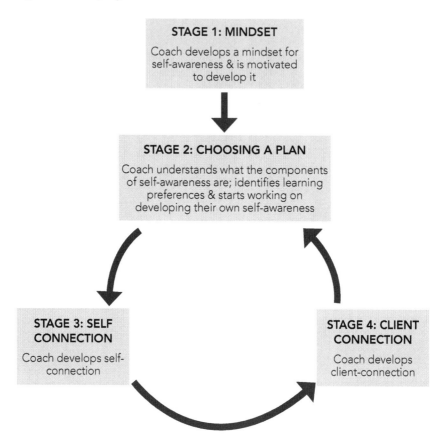

Figure 47.2: Developing self-awareness

There is no one 'best' method or approach to developing self-awareness. It is important that you find what works best for you and what provides you with the deeper insights. Here are a few ideas:

1. **Receive coaching and therapy:** Therapy can be useful to help us understand how past relationships and/or events have influenced and shaped who we are today. Coaching can provide us with a space to reflect, identify patterns of behaviours, triggers to behaviour, deep motivations and how we might want to change.

2. **Engage in coaching supervision:** Coaching supervision is a process of helping you step back and take a 'helicopter' meta perspective of your

coaching work and practice. Your coaching supervisor can help you identify habits, patterns of behaviours and assist you in managing your own 'triggers'.

3. **Engage in self-reflection:** Think about keeping a journal to track your thoughts, feelings, insights and reactions before and after coaching sessions, and in other day-to-day events. After a few weeks, look back and review to identify themes.

4. **Participate in mentor coaching** where your coaching sessions are reviewed against the ICF coaching competencies (Norman, 2020).

5. **Practice mindfulness:** Practising mindfulness has been proven to increase levels of self-awareness and emotional intelligence.

6. **Psychometric profiling:** Complete a psychometric profile e.g. Saville Wave, Hogan Development Survey, 16Personalities or VIA. These profiles can help you identify and understand personality traits, types and preferences.

7. **Identify your values and beliefs:** Values are the things we hold most dear. They, along with beliefs, guide our choices and the way we understand the world and those around us. They are often unconscious, but if we can become more conscious of what our values are, we can understand why we make decisions in a certain way, how we have made choices and how we behave in certain situations.

   ■ What are your most important values (perhaps the top 10)?
   ■ When and why did these values become so important to you?
   ■ How does each of these values affect who you are?
   ■ How might each of these values affect your behaviour and how others might view you?

8. **Reflect on personal strengths:** Undertake a strengths profile assessment – for example, www.viacharacter.org/www/Character-Strengths-Survey

9. **360 feedback:** Gain 360 feedback from a diverse range of respondents, then look for themes to gain an understanding of what your impact on others might be.

10. **Think about your purpose:** Your purpose should be an expression of your true self (Inam, 2015).

Conclusion

The development of self-awareness enhances coach effectiveness because it enables them to work at a deeper level with clients, be more flexible in their approach and ensure they are minimising their own, personal impact on the coaching outcome. However, the development of self-awareness is not a one-off activity, but an ongoing piece of work requiring effort and focus – it's a developmental journey.

References

Bachkirova, T (2016) The self of the coach: conceptualization, issues, and opportunities for practitioner development. *Consulting Psychology Journal: Practice and Research* Vol 68 (2) 143-156.

Carden, J (2019) *Self-awareness in Coaching: A Systematic Literature Review.* Unpublished thesis, Henley Business School.

Carden, J. Jones, R., and Passmore, J. (2021). Defining self-awareness in the context of adult development. *Journal of Management Education.* https://doi.org/10.1177/1052562921990065

Collins, J (2001) *Good to Great.* London, UK: Random House Publishing.

Goffee, R & Jones, G (2006) *Why Should Anyone be Led by You?* Boston, USA: Harvard Business School Press.

Goleman, D (1996) *Emotional Intelligence.* London, UK: Bloomsbury.

Hardingham, A (2004) *The Coach's Coach.* UK: CIPD.

Inam, H (2015) *Wired for Authenticity.* Bloomington, USA: iUniverse Books.

Jung, C (1957) *The Undiscovered Self.* New York: American Library.

Laske, O (1999) An Integrated Model of Developmental Coaching. *Consulting Psychology Journal: Practice and Research* Vol 51 (3) 139-159.

Norman, C (2020) *Mentor Coaching: A Practical Guide.* London, UK: Open University Press.

Silvia, P J and O'Brien, M E (2004) Self-awareness and constructive functioning: revisiting 'the human dilemma'. *Journal of Social and Clinical Psychology* 23 (4) 475–89.

Chapter 47: How should I plan my personal development as a coach?

Jonathan Passmore

Introduction

Continuous professional development is a requirement of most of the professional bodies, as well as being an essential ingredient for professional coaches who want to stay up to date. But what is the best way to stay up to date? What does an ideal personal development plan look like? The answer is there are a variety of ways and for most coaches having a mix of these different ways of engaging in learning is best. In this chapter, we will explore how both novice and experienced coaches can identify and plan their annual learning and review their progress.

What is professional development?

We live in a dynamic and fast-changing world, where research and ideas are emerging all the time. Personal development is a process engaged in by all professionals as a means to keep up-to-date with changing ideas, practice and research. Without professional development, it's easy for the coach to become out of date.

Professional development is best seen as a continuous process, based on specific aims and objectives. It is also best seen as continuous, as it should not be a single event, but is an activity that the coach engages with on a frequent and regular basis, after completing their formal training. Secondly, it is goal-focused, as identifying gaps in our knowledge, or following specific areas of interest or curiosity, leads to more focused and motivated learning.

> **Box 47.1: Definition of continuing professional development**
>
> 'Continuing Professional Development (CPD) is a combination of approaches, ideas and techniques that will help you manage your own learning and growth. The focus of CPD is firmly on results – the benefits that professional development can bring you in the real world.' (CIPD, 2020)

How can I continue to develop as a coach?

Some might think that having completed their coach accreditation or achieved a master's degree in coaching, learning can stop. After all, what else is there to learn? The danger is the coach who stops learning today is tomorrow's dinosaur: out of date, out of touch and out of business.

Instead, coaches need to see themselves as continual learners. This should involve developing an annual personal development plan containing four or five new goals to explore or learn during the forthcoming year.

Creating a routine to review and write the annual plan is a good idea. Add this event to your personal diary. The new year offers one option – taking time over the holiday season to reflect on the past year of work, think about emerging trends and the needs of your clients and consider the question: 'What am I curious about now?' Based on these elements write down four or five headings – and develop these into learning outcomes (something you can measure). An example of a simple annual plan is contained in Table 47.1.

Table 47.1: CPD annual plan

Topic	Learning outcome	How and when
Motivational Interviewing (MI)	1. To better understand MI, its spirit principles, underpinning model of change. 2. To be able to use five MI based tools in my coaching practice consistent with 1.	1. Read 3rd edition of Miller and Rollnick *Motivational. Interviewing* by 1st February. 2. Attend a one- or two-day workshop on MI by 1st June. 3. Reflect on my application of tools in my journal and with my supervisor.
ICF 2019 Competencies	1. To better understand the competencies. 2. To be able to bring the competencies alive in my coaching practice.	1. Review the new framework. 2. Read *Becoming a Coach – The definitive ICF Guide* by 1st April 3. Undertake four hours of mentor coaching to review recordings of my practice, and discuss my application of the competencies by 1st July. 4. Continue to reflect on this in my supervision sessions throughout the year (December).

Once a plan has been created, the coach can establish a six-month review point – to check on their progress, amend or add to the plan, before completing the year. At the year-end, the coach can review their achievements, capture these in their journal, as well as plan the coming year ahead. It's a good idea to keep a record of the learning as evidence for reaccreditation, including CCEU, CPD points or certificates of attendance.

What types of development should I consider?

Most people have their preferences for how they learn – reading, talking to others or reflecting. However, we would advocate that you should use all three in your personal development. For example, say you want to learn more about 'chairwork'. You might start by setting a personal learning objective, which includes understanding what it is, how it works and how others use it in coaching and therapy, with the aim of making greater use of the approach in your own coaching. You might move closer to the goal by firstly reading a book such as Matthew Pugh's *Cognitive Behavioural Chairwork* (Pugh, 2020) or an article, *Pull up a chair* (Pugh, 2017).

The next step may be to begin to explore the use of the tool and one's feeling about testing it out in a discussion with a mentor coach or supervisor. What thought or emotions arise as one thinks about using it with a client? What assumptions or beliefs do we hold about the impact of the approach? What does the coach need to do to prepare prior to using the tool?

The next step might be to test out this new approach in practice. However, application is not the end of the process of learning, as to ensure effective use the coach should reflect on the process and gather client feedback. They might, for example, write up their experience in their journal, or use the Henley8 model of reflection to guide their reflective practice.

Finally, the coach might engage with their supervisor or mentor, to explore the experience, the data and their insights. This may lead to both new insights about themselves, and how they are setting up the exercise, using it with clients and how they help clients gain insights looking back on the tool at the end of the session.

In this way, professional development of this one skill also becomes a continuous process of plan, do, review, as the coach repeatedly practises and refines this skill.

Training

Attending training courses is possibly the most obvious form of professional development. All coaches undergo training as part of their journey to becoming an accredited coach (Passmore & Sinclair, 2020), and many continue this by attending masterclasses, webinars and additional qualification training. Including formal training is an important part of CPD, but should not be seen as the only route to personal development.

Supervision

Supervision has a key role to play in continuous professional development. Most coaches now accept that supervision is a helpful practice (Hawkins *et al*, 2019). Further, most of the main professional coaching bodies now actively encourage the use of supervision. Supervision plays a number of roles, one of which is to encourage reflection and a second is to support coaches in maintaining best practice. As we have noted above, both are important aspects in continuous professional development. For this reason, we believe supervision is an essential ingredient in planning, reflecting and implementing a professional development plan.

Mentor coach

Mentor coaching is a more hierarchical relationship than supervision and, for some professional bodies, such as the ICF, it is a way to support development, refinement and integration of the coach competencies. The mentor, as a more experienced professional, shares their views, insights and knowledge to support the coach to engage with and apply the ICF competencies in their practice. In this way, for those engaged in a competency-based approach to learning, the mentor model is also a key ingredient in a personal development plan.

Personal board of directors

A third method is the role of a 'personal board of directors'. These are the coaches go-to team of experts, advisers, experts and cheerleaders. The coach may approach these individuals to ask for their support, or they can be imaginary, and simply called to mind as a problem would emerge: 'What would Gandi advise in this situation?'

Alternatively, the coach may prefer to have a small but real board of individuals who they can approach. This real group of mentors can provide positive encouragement, advice, as well as to challenge the coach in their practice. These individuals should be people who the coach respects, and whose advice they value, as well as individuals who are accessible and have agreed to support or mentor the coach.

Reading

The fourth option for personal develop is reading. This includes books and peer-review research. If, as coaches, we believe in evidenced-based practice, then as any profession we should read the relevant research journals and science associated with our field. In coaching this is likely to include the

International Coaching Psychology Review and *Coaching: An International Journal of Theory, Practice and Research*. Accessing journals allows us to keep our practice both up-to-date and informed by the latest research. Wider reading of books and coaching magazines, such as the ICF's *Coaching World*, the AC's *Global Coaching Perspectives* or *The Coaching Psychologist*, enables the coach to acquire new knowledge, while reflecting on how others applied familiar models or approaches. While not a replacement for journals, books can also be a source of more in-depth practice-based knowledge and provide engaging material often with case studies, stories and examples to bring alive the model or ideas.

Conclusion

Professional development is an essential aspect of being a professional coach. Having a plan consisting of reading, training, supervision, mentoring and your personal board of directors can help you keep up-to-date in your practice and remain in the service of your clients.

References

CIPD (2020) *CIPD definition of personal development*. Available at: https://www.cipd.co.uk/learn/cpd/about (accessed 1 June 2020).

Hawkins, P, Turner, E and Passmore, J (2019) *The Manifesto for Supervision*. Henley-on-Thames: Henley Business School. ISBN: 978-1-912473-24-3

Passmore, J and Sinclair, T (2020) *Becoming a coach: The definitive ICF guide*. London: Pavillion.

Pugh, M (2020) *Cognitive Behavioural Chairwork*. Abdingdon: Routledge

Pugh, M (2017). Pull up a Chair. *The Psychologist* 30 (7) 42-74. Available at: https://thepsychologist.bps.org.uk/volume-30/july-2017/pull-chair (accessed 1 June 2020).

Chapter 48:
How can I develop towards being a wise coach?

David Clutterbuck

Introduction

Wisdom is the product of reflection on and learning from experience. It is one of the characteristics that distinguish run-of-the-mill coaches from masterful coaches. It's not just about having lots of experience to draw upon. It's about the quality of learning that comes from depth of reflection and integrating learning across a multiplicity of experiences. In this guide, I will explore reflection and how coaches might develop coaching wisdom.

The absurdity of education

> 'I gladly come back to the theme of the absurdity of our education: its end has not been to make us good and wise, but learned. And it has succeeded. It has not taught us to seek virtue and embrace wisdom: it has impressed upon us their derivation and etymology' (Montaigne, 1993).

Montaigne's words, written originally more than 400 years ago, ring very true today. Commentators point to a crisis of leadership, by which they mean an absence of wisdom in leaders, whether they be in politics, business or many other fields (e.g. Pearse, 2007). As the roles of leaders and executives become more complex and unpredictable, they require increasing complex thinking and judgement. In other words, wisdom is an increasingly scarce skill that leaders need to cope with their job roles. If coaches are to help leaders acquire wisdom, they must achieve wisdom themselves.

What is wisdom?

Human history first encounters wisdom in the persona of Athena, the Goddess of Wisdom, accompanying Odysseus in his travels and helping him interpret his experiences in the light of his desire to be a virtuous and strong leader. With each encounter, Odysseus becomes wiser – more self-aware, less impulsive and more in touch with his values – until he returns home a very different person than when he embarked on his adventures.

There are several ways of defining wisdom. The Ancient Greeks distinguished between:

- Sophia, searching for truth, from which derives the word philosophy
- Phronesis, practical wisdom
- Episteme, the equivalent of scientific knowledge.

Dilip Jeste (2019), one of the world's leading authorities on wisdom studies, defines wisdom as a complex construct with at least six components:

Social decision-making – such as the village elder, being the person people turn to for guidance when they are in conflict about what to do. This is sometimes referred to as *the wisdom of Solomon*.

Emotional regulation – the ability to manage and sometimes employ our emotions.

Prosocial behaviours – things that we do for others rather than for ourselves. This typically involves compassion, empathy and altruism.

Insight – which includes high self-awareness and self-understanding, both the result of self-reflection.

Acceptance of uncertainty – not needing to know everything, or to be right; accepting other people's opinions, values and perspectives as equally valid compared to our own.

Decisive – working through uncertainty to act, rather than sit on the fence; deciding what, in this instance, is the right thing to do and getting on with it. Jeste describes it as 'being aware of, but not paralysed by, uncertainty'.

Three other components have been proposed in the literature (Bangen *et al*, 2013):

- Spirituality
- Sense of humour
- Openness to new experiences.

To add to the complexity, Clutterbuck (2019), in a series of papers and webinars comparing human coaches with artificial intelligence counterparts, posits three kinds of wisdom:

- Lean wisdom – context (task) specific
- Broad wisdom – reflection on life experience (personal and vicarious)
- Meta-wisdom – brings together multiple, shifting perspectives.

Of these, only the first is (so far) accessible to machines.

How can coaches develop greater wisdom?

Wisdom is closely associated with adult maturity (Kegan, 1982) and the evolution of socio-emotional perspectives and cognitive complexity. Ongoing studies into coach maturity, at Henley and elsewhere, suggest that there are four stages of evolution in coaches' mental models (Clutterbuck & Megginson, 2010):

- Models-based coaches apply a prescriptive formula – doing coaching to the client

- Process-based coaches hand some control to the client – doing coaching with them

- Philosophy-based coaches integrate what they do as a coach with who they are – being a coach rather than doing

- Systemic eclectics see the complexity of the client in their systems – they 'hold the client while the client has the conversation that they need to have with themselves'.

The critical factor in this evolution appears to be the quality of reflection on experience – both as a coach and more broadly (the ongoing studies are, in part, aimed at testing this assumption). Broad wisdom and meta-wisdom evolve from the quality of both how we experience (being mindful) and how we review and learn from each experience. Coaches wishing to become wiser can therefore:

- devote time regularly to reflection and to learning how to reflect more deeply and more diversely

- choose a supervisor who will challenge their assumptions and who is sufficiently further along the path of wisdom to lead them gently into imagining what the next stage of their journey might be like

- cultivate diverse perspectives – for example, by reading widely, or by choosing clients from worlds radically different to their own

- continuously let go – for example, of the need to ensure the client reaches a solution, of one's own judgements and replacing these with 'naïve curiosity'.

How can coaches help clients become wiser?

As Montaigne observed, modern approaches to education, both at school and in the workplace, focus on making people clever (intelligent), but not wise. Yet, intelligence on its own cannot enable good decisions. Coaches can help create wise leaders by giving them the time and space to reflect deeply on their experiences, their values and their identity.

The coach uses his or her wisdom to help the client develop their own (so, the client's wisdom may be different from that of the coach and equally valid).

They do this by:

- helping the client assess, analyse and draw patterns and inferences from their experience
- raising the client's awareness of their own values and how these are (or aren't) expressed in what they do and what they aspire to
- offering insights from the coach's experience where appropriate
- asking challenging questions that lead the client to insights of their own
- helping identify and consider a wider range of perspectives and options than would normally be the case – for example, in being comfortable with polarities and other forms of complex thinking (Boston & Ellis, 2019).

To become more effective at helping the client reflect on experience, the coach can encourage them to:

- think about how they think
- feel about how they feel
- think about how they feel
- feel about how they think.

A thoughtful analysis of how effective leaders help others acquire wisdom (Aubrey & Cohen, 1995) has relevance to the coach's role. They identified five core skills or stages:

- Accompany – taking the path with the learner
- Sow – preparing the ground before the learner is ready to change by offering insights that they may not understand now, but will become increasingly meaningful to them
- Catalyse – when the learner reaches a critical level of turbulence or chaos, helping them accelerate through it
- Show – making knowledge visible and intellectually understandable; revealing one's own values and beliefs
- Harvesting – clarifying the learning and how it can be used.

Wisdom and ethicality

Warren Bennis' distinction that 'managers do things right; leaders do the right thing' has relevance to coaching in that coaches help people access values in making complex decisions. These values are not just their own but also those of the organisation, society and beyond. A growing role for coaches within organisations and externally is that of 'ethical mentor' –

using their own wisdom to help clients unpack difficult ethical dilemmas and conflicts of values. Coaches typically think of ethics only in the context of adhering to a professional code of conduct, but it is much more than that. By understanding and challenging our own ethical decision-making, we equip ourselves better to help others with their ethical conflicts. This is truly using your wisdom to help another become wiser.

Conclusion

If this sounds very like the role of a mentor (in the correct meaning of the word, as someone who uses their wisdom to help another develop their own wisdom), it is because at this point the roles of mentor and coach tend to merge. Indeed, mentoring is sometimes described as 'coaching plus', because the mentor uses their experience not to suggest or direct, but to provide context and ask more penetrating questions. Of course, it takes wisdom to do this.

References

Aubrey, R and Cohen, PM (1995) *Working Wisdom* (pp 22-23), Jossey-Bass, SF.

Bangen, J K, Meeks, T W and Jeste, D V (2013) Defining and Assessing Wisdom: A Review of the Literature, *American Journal of Geriatric Psychiatry* 21 (12) Dec 1254-1266.

Banicki, K (2009) The Berlin Wisdom Paradigm: A Conceptual Analysis of a Psychological Approach to Wisdom *History & Philosophy of Psychology* 11(2), 25-35

Boston, R and Ellis, K (2019) Upgrade: Building your capacity for complexity, *Leaderspace*. London.

Clutterbuck, D (2019) *Coaching and Mentoring: The antidote to rampant technology*, paper to Australian Human Resources Institute, Brisbane.

Clutterbuck, D and Megginson, D (2010) Coach Maturity: An emerging concept, *The International Journal of Mentoring and Coaching* 8(1).

Jeste, D V and Lee E E (2019) The Emerging Empirical Science of Wisdom: Definition, Measurement, Neurobiology, Longevity, and Interventions, *Harvard Review of Psychiatry* 27(3) 127-140.

Kegan, R (1982) *The Evolving Self*. Harvard Press.

Montaigne, M (1993) On Presumption, *The Complete Essays*, ed. MA Screech. London: Penguin Books, Penguin Classics edition. Book II, Essay 17, 749-50.

Pearse, C (2017) 5 reasons why leadership is in crisis. *Forbes*. Available at https://www.forbes.com/sites/chrispearse/2018/11/07/5-reasons-why-leadership-is-in-crisis/

Peterson, C and Seligman, MEP (2004) *Character strengths and virtues: A handbook and classification*. New York: Oxford University Press.

Torbert, WR and Rooke, D (2005) Seven transformations of leadership. *Harvard Business Review* 83 (4) 66-76.

Sternberg, RJ (1998) A Balance Theory of Wisdom. *Review of General Psychology* 2(4) 347-365.

Chapter 49:
How do I develop my own integrated approach as a coach?

Jonathan Passmore

Introduction

Coaching has grown dramatically over the past two decades to the point where most managers, trainers, facilitators and consultants describe part of what they do as 'coaching'. However, any examination of practice reveals many coaches are using a one-size-fits-all approach: a standard formula for every person and every problem.

Research with the most experienced coaches (Passmore, 2007) suggests these coaches use a range of different approaches, selecting the appropriate tool for the person and the problem they are working with. They adapt and flex to meet their client's needs and select the most effective approach to help. But how can coaches integrate the wide range of different coaching approaches available to help their clients become the best they can be?

In this chapter, I offer one way to bring together different approaches, which enables the coach to offer an integrated practice, allowing them to flex and adapt to their client's needs.

What is integration?

Most of us would agree, when asked, that people are all different. They have different personalities, different interests and have had different experiences. It may be not surprising that these different people and the vastly different problems they experience require different approaches. Not every DIY job at home requires a hammer – but when we only have a hammer, every problem looks like a nail.

Integration involves bringing together different approaches to create a coherent way of working, while having the flexibility to adapt to different clients. Integration involves synthesising our mass of learning of multiple models, ideas about change, and different tools and techniques, to create a unified whole that is consistent with our values and beliefs.

An integrated model for coaching practice

There are many ways of bringing together different approaches or models within coaching. The Seven Streams Integrated Coaching Model is just one way (Passmore & Sinclair, 2020). As your coaching experience grows, you will develop your own way of making sense of what you do. This particular framework is based on a series of streams in which the coach can work, moving between streams as required. The model was originally developed in 2006-7 (Passmore, 2007) and has been developed over time, the original model contained six streams and is now presented as a seven-stream model.

In the classic version of the model, the first two streams are the coaching partnership. This term can be used to emphasise the collaborative and equal nature of the relationship. If either party is overly dominant, the coach is likely to feel restricted in their ability to act, or the client may be less open and willing to talk about intimate issues. Within this pair of streams are a series of approaches, which the coach can employ, working with the different facets of their client – behavioural, cognitive, emotional and physiological. All of this work takes place within a cultural, or systemic, context. Let's look at each stream in turn.

Streams one and two: The coaching partnership

Before any coaching to enhance performance can begin, the coach needs to build a working relationship with the client. Stream one involves the coach working with the client to develop a relationship of mutual trust and respect. To create the right conditions for coaching, the coach needs to invest in the relationship. This may take a few minutes or many sessions, depending on the individuals and the nature of the conversation the client is bringing to coaching. In working in this stream the coach draws in ideas from person centred psychology, and validates the research evidence that an effective working alliance is essential before any work is done in the coaching assignment.

However, once established, this work on the relationship cannot stop. The coach needs to continue to invest in this relationship. The focus, though, can begin to shift to start to undertake the work required in the session.

The coach thus seeks to create and maintain a safe container for the coaching work. If that container breaks, or is not created in the first place, the coach will be unable to progress the work the client needs to undertake.

Stream three: Behaviours

The third stream relates to the work that the coach can undertake with the client at a behavioural level. This can often be a useful place to start, helping clients to understand and gain confidence in the coaching process. In this stream, the coach encourages the client to use a simple problem-solving approach: to set a clear and measurable objective; think about their current issue; critically review alternative options; and develop action plans (usually things to do) that enable them to move closer to their goals. Models such as GROW (Whitmore, 2004) are well suited to this, being primarily behaviourally focused. Such frameworks direct clients to use problem solving and creativity techniques to generate actions they can take to solve the problem, while putting in place project management mechanisms to track progress and mitigate risks.

Streams four and five: Cognitions

The fourth stream is centred on the client's thoughts and beliefs. How do these help or hinder the client in their journey to achieving their goal? In this stream the coach will typically draw upon cognitive behavioural approaches (Beck, 1991; Ellis, 1998; Gilbert, 2009; Hayes, 2004) that have been refined by coaches to make them more suitable for the work of the coach than the therapist (Anstiss & Blonna, 2014; Anstiss & Gilbert, 2014; Edgerton & Palmer, 2005; Neenan & Dryden, 2001).

The coach's aim is to help their client to recognise the relationship between their thoughts, feelings and behaviour. Through this, the coach can help the client develop more helpful, supportive or evidenced-based beliefs, or simply become more accepting and compassionate towards themselves, and, through this, change their thinking to improve their performance or reduce their anxiety.

The fifth stream is the work with unconscious cognitions. In stream four, the client may quite easily bring to mind the beliefs they hold and the words used by their inner critic that inhibit their performance or are a trigger for their anxiety. In stream five, the client's thoughts, beliefs and attitudes, and their relationship with their current situation, are not part of their conscious awareness. Often what has brought them to coaching can be something completely different. The aim of the coach in this space, working sometimes over many sessions, is to help the client to explore the topic from multiple perspectives. Through this, a greater self-awareness may emerge and ultimately a desire to address the issue. Approaches such as psychodynamic coaching or motivational interview can be particularly useful in this stream.

Stream six: Working with the body

In this stream we will aim to work with the body. While some clients may be naturally drawn to this stream, others will more strongly push away from it, in a more dramatic way that the other streams. In this stream the coach works with the client to become more aware of their body, and how this communicates with them to give an understanding about emotional responses, both in the moment (for example, feelings expressed as butterflies in their stomach) and in the longer term, (for example how the body carries stress, expressed in neck ache). Working with the body can also help with performance, and includes encouraging clients to participant in mindfulness body scans pilates or yoga, as well as looking after physical health through engaging in a HIIT workouts or jogging.

Stream seven: Systems

The seventh and final stream, surrounds and influences all of the others; this is the cultural or systemic stream. Culture is often unseen and unspoken, but influences how we do the things we do at this point in human history, in our national society, in our regional culture, in our city, in our sector, in our organisation, in our team and in our family. The aim of the coach is to bring these unspoken forces into the client's awareness, so they can recognise that systemic forces are powerful and influence both them and others. Writers in this space, such as Oshry (2007), have provided fascinating insights into how organisational forces can impact individuals and what individuals can do to both accept and manage these forces.

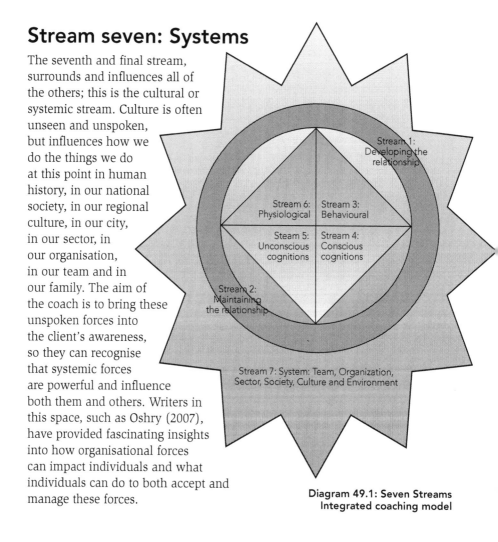

Diagram 49.1: Seven Streams Integrated coaching model

How can you develop your own integrated approach?

While using a diverse range of approaches can help coaches to be able to adapt and flex to meet the different needs of individual clients, how should the coach go about developing their own integrated approach? The answer lies in what beliefs hold together the different approaches that the coach uses with their clients. The starting point is a belief in equality; that the coach and client are equal. Secondly, that the coach is working solely in favour of their client, but with a rider, a recognition that the client does not always know what they want all of the time, and that sometimes the coach needs to encourage the client to explore more challenging spaces or be confronted by unpleasant emotions to create a change. However, this must always be done in service of the client. Thirdly, that change is difficult, and that falling off your bicycle and getting back on are part of learning. In essence, coaches need to equip their clients to be able to cope with lapses and relapses, and to stay focused on the goal. This is best achieved through a positive and encouraging approach, where the coach is willing to go on the journey with their client. Finally, that coaching is a brief affair and thus, each assignment is working towards an ending. It is not an indefinite, ongoing relationship that rolls on for years. In short, coaching starts with the end in mind – in thinking about your own approach.

Table 49.1: Three key questions

1. What beliefs underpin your work with clients?
2. Which approaches have you been trained in?
3. Which approaches do you feel competent to use and have found helpful with your clients and their issues?

For some, writing answers to these questions is the best way to think through and develop their own model. For others, drawing their model works best. Either way, as an integrated coach, be able to describe what and how you work.

Conclusion

Each coach needs to develop their own approach – how they can sense of, and articulate what they do. The best coaches are able to draw from a range of different philosophical traditions, while underpinning these with a uniting set of values or beliefs. As you continue your journey, continue to reflect on your practice to develop your personal philosophy of coaching.

References

Anstiss, T and Blonna, R (2014) Acceptance and commitment coaching. In: J Passmore (ed) *Mastery in Coaching: A Complete Psychological Toolkit for Advanced Coaching*. London: Kogan Page.

Anstiss, T and Gilbert, P (2014) Compassionate Mind Coaching. In: J Passmore (ed) *Mastery in Coaching: A Complete Psychological Toolkit for Advanced Coaching*. London: Kogan Page.

Beck, A (1991) *Cognitive Therapy of Depression*. New York: Guildford Press.

Edgerton, N and Palmer, S (2005) SPACE: A psychological model for use within cognitive behavioural coaching, therapy and stress management. *The Coaching Psychologist* 1 (2) 25–31.

Ellis, A (1998) *The Practice of Rational Emotive Behavioural Therapy*. London: Free Association Books.

Gilbert, P (2009) *The Compassionate Mind. A New Approach to the Challenges of Life*. London: Constable and Robinson.

Hayes, S (2004) Acceptance and commitment therapy, relation frame theory and the third wave of cognitive behavioural approaches. *Behavioural Therapy* 35 639–65.

Neenan, M & Dryden, W (2001) *Life Coaching: A Cognitive Behavioural Approach*. Hove: Routledge.

Oshry, B (2007) *Seeing Systems Unlocking the Mysteries of Organizational Life* (2nd edition). San Francisco: Berrett-Koehler.

Passmore, J (2007) Integrative coaching: a model for executive coaching, *Consulting Psychology Journal: Practice and Research*. American Psychology Association 59 (1) 68-78.

Passmore, J and Sinclair, T (2020) *Becoming a coach: The essential ICF guide*. Worthing: Pavilion

Whitmore, J (2004) *Coaching for Performance: Growing People, Performance and Purpose* (3rd edition). London: Nicholas Brealey Publishing.

Chapter 50:
How can I develop a coaching culture in my organisation?

Jonathan Passmore

Introduction

Coaching is now widely used across business. But having a coaching culture is more than just using coaching. We close this book by thinking about how coaches and those responsible for business coaching in their organisations develop a high-performing culture by integrating coaching into their wider human resources strategy. This involves understanding how coaching can be used to leverage improved performance, through growing high-potential employees and supporting high performers. In this final chapter, we explore what a coaching culture is and how organisations can go about developing one through a 10-step plan.

What is a culture?

The term 'culture' is widely used, but, like coaching, has a wide variety of definitions that are applied by different leaders, organisations and sectors. One of the clearest and shortest definitions is by Terence Deal and Alan Kennedy: *'the way things get done around here'* (1982). A more academic definition was offered by Ed Schein:

> *'A pattern of shared basic assumptions that was learned by a group as it solved its problems of external adaption and internal integration, that has worked well enough to be considered valid and, therefore, to be taught to new members as the correct way you perceive, think and feel in relation to those problems.'* (Schein, 2004: 8)

Drawing on this thinking about organisational culture, I define coaching culture as:

> *'An organisation that aims to maximise the potential of all who work with it, through its use of coaching as the default style of leadership, and where individuals are supported and challenged to become more self-aware, with increased responsibility to deliver organisational goals.'*

To bring a new culture alive the organisation requires a planned approach; one way of delivering culture change is a three Cs approach (see Figure 50.1):

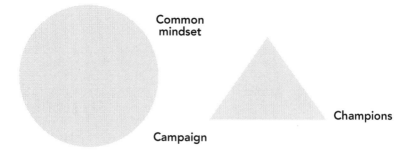

Figure 50.1: A three Cs approach to a coaching culture

The first of the three elements is a Common mindset. This is a shared view about the role of coaching within the organisation from the senior team to supervisors. Secondly, creating Champions. This requires the leadership team of the organisation having a vision for the role coaching can play in achieving the organisation's strategy objectives. Finally, it requires a Campaign to communicate to each and every employee what coaching is, what role it plays in the wider business strategy and how they can use and access coaching.

Old-style approach to coaching

While coaching has been actively used by managers for more than three decades, in many organisations it has remained a personal perk, almost like a parking space in the company offices car park: disconnected from the wider organisational activities. This approach to coaching is typified by a number of common features we have summarised in Table 50.1.

Table 50.1: Old-style approach to coaching

1. **'Why' of coaching:** the organisation understands that coaching is valuable to its executives, but not how to integrate it into the wider HR or wider business strategy.
2. **Appointments:** the selection of the coach and their appointment is undertaken by the individual manager, often without due process and frequently based on personal relationships or a recommendation.
3. **Assignment focus:** the focus of the assignment is decided by the individual manager with little or no reference to the wider organisational perspective.
4. **Coaches:** the coach is seen exclusively as an external contractor, responsible for their own development and standards.
5. **Evaluation:** the evaluation is based on the perceptions of the manager as to how they felt the coaching went, with little consideration of metrics or alternative perspectives.

Each of these five aspects reinforces the personal rather than the strategic nature of coaching, keeping the focus on personal needs and impact. While such a focus may benefit individual managers who receive the coaching, much can be gained by linking the coaching process more closely to the organisation's needs and objectives, to ensure the wider organisation's benefits too.

The coaching culture model

The LEAD coaching culture model is a framework that can help organisations to move away from the approach of an old-style personal coaching to a more integrated strategic approach (Passmore & Crabbe, 2020). The model is based on earlier work by Passmore and Jastrzebska (2011) exploring the work of organisations in developing coaching cultures. The LEAD framework suggests that to develop a coaching culture, organisations need to consider coaching as containing four zones (see Figure 50.2). Each zone contains a checklist that the organisation can apply to evaluate its progress towards full implementation of a coaching culture.

Figure 50.2: LEAD coaching culture model

Zone 1: Leaders

In this zone, the focus is on how the organisation uses coaches to develop and support its top talent, specifically the board, senior managers and leaders. This is usually through the engagement of external executive coaches. The framework advocates that instead of a passive role for the organisation, the organisation actively engages, manages and evaluates the delivery of coaching to ensure it is aligned with wider organisational strategy.

Zone 2: Everyone

In this zone, the focus is on how coaching can be extended from the top team to all managers and supervisors throughout the organisation. One common way of achieving this goal is through developing an internal coaching team. A second route is to engage with an online coaching programme, like CoachHub and BetterUp, which provides online coaching services at low cost. The framework provides guidance of the selection, training, management, support and evaluation of the coaching pool, as well as how managers can access the pool, and criteria to consider when seeking an external provider.

Zone 3: Approach

In this zone, the focus is on how a coaching style of management can be adopted as the 'default leadership' approach of the organisation. This requires coaching skills to be an integral part of all leadership, management and supervisor training programmes, helping managers to understand what coaching is, when to use it and how to use it to best effect within a line management role. What also needs to be made clear is that coaching is not a silver bullet for use in all situations to solve all problems. It is simply one of a number of styles of leading, and the one that the organisation favours as its 'go to' style.

Zone 4: Distributed

In this zone, the focus is on extending coaching beyond the organisational boundaries. Most organisations use multiple partners and suppliers to deliver their services or products. In this zone, the organisation looks for ways to extend a coaching style to these relationships. This may mean for a public-sector organisation, creating cross-boundary training and cross-boundary coaching delivery. In other sectors, it may mean adopting a win–win development approach to project delivery, where project issues are worked through using a coaching style.

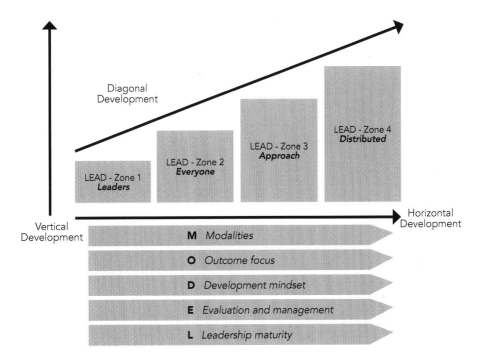

Figure 50.3 Lead model components

Developing a coaching culture

At a practical level, what can organisations do to move closer to a coaching culture? Few of the books on coaching culture offer practical advice on how to build a coaching culture, preferring to stick to the benefits that might arise. In Table 50.2, we offer 10 steps that organisations can apply to help them move closer to a more strategic and integrated approach to coaching.

Table 50.2: 10 practical steps towards a coaching culture

1. Integrate coaching into your HR strategy
2. Commission, manage and supervise external coaches, not firms
3. Build an internal coaching pool
4. Managers select their coach from the pool
5. Pool reflects the organisation
6. Enable coaching outside line relationships (or the organisation)
7. Train all managers in coaching skills
8. Develop coaching as the default management style
9. Use team coaching to develop team performance
10. Develop a coaching style of working with suppliers – focusing on win–win

Conclusion

The LEAD coaching culture model offers a practical tool that organisations can use to audit their own coaching practice and to plan their next step in the developmental journey towards building a successful coaching culture: using coaching as a strategic element of the organisational strategy. We close the chapter with 10 practical steps for those responsible for coaching leadership to take away.

References

Deal, T and Kennedy, A (1982) *Corporate Culture: The Rites and Rituals of Corporate Life*. San Francisco: Perseus Books.

Passmore, J. (2020). Building a coaching culture. Greek Coaching Conference, 26th September 2020.

Passmore, J and Jastrzebska, K (2011) Building a coaching culture: A development journey for organisational development. *Coaching Review* 4 (2) 123–7.

Schein, E (2004) *Organizational Culture and Leadership*. San Francisco: Jossey Bass.